Grief and the Meaning of the Funeral

Grief and the Meaning of the Funeral

Edited by Otto S. Margolis, Howard C. Raether,
Austin H. Kutscher, Robert J. Volk,
Ivan K. Goldberg, and Daniel J. Cherico

With the editorial assistance of Lillian J. Kutscher

A Volume in The Foundation of Thanatology/
MSS Information Corporation's continuing
Series on Thanatology

MSS INFORMATION CORPORATION, 655 Madison Avenue
New York, New York 10021

Library of Congress Cataloging in Publication Data

Main entry under title:

Grief and the meaning of the funeral.

(MSS' series on Thanatology)
1. Funeral rites and ceremonies — Psychological
aspects. I. Margolis, Otto Schwarz, ed.
BF789.F8G74   393'.01'9   74-32076
ISBN 0-8422-7267-4

Printed in the United States

Table of Contents

THE FUNERAL HOME: A COMMUNITY RESOURCE

GRIEF AND THE PUBLIC IMAGE

OVERVIEW

List of Contributors

Reverend Marbury E. Anderson, Pastor, Augustana Lutheran Church of Denver, Denver, Colorado

Howard Barnard, Editor, *Casket and Sunnyside,* New York, New York

Linda Bove, Editorial Associate, The Foundation of Thanatology, New York, New York

G. David Burton, Funeral Service Director, Erie, Pennsylvania

Daniel J. Cherico, Ph.D., Assistant Professor, Queensborough Community College, Bayside, New York; Administrative Director, The Foundation of Thanatology, New York, New York

Paula J. Clayton, M.D., Associate Professor, Department of Psychiatry, School of Medicine, Washington University, St. Louis, Missouri

Linda Colvin, Associate Director, John F. Kennedy NATO, Erie, Pennsylvania

Terrance M. Copeland, Funeral Service Director, New Paltz, New York

John J. Curran, Funeral Service Director, Rochester, New York

Reverend Buell W. Dalton, Wesley Chapel United Methodist Church, Fort Lauderdale, Florida

Frances I. Delany, Ph.D., Chief of Psychological Services, League School for Seriously Disturbed Children, Brooklyn, New York

Robert E. Delany, J.D., New York, New York

Eugene I. Dyszlewski, M.A., (Doctoral Candidate), Teacher College, Columbia University, New York, New York

Reverend E. T. Eberhart, Chaplain, Salem Hospital, Salem, Oregon

Elaine A. Finnberg, Editorial Associate, The Foundation of Thanatology, New York, New York

Jerome F. Fredrick, Ph.D., Director of Research, Dodge Chemical Company Research Laboratory, Bronx, New York

Ivan K. Goldberg, M.D., Associate in Clinical Psychiatry, Department of Psychiatry, College of Physicians and Surgeons, Columbia University, New York, New York

Patricia P. Hannaford, Doctoral Candidate, Department of Sociology, Graduate School of Arts and Sciences, Columbia University, New York, New York

Reverend Edgar N. Jackson, Author, Corinth, Vermont

Baheej Khleif, Ph.D., Associate Professor, Department of Sociology, Worcester State College, Worcester, Massachusetts

Samuel Klagsburn, M.D., Director, Psychiatric Consultation Service, St. Luke's Hospital, New York, New York

Austin H. Kutscher, D.D.S., Associate Professor and Director, New York State Psychiatric Institute Dental Service, School of Dental and Oral Surgery, Columbia University, New York, New York; President, The Foundation of Thanatology

Lillian G. Kutscher, Publications Editor, The Foundation of Thanatology, New York, New York

Martin L. Kutscher, Columbia College, New York, New York

William L. Lamers, Ph.D., Author; Member, American Board of Funeral Service Education, Wales, Wisconsin

Otto S. Margolis, Ph.D., Dean, American Academy McAllister Institute of Funeral Service, New York, New York

William Matthews, Coordinator, Mortuary Science Curriculum, McNeese State University, Lake Charles, Louisiana

J. Sheridan Mayer, Chairman, Department of Restorative Art, American Academy McAllister Institute of Funeral Service, New York, New York

Joseph L. McCracken, Past President, National Funeral Directors Association, Pana, Illinois

Charles H. Nichols, Director and Trustee, National Foundation of Funeral Service, Evanston, Illinois

Roy Vaughn Nichols, M.Ed., Funeral Service Director, Chagrin Falls, Ohio

Robert W. Ninker, Executive Secretary, Illinois Funeral Directors Association, Springfield, Illinois

Paul R. Patterson, M.D., Professor of Pediatrics, Albany Medical College of Union University, Albany, New York

Raoul L. Pinette, M.A., Immediate Past President, Board of Governors, National Funeral Directors Association, Lewiston, Maine

Howard C. Raether, J.D., Executive Director, National Funeral Directors Association, Milwaukee, Wisconsin

John E. Schowalter, M.D., Associate Professor of Pediatrics and Psychiatry, Yale University Child Study Center, New Haven, Connecticut

Murray Shor, Funeral Service Director, New York, New York

Phyllis R. Silverman, Ph.D., Director, Preventive Intervention Unit, Laboratory of Community Psychiatry, Department of Psychiatry, Harvard Medical School, Boston, Massachusetts

ix   **Contributors**

Dale W. Sly, President, San Francisco College of Mortuary Science, San Francisco, California

Jeanette Scaros, Hunter College, City University of New York, New York

Margot Tallmer, Ph. D., Associate Professor, Department of Psychology, Hunter College, City University of New York, New York

Walter K. Thorsell, Director, Department of Funeral Service Education, Mt. Hood Community College, Gresham, Oregon

Susan Trachtenberg, Englewood, New Jersey

Willadean W. Turner, Funeral Service Director, Brooklyn, New York

Robert J. Volk, Funeral Service Director, Teaneck, New Jersey; Chairman, Funeral Service Section, Foundation of Thanatology, New York, New York

Sumner James Waring, Jr., Funeral Service Director, Fall River Massachusetts; Member, Board of Governors, National Funeral Directors Association

Grief and the Meaning of the Funeral: An Introduction

Austin H. Kutscher and Lillian G. Kutscher

Both grief and the funeral are components of a sequence of events that follows the death of a loved or significant person. A death provokes emotional reactions among those who have been bereaved and, at the same time, initiates activities which mark it as a community event. Within a limited number of hours after a person has died, principal survivors must observe certain procedures specified by law for the well-being of the community at large; they must conform to the rites and rituals of an ethnic, cultural, or religious nature observed by the smaller community of family and friends; and they must simultaneously take the first painful steps toward the restoration of normal patterns of living.

It is therefore customary for society and the bereaved to respond to a death with activity, despite the paralyzing emotions of acute grief. The nature of this response is shaped by the legal requirements for disposal of the body and by the structured activities which comprise the psychosocial and pragmatic aspects of grief. In most situations, the ceremony of a funeral service, which terminates with the interment or cremation of the deceased's remains, is involved. The funeral then becomes, and gives, a focus and a setting for experiencing one of the most profound and complex of human emotions, acute grief. And it is this emotion that gives functional validity to the funeral, which in and of itself serves as the mechanism for those who mourn the loss to share and ventilate emotions and thoughts with their family, friends, and community.

Preceding, during, and following the funeral rites, the grief reactions are not only respected but also are granted a very special sanction for almost unrestricted expression. Traditionally, society has recognized that the mourners should be comforted and made to feel that their loss is being shared. A socially supported respite is granted so that the primary mourners — the members of the deceased's immediate family circle — may start the processes of replenishing their severely depleted emotional resources, reorganizing their lives, and often assuming new responsibilities. When funeral rituals, whether secular, religious, or humanistic, are acted out, they serve to reinforce the reality of loss and help to dispel those forms of denial which, if not dealt with appropriately, may result in pathological grief. Dramatic testimony is presented that a death has taken place, that a loss has been sustained, that people are mourning that loss, and that these facts cannot be changed.

This period of acute grief permits the realities of loss to fall into a perspective that relates not only to what has been in the past but also to what will be in the future. As part of the sequence of postmortem events, the funeral gives the bereaved a kind of "time out" as well as some "time off." In the hours and days of specified activity, temporarily divorced from day-to-day living and working, it relieves the grief stricken from accustomed routines. Orderly memorialization is encouraged, and a creative kind of grief can be fostered which at a later time transforms the energies of sorrow into potentially productive endeavors.

Each funeral serves each grieving individual in its own way; yet all funerals serve a common purpose in satisfying the common needs generated by sorrow. Whatever the circumstances surrounding the death — such as those associated with a long-term chronic illness when the bereaved have had a period of anticipatory grief or those encountered following death through accidental or natural trauma wherein no preparation for acceptance of the loss is available to the bereaved — adjustments to the changes within a family and within a community must be made. In every situation these changes occur: roles are altered for many people; valued and trusted professionals are replaced by other professionals; scenes of activity are shifted to other and often unfamiliar sites.

At the hospital, the home, the church, the funeral home, or the cemetery, each individual confronts a new status quo and a new environment and plays out his own role in accommodation to these. Before the death, the hospital or other institution had attempted to provide a secure and stable setting for moments of hope, perhaps for prayers for cure, and finally, the ultimate in care from physicians, nurses, social workers, clergymen, family members, and friends. Thanatological studies have shown that team effort can, indeed, be most effective in giving therapeutic support to the dying patient and his family. When death occurs, the survivors must seek out a different team; although this group may be from their own cultural, religious, social, or family milieu, it often cannot function as well or be as helpful as the one it replaces. Frequently, the transition is excruciatingly painful. At this time, the survivors must also engage the services of the funeral director who, by virtue of his education, his license, and his experiences, functions as a major member of a new care giving team. His entrance is rarely seen as the useful intermediary step it usually turns out to be; more than likely it is assessed initially as an unwanted, disagreeable intrusion which provokes extreme anxiety.

The funeral director responds to calls for his services at any hour of the day or night. He is with the bereaved at the most shocking moments of intense

sorrow and decision making. Physicians, clergymen, and those in the allied health
professions are trained to serve the needs of the dying and the living; funeral
directors are trained to assist the bereaved with service and counsel, to give
guidance during the period of acute grief. The funeral director's role is multifaceted: he is a technician, a coordinator, a counselor, an observer, a comforter,
and very often a friend. During hours of turbulence and stress, he is a figure of
substance and direction in the lives of the grief stricken. The performance of
the ritual of the funeral extends far beyond the rigid enforcement of legalities;
and if extraneous trauma can be avoided while realities are faced, the period of
acute grief can signal the beginning of restitution for those who have been
bereaved.

    The process of recovering from bereavement is aggravated by internal con-
flicts that must be resolved. Harsh memories from the days of illness and suffering, feelings of guilt — classical symptoms which may be experienced during
acute grief — should begin to yield to a strong sense of not unremitting loss,
then eventually to the acceptance of that loss, and finally to an amelioration of
emotional symptoms. What is to be hoped for is not the repression of emotions
but their therapeutic expression. From this should develop resolution of both
the emotional and practical problems caused by the fracture in the family
structure, a constitution of the significant survivors' lives into new patterns,
and the emergence of new relationships.

    Usually, only those closest to the deceased suffer the crucial components
of this experience or comprehend fully through self-involvement the magnitude, intensity, and total pervasiveness of acute grief and the disintegrating
impact of the frequently ambivalent emotions which form the essence
of the "acute grief syndrome." The balancing effects of objective thoughts from
those who are removed from emotional involvement by either relationship or
professional distance are important to the bereaved. With concern, knowledge,
and all the material symbols and necessities he is capable of providing, the funeral
director gives guidance, service, and comfort in a setting that can give meaning
to a ceremony and allow for the emotional catharsis so needed in periods of
heightened stress. He has elected to serve his community in a specific way; he has
succeeded as a professional when his image of himself can be projected meaningfully into therapeutic care giving for those who have been bereaved.

    When questions about death and dying, loss and grief, and recovery from
bereavement are posed, physicians. psychologists, nurses, social workers, clergymen, funeral directors, philosophers, scholars, and students in many disciplines
seem to provide the definitive answers. For almost a decade these workers have
tried to stimulate productive thinking about topics which most people try to
avoid. Investigating as pioneers in the field of thanatology, they have been able
to break down certain of the barriers which have inhibited open discussion of
death and aggravated the death-fears of many. They have exposed and opened

for examination the ethical and moral issues that a highly sophisticated medical technology has forced families to confront when making decisions for the care of terminally or critically ill members. Terminal illness can strip a patient of every ounce of his dignity; bodily disfigurement can affect the patient, his family, and even hospital staff; the aftermath can bring a plague of additional suffering upon those survivors who are unable to cope with the decision making forced upon them and with the tragedy of bereavement.

Health science professionals seek to serve with honor and integrity, to recognize the rights of all human beings in sickness or health, and to make every effort to preserve the dignity of the person. The average citizen does not involve himself in clinical hypotheses, mainly because he is not oriented in that direction. He is concerned primarily with the realities that affect his own life and those of his intimates — the realities that can disrupt what he has established as his way of life. When he avoids talking and thinking about death and its consequences or avoids preparing for these in practical ways, he is displaying his phobias and surrounding himself with a shield of denial. All too often he refuses to talk about, contemplate, or even go to a funeral. At the time when he is forced to drop his defense mechanisms, he needs all the support that psychosocial insights, scientific information, medical care, and humane care giving can provide for him. In a state of shock, he finds it easier to conform to what is comfortable, comforting, and compatible with his emotional situation than to be a nonconformist. Mourners seek sanctuary in what has been traditional and safe or in those activities or thoughts which can be summoned up for or adapted to their emotional needs from moment to moment.

In conclusion, or by way of introduction, it seems crucial to recall the fundamental thesis that is the core of positive thinking about acute grief and the funeral: as the elements of acute grief are subjected to analysis, the series of events which we generalize as the funeral invariably emerge as central and important. Likewise, as the funeral is analyzed, this event cannot be conceptualized without perceiving that it can never of itself be more than a profoundly effective, but time-limited, event in the larger spectrum of acute grief. However seen or by whom, the funeral appears to symbolize the termination of human relationships while it reinforces the reality of individual and societal evolution.

GENERAL OBSERVATIONS

The Wise Management of Grief

Edgar N. Jackson

INTRODUCTION

It is usually assumed that grief is a universal emotion. This is not necessarily the case. Only those who are capable of love experience grief. The socio-
path with his inadequate inner being seems to be unable to feel the deep emotion
equated with grief. Grief is the other side of the coin of love. Those who love
deeply accept a special type of vulnerability and become those for whom a special need exists as far as the wise management of their deep emotions is concerned.

It is important, then, to make some verbal distinctions. In the context of
our thinking, death or bereavement is the event in one's personal history that
precipitates the emotion of grief. Mourning is the process that works through the
emotion to retrieve the emotional capital invested in the life and love of the one
who has died. The mourning process, then, is a way of managing grief that re-
stores the vulnerable person to wholeness.

THE VULNERABLE PERSON

People in acute grief may be highly vulnerable. I say "acute grief" for there
are other types. The patterns in which we experience death may modify the
nature of our grief. At the turn of our century, more than half the deaths were
among children. Now, the figure is less than 7 percent. At the turn of the century,
average life expectancy was under 47 years. Now, almost a generation of life expectancy has been added. That means that in less than 100 years, we have moved

1

from a culture where death was usually tragic and untimely to a culture where the majority of people live to the end of a normal life span, three score years and ten. When death can be foreseen and approached gradually, the defensive stance makes it possible to do anticipatory grief work, and so the acute response is reduced. However, our experience with acute deprivation is also reduced, and so people can be more vulnerable when tragic and untimely death occurs. These are the people who need special help.

Recent researches indicate how vulnerable the person in acute grief may be. One study shows that the death rate among widows the first year after the death of a husband is 700 percent higher than among other women in comparable age groups. A hospital study shows that admissions to a general hospital are 600 percent higher among those in acute grief than in the general population. A study of parents of leukemia victims shows that 50 percent of them were in psychotherapy before a year was over. So it is obvious that these persons are in a highly vulnerable state as far as their own death, illness, and emotional stress are concerned.

THE ROOTS OF VULNERABILITY

To understand the needs of these vulnerable people, it is also important for us to realize that the capacity for grief is a great achievement as well as a great burden. This helps us to perceive the resources we can use in grief management and to understand the deep distress that characterizes these powerful emotions.

It took millions of years of long, slow development to come to the place where social or other consciousness was refined enough to produce the heightened sensitivity for another that we call love. The writings of Pierre Teilhard de Chardin, Eilhard VonDomaris, and Erik Erikson stress this process and the meaning of the identity relationship that can become the identity problem or the identity crisis.

It is obvious that when you love someone you identify with him and so become vulnerable. When something good happens to him, you feel pleased, but when something devastating happens to him, you can feel devastated. It is this devastation that we are concerned about in acute grief.

There is also an anatomical or physiological dimension to this acute emotion. Deep in the nervous system and mental structure of each individual are the mechanisms that can be employed to protect the self against the intense stress of life or its intolerable pains. With the severe suffering of intense deprivation, the subthalamic regions of the brain may be activated, causing the spontaneous and irrational behavior that is related to the mechanisms of self-defense and self-preservation. The ancient equipment of the nervous system that was apparently employed originally to preserve life may now be used to react to acute psychic pain in a similar manner. This not only increases the need for understanding, but also in a highly organized cultural setting, may increase the vulnerability of the individual who feels constrained to modify his feelings to fit his environment.

When we add to that condition the atmosphere of a death-denying, death-defying society, we begin to see how heightened vulnerability is so significant a factor in contemporary grief management. If it is difficult or impossible to move from the pain of grief to the health-restoring process of mourning, the grief-stricken individual is thrust into a chronic state of emotional stress with all the physical and psychological effects related to this prolonged disturbance.

THE NATURE OF VULNERABILITY

When emotions cannot be dealt with as emotions, they may find other and perhaps more damaging means of expression. Dr. James Knight, Professor of Psychiatry at Tulane Medical School, says that the major area of psychosomatic research now is in the side effects of unwisely managed emotional crises. When a person is unable to pour out his feelings wisely, they may become impacted and show up in physical symptoms that can be life-destroying. E. Lindemann alerted us to this possibility years ago with his pioneer study of ulcerative colitis (1944).

LeShan (1961) has dramatized this process by his study of emotional factors related to the onset of neoplastic tissue growth and the mechanisms of spontaneous regressions. In papers on treatment of cancer by psychotherapy (1958, 1961), he points out that almost invariably the onset of the disease was related to an emotional crisis that became chronic and produced a long-term modification of body chemistry and that the spontaneous regression, so called, began when the emotional crisis was dealt with in a psychotherapeutic process. This study brings into focus some of the cause-and-effect factors related to the vulnerability we have been mentioning.

Recent studies, then, verify the physical and psychological hazards faced by those in acute emotional crisis and, further, they indicate some of the cause-and-effect elements at work that compound the vulnerability of the crisis victim. Is there any comparable research that could help us to understand how we might cope with the human problems that are related to these crises in our work with people?

Yes, there is some rather significant work that has been done in the last couple of decades, and in the rest of my presentation these will be spelled out. I shall explore these researches under three headings: talking out, feeling out, and acting out.

TALKING OUT

No one has to be convinced of the therapeutic value of talking out. It has become basic to the perception we have of dynamic healing processes emotionally. In coping with the anticipatory grief that a person feels in facing his own death, the work of Cicely Saunders has been imaginative and important. She has found that the free expression of feelings verbally has been physically as well as psychologically useful. In her treatment centers in London, she has encouraged free communication as a way of life. She has found that this process relieves the anxiety that causes muscular spasticity and stress on lesions so that the result is reduced pain. Also, the ability to talk freely about anything that may be troubling the patient brings things into focus and tends to reduce the threat of the material that would otherwise be repressed or magnified out of proportion. In response to my request, Dr. Saunders gave me permission to interview 20 patients at random. The common expression of these patients was that it was wonderful to be in a place where everyone was honest and one could talk about anything at any time. Repeatedly, there were contrasts with treatment centers where they had been previously and had experienced quite a different atmosphere regarding communication.

One of the dangerous trends I see in the management of acute grief is the retreat from therapeutic communication. The use of private or limited types of funeral services diminishes the opportunity to talk about what has happened and thus curtails sharply the whole purpose of the funeral process. The user of private or limited processes seems to be unaware of the purpose of the funeral. Basically, the funeral is a time to relate the grieving individual to the multiple resources of a larger community which can serve as a resonant sounding board for talking out deep feelings at a time and place that are appropriate and meaningful. The private process limits the opportunity for talking out and so proportionally reduces the healing benefits of the process.

Where the atmosphere necessary for socially centered talking out may not be possible for any number of reasons, the specialized forms of counseling may be employed to take its place. But here it is often found that the counseling is delayed until a person has experienced excessive and unnecessary psychic pain. If the talking-out process can take place as quickly as possible in an accepting setting, the additional and needless suffering may be avoided and a healthier direction for the mourning activity may be provided earlier in the time sequence.

FEELING OUT

Feeling out adds another dimension to talking out. We have some unfortunate attitudes toward feelings in our culture. If, as we believe, grief is essentially a feeling, these unfortunate attitudes can do people real damage.

For instance, some people feel that emotions are a sign of weakness and should be repressed or denied. We assume that if we can build a better world through chemistry, there should be some ingestible chemical to take away the pains that come with our personal crises. The use of sedation and tranquilizers to suppress the discomforts of acute grief appears to be therapeutically unsound except for certain special medical problems.

Certainly, all the strong feelings incident to acute grief cannot be expressed at once, but the creating of an atmosphere where valid feelings can be expressed with confidence and accepting reassurance may be an important starting point in the wiser management of the strong emotions equated with grief.

The type of highly intellectualized behavior that tends to deny the validity of feelings may be prevalent, but it is not necessarily sound. Some disciplined activity only creates detours for feelings. Air Force physicians tell me that military jet pilots are among the most highly disciplined athletes, mentally, physically and emotionally. They are carefully selected for these qualities. But these same physicians say that stomach trouble is an almost universal symptom among these pilots. No matter how firm the external controls may be, there is an inner core of emotional response that asserts itself in its own way. With those who are less highly disciplined, it may be even more important to pay closer attention to the need for wise management of the emotions of acute grief.

We do not choose whether or not we will have feelings. The only choice we have concerns how we will manage them. If the grief-stricken person is encouraged to deny his feelings, he is apt to marshall his strength to repress this important part of himself. However, these feelings will continue to exist and they will be apt to express themselves in personality changes, psychogenic ailments, and social disorientation. This is a high price to pay for the unnecessary mismanagement of strong emotional responses to life crises.

Often, the more intellectually oriented members of the community try to prescribe, in the absence of acute feelings of their own, what they consider to be proper behavior for those who are experiencing acute grief. This explains why some of the more unfortunate guidance given in grief situations comes from educators, clergymen, physicians, and funeral directors—all of whom should know better. Their efforts to intellectualize, spiritualize, anesthetize, or generalize about death and grief may serve as protective devices for the professionals, but they are not usually valid guidance for the persons suffering the acute forms of grief. It may well be that those who have known grief and are resonant to the feelings may most easily understand and help the bereaved. These are the persons who can be made accessible through such processes as wakes and visitations, where the atmosphere is valid for meaningful communication and an honest expression of deep feelings.

ACTING OUT

Acting out of feelings is an ancient resource in managing crises. According to Geoffrey Gorer (1965), it may still be the most valid and useful resource for helping the grieving person to manage his feelings constructively.

Every culture has provided a cluster of rites, rituals, and ceremonials around the crisis events of life. These rites of change are usually centered about events like childbirth, the onset of adolescence, marriage, and political, historical, educational, and religious events. The ceremonial acting out related to death is also a significant resource for managing the changes wrought by death.

These ceremonial events provide a time and place for the expression of feelings, the creation of both intellectual focus and large-muscle activity. Most ceremonials incorporate a parade, an emotional climate, and a meaningful expression of traditional ideas. Ceremonials use a variety of art forms to increase communication. They do not need to be explained, for everyone understands what is going on and why. They communicate in depth to the person who is feeling in depth. And, usually, they use a large, knowing, and supporting segment of the community.

Gorer says that the more ceremonial acting out there is at the time of death, the more readily the acutely bereaved seem to manage their grief. When the ceremonial acting out is curtailed either by choice or accident, the grieving persons tend to become withdrawn and maladaptive in their behavior and develop neurotic patterns of action. With more and varied ways for acting out, Gorer indicates, people more quickly work through their grief and are more readily restored to what might be called normal behavior.

Alvin Toffler (1970) says that one of the hazards of rapid change is the possible loss of the meaningful ceremonials that tend to cushion the impact of rapid or painful change. It may be that each age, especially an age of rapid change, has to examine and rebuild the ceremonial forms that help the person to adapt and adjust to the traumatic events of his life. This process would require an understanding of the needs, the values, and the methods that would be central to therapeutic acting out.

In relation to grief and death, some form of funeral practice has always been available to provide a climate for expressing feelings, talking out ideas, and finding supportive group action that verifies reality and accepts appropriate feelings. When times change rapidly so that old ways of doing things may have lost their value, it is important to discover new and meaningful forms of group action to accomplish the purposes fulfilled by the acting-out techniques of the past. Jettisoning old forms without replacing them with adequate substitutes may well leave vulnerable people doubly exposed to the impact of their grief. It appears that people in our age may need the values of sound funeral processes more than ever before to compensate for deficiencies that have developed socially and psychologically. It would be unfortunate if they came asking for bread and we gave them stones.

SUMMARY

What have I been trying to say? I have been trying to bring into focus the research in the personality sciences that bears on our understanding of grief and its wise management. I have been pointing out the vulnerability of the bereft in our culture. I have been trying to indicate some of the reasons for this vulnerability as well as some of the resources we can use in more helpfully managing our approach to these acute needs. And, in conclusion, I have tried to assess our ways of doing things so that we can learn to act more wisely.

As we look at the funeral as a form of acting out of deep feelings, we can see that we have been encouraging some unwise and psychologically unsound practices. But we can also see that the funeral or its emotional equivalent remains the most easily accessible and the most valid resource for meeting the whole range of emotional problems that modern man experiences as he encounters the acute loss that death imposes. Any useful changes in funeral practice must start from an awareness of the needs and move toward the most adequate social, psychological, and spiritual resources available. To these tasks we set ourselves during these days we spend together.

REFERENCES

Gorer, G. "Death, Grief and Mourning." New York: Doubleday (1965).

LeShan, L. L. A basic psychological orientation apparently associated with malignant disease. Psychiatric Quarterly, 35:314 (1961).

LeShan, L., and M. Gassman. Some observations on psychotherapy with patients suffering from neoplastic disease. American Journal of Psychotherapy, 12:723 (1958).

LeShan, L., and E. LeShan. Psychotherapy and the patient with a limited life span. Psychiatry, 24:318 (1961).

Lindemann, E. Symptomatology and management of acute grief. American Journal of Psychiatry, 101:141 (1944).

Toffler, A. "Future Shock." New York: Random House (1970).

Considerations for Our Funeral Evaluations

Marbury E. Anderson

There is a power of positive thinking as well as a power of negative thinking. Both currently are operating in regard to the funeral and funeral practices.
Those taking the positive stance on behalf of present practice are ready to defend.
Those with negative feelings are quick to find fault. The development of these
two camps of thought is unfortunate because taking sides tends to close the mind
to the other point of view and puts individuals on the defensive.

It would appear that two questions must be faced in order to evaluate
funeral practice today. "Is there something in the funeral which is done for the
well-being and benefit of the deceased?" If you believe there is, then your feelings about the funeral and its importance are governed by those convictions and
those theological presuppositions. In a society and state which respect the convictions of each individual, it should be understood that people have a right and
privilege to proceed to do that which they believe to be of benefit for the individual who has died.

But, "What are the needs of the bereaved?" It is to this question that a
society can more freely address its attention, for it is not answered by fixed systems of thought. The needs of the bereaved are multiple, complex, and ever
changing. Not to be overlooked is the fact that social structures exist in part because of the needs which exist in society. Social practices are created to answer
human needs and to render assistance where these needs exist. The funeral and
funeral practices as they are known today are ceremonies which in part at least
have emerged because death brings to the fore certain human problems. Present

9

funeral practices are intended to help alleviate these problems or to assist individuals in working through certain of them.

We can assume that the funeral and present practices related to it today represent a clinging to the forms which evolved because of that which society in past times thought to be beneficial for the bereaved. It is my conviction that we need to assess carefully the special needs of the bereaved today. Observing what these needs are and evaluating what can be done to meet them, we will be in a better position to evaluate contemporary funerals and funeral practices.

It is not my intention to argue for or against present funeral practice. It is rather my intention to talk about some needs which seem almost universal among the bereaved. It is my hope that when we as a society evaluate funeral practice we will do it with an eye to the bereaved and with a concern that what is done is done with the maximum desire to assist individuals in the resolution of those needs.

Obviously, when death strikes, one of the first needs that arises is the disposition of the deceased's body. Whatever else the body represents it is a symbol of the person who has expired. It is a symbol of a person whose life carried within itself dignity and worth. The disposition of that body should reflect that dignity and worth. Death is not the cord which snaps our estimate of human value. Death is rather an opportunity to demonstrate the regard, the reverence, even the awe with which we relate to one another. The bereaved is in a strange position. Death, which he didn't want, has invaded his life, and he is left with the responsibility to dispose of the body of his "loved one." His action in this regard is a responsibility of no small magnitude. What he does is more than a disposition of a "dead carcass." What he does is related to what he thinks not simply of death but also what he thinks of life. It is intricately tied to what he thinks of a person. In the midst of death he faces the age-old question of the Psalmist:

> What is man that thou art mindful of him,
> and the son of man that thou doest care for him? (*Ps:8:4*)

When death strikes there is the need to accept the fact of death. Relationships once enjoyed are now permanently altered. That which has been can no longer be. However, in an era called by some "the era of cushions unlimited," we can tamper with reality. We can seek in the midst of our bereavement a "dream world," and we can begin to live with an illusion. We may in part do it to evade the pain. In the process of doing it, however, we create a situation which lacks reality and which tends to corrode the rest of life. What is needed is an acceptance of the hard fact and the frightening truth that death has come and death brings changes. What makes all this especially challenging is the fact that there are different ways in which this acceptance can be gained. Also, we need to remember there is no point in making the acceptance more difficult than is necessary. All that is really important is that there is acceptance so that artificiality is not allowed to prevail and that the hard work and healing work of grief are made possible.

When death strikes there is a need to give opportunity for the community to express its feeling and to give support to the bereaved. Death is a private affair. Yet at the same time death is a community affair. In one instance, the community is the whole of a people in a given geographic area. In another, the community is a portion of the people in a given area. In still another, the community may be a small group of select persons with whom the life of the deceased has entwined. In some instances, the community is large. In others, it is small. Whatever the community, whatever its size, the death of a specific person has an effect. Generally, the community desires to express itself. Furthermore, the community needs to express itself, for in that expression there is also healing and help not only for the bereaved family members, but also for the persons in the community. The latter fact is made evident in the comment of a friend to his grief-stricken companion: "It makes us feel better if you let us do something."

When death strikes there is a need for a climate in which mourning can take place. Months after his wife's death, a husband related how he had retired to the basement of his home and there wept long and hard. It was a catharsis for his inner self that started the long road to the recovery of his life without his wife. In recent years, there have been studies and the publication of articles speaking of the "hard work of grief." One such article more than a decade ago called grief "the hurt that heals." If there is to be a healthy working through, if there is to be healing, if there is to be the adjusting to a new life, then there must be the climate in which these can take place. Such a climate provides a chance to unburden and promotes the expression of feelings rather than their repression. It is a climate in which supports are allowed rather than rejected, which moves the bereaved from his state of shock, loss, and loneliness to a state in which he is both unafraid and happy to be alive. It is a climate in which the bereaved can build ways of finding continued meaning and worth in life.

When death strikes there is a need for ceremony. Fredelle Maynard (1969) states the case for ceremony:

> I am reminded of a haunting story about a man whose ugliness produced in others reactions of fear and revulsion. Desperately unhappy, he commissioned an artist to make for him a lifelike mask. The mask represented a face beautiful, sensitive, compassionate. From the moment he adopted it, he observed a change in his relations with the world. Fear was replaced by trust, revulsion by sympathy and attraction.
> Years passed. Surrounded by friends, he worried about the innocent deception. Would these friends love him if they knew his real face? One day he strode to a mirror, ripped off the mask—and saw that mask and face were now the same. The tale suggests, I think, a

profound human truth: Practicing the outward forms may in time create an inner and spiritual grace.

The function of ceremony in human life is surely to do for the individual what mask and buskins did for the Greek tragic actor—to raise him above himself. Science may suggest that man is a chance collocation of atoms, an organism at the mercy of unconscious forces. When we participate in traditional ceremonies—from minor social amenities to the rites of birth, marriage, death—we sense another truth. . . .

This, however, we *can* do: we can oppose fragmentation by cultivating those rituals which give continuity and pattern to our lives. A young man once explained to me why, though he had abandoned his mother's religion, he continued to observe the anniversary of her death. "When I light the candles," he said, "she becomes real to me again. I remember her lighting candles for her mother—and I think of candles lighted through the centuries."

Isn't this, in a sense, what meaningful ceremonies do for us all? They light candles in a changing world, creating that sense of order and continuity without which security is impossible.

When death strikes there is a need for comfort born of a living hope and strengthened through a collective remembrance. In the fabric of every life is the potential thread of hope. "I live on hope," wrote Robert Bridges in *The Growth of Love.* "All human wisdom is summed up in two words—wait and hope," said Alexander Dumas the Elder in *The Count of Monte Cristo.* "Everything that is done in the world is done by hope," declared Martin Luther in his *Table Talk.* A man's religion and what it has to say about death need to be expressed, affirmed, and refined in the hour of his grief. Hope is vital. Hope provides the props and sustenance of comfort. Hope is nurtured and strengthened in worship.

A study of the Old Testament is a study in the power of remembering. The sermons of Moses in the book of Deuteronomy, for example, are a call for the people of Israel to remember. In the collective memory of the people, Moses projects an encouragement which would have continued salutary effects on the behavior of the people. In the reaffirmation through remembering, Moses envisions renewal and restoration.

The New Testament likewise accents the importance of remembrance. The central act of Christian worship, the Sacrament of Holy Communion, pivots on the words of Jesus, "this do in remembrance of me." A central fact of the Christian faith is the resurrection of Jesus Christ from the dead. The remembrance of that fact undergirds the promise conveyed by the apostle Paul in Romans 8:18:

> I consider that the sufferings of this present time are not worth comparing with the glory that is to be revealed to us.

When death strikes there is the need to learn to live without the "departed." Something of the complexity involved in doing this is evident in the statements of two parents who have related their own personal crisis.

The first, a young mother (1973), has written:

> The beautiful habit of sharing our daily lives with our son had to be broken.
>
> Through our experience I have learned that grief involves the total person. My body, mind, and spirit all experienced change. Physically I felt so fragile—like a wounded bird. I lost weight and my stamina was half of its normal capacity. I felt the need to be held and touched. I didn't have the strength to reach out or give myself to others. It was too much of a drain to be with many people for a long period of time. My home was my nest where I could turn off the noise and confusion of the outside world and allow my wobbly legs to regain strength.
>
> While my physical condition was fragile, my mental state could be described as having narrowed in scope. For several weeks it was as if my mind could handle only one subject—Todd. Thoughts of him were hanging out of the top of my head and constantly dangling in front of my eyes. Because Todd had been in a peak growth period of life, the cancer also grew rapidly. The autopsy showed that he had cancer in every part of his body—skin, bones, muscle, organs—everywhere, except the brain. His strong heart had continued to beat and his good mind had continued to function in spite of his body's extremely emaciated condition. Consequently, his seven months of suffering left a vivid picture in my mind. To attempt to handle any additional mental strain was a burden too heavy to manage. I found it difficult to make decisions or to plan for the future because of my inability to concentrate. My mind was busy dealing with the most important thing that had happened to me.
>
> In working through grief the most deeply involved part of my total being was my spirit. The word "tender" does not adequately describe the delicate condition that I found my spirit to be in. I felt like a dandelion in the seed stage, where one wisp of wind would have the power to scatter my "whole" into many parts. Emotional issues other than my immediate one were like the winds of a mighty storm and completely overpowering. I found it necessary to avoid insensitive people whom I knew were capable of causing further damage to my spirit.
>
> Perhaps it is good that the total person—body, mind, and spirit— deals with grief. How much better it is that all three slow down. Think of the frustration and defeat which would be experienced if one part were capable of racing on while the other two dragged behind.

The second, Dr. Alvin N. Rogness, president of Luther Theological Seminary in St. Paul, Minnesota, wrote:

> The weeks following the death of our son found me embracing grief as a virtual duty. If, indeed, I have loved him, must I not grieve? If I should stop grieving, would this not mean I had not really loved him after all?
>
> It was at this point that the bleachers came to my help. I pictured him among the "great cloud," the sea of indistinguishable faces, cheering me on. I could imagine him shouting, "On with the race, Dad," and when I was able to turn again to the common task and away from my grief, I imagined him cheering me with, "Atta boy, Dad, now you're making it." I was honoring him by dropping grief and turning to people and enterprises yet within my reach.

When death strikes there is the potential of working through some of the problems we harbor in relationship to our own death. If indeed Karl Jaspers is right in saying, "To learn to live and to learn how to die are one and the same thing," then working through the loss sustained in death can be learning to die so that we better learn to live.

We have discussed seven needs which seem apparent when death strikes. There are others which might have been included. For example, when death strikes, many individuals are in need of forgiveness. They have feelings of guilt about what they have done to or failed to do for the dead. Our partial summary at least highlights the fact of the universality of need in the face of death and the potentiality of a service being extended to the individuals involved. Everyone agrees that death causes extremely trying and agonizing experiences. Perhaps everyone does not realize that death demands from society help which is neither second rate nor hastily conceived.

Caution is needed in what is proposed and practiced, for in death we deal with individuals at a time when their emotional framework is likely to be most fragile. The bereaved need empathy. The bereaved need an openness which is not likely if the community gets caught taking sides. For this reason we propose that when society evaluates the funeral and funeral practices, the starting point for that evaluation be the needs of the bereaved. Society needs to assess whether through present practice or proposed change of practice a wholesome benefit accrues for the bereaved.

REFERENCES

Johnson, V. In Event (December 1972), p. 14.
Maynard, F. In The PTA Magazine (April 1969), p. 23.
Rogness, A. N. Appointment with death. Eternity Magazine (February 1973).

The Kinship of Sorrow

E. T. Eberhart

The funeral exists within a matrix of human relationships and is not a thing apart, an event unto itself. It is a specialized activity relating to human emotions and belongs to a process which is initiated prior to the funeral's beginning and which will continue long after the funeral is ended. The value of the funeral will be determined in large measure by the quality of relationships surrounding it— the personal responses made by friends, neighbors, and professionals to the individual suffering grief.

The more significant responses come from those who enter honestly into the grief experience, those whose presence becomes a part of the healing process, thus creating a kinship of sorrow with the bereaved.

We need only recall our own moments of suffering and sorrow to appreciate what these responses mean to the grieving spirit. For the help we found came not from him who had never sorrowed; nor from him who had forgotten his grief; rather it came from one who remembered what it was to suffer and sorrow.

How precious is such a person. He knows our feelings of loss, despair, helplessness; he understands our anger, our dismay, our confusion. In the presence of one like this we feel understood. It comes in the simplest of ways: the touch of a hand, the look in the eyes, the embrace and the quiet whisper, "I know. I know." From this kinship we find hope, strength, courage—the very qualities we need to meet the sorrow that floods our souls.

In this kinship the noblest human qualities are given and received. Compassion, understanding, sympathy, love. These and many more are made manifest between the one who sorrows and the one who remembers his own sorrow.

Unfortunately, many who want to enter into a helping relationship with the bereaved become ensnarled in their own network of fears and anxieties. They are incapacitated in their ability to give a genuine response. Some will avoid personal contacts altogether, while others try, only to falter along the way.

An example of the latter was the lady making a condolence call on a close friend whose son was killed the day before in an accident. She drove to the friend's home with food she had prepared. But beyond this compliance with local custom she was uncertain about what would happen and about what her own actions and feelings would be and should be. When she reached the home she was quite nervous, but she needn't have been. Much to her relief no one was home. She felt obliged to wait for a while, having 30 minutes before her next appointment. As she waited, she began hoping that her friend would not return before she had to leave. (How many of us can identify with this?)

Her hopes were realized. She left the food and drove away assured that her friend would know that she had been there and was aware of her concern.

Yet later, as she related this experience, she was not satisfied with her actions. They were expressions of escape and avoidance, not of involvement. She knew she had failed both her friend and herself.

Ironically, the appointment she had been so eager to keep was to attend a class on understanding the feelings and emotions surrounding death, dying, and grief.

The distinction between this type of involvement and that of one who enters into a kinship of sorrow is analogous to the difference between the role of a cook and of the ingredients in the baking of a cake. The cook does many important things, but her "person" does not become a part of the finished cake. She stands outside of it, more as an interested observer. The ingredients, however, are in the cake. Their inherent qualities are used.

The lady who made the condolence call did some important things that were no doubt helpful to the bereaved. She prepared food and called at the place of residence. But she did not enter the grief experience with her person.

The kinship of sorrow is created by those who personally enter into the experience. Their presence has something to do with bringing wholeness out of the bereaved's broken life patterns. These persons are different from those who are interested observers.

The funeral carried on in the context of this kinship will have a value for the bereaved that cannot be found in the funeral where this quality of human interaction is weak or absent—regardless of the technical perfection of the funeral itself. Many "poor" funerals have performed their task admirably because of the quality of shared relationships on that occasion.

This poses a major problem for those who are serious about making the funeral an effective resource for the bereaved's grief needs. While the funeral should provide the opportunity for the expression of these significant responses, it cannot insure their presence. In other words, the funeral cannot in and of itself create the needed human responses that will be most helpful to the bereaved. But if these responses are absent, the funeral is irrevocably handicapped.

Therefore, to insure that the funeral be carried on within the dynamics of the healing process and not apart from it, responsible attention must be given to the community's ability to respond appropriately to the bereaved in times of grief. However, there are strong factors at work in our society which inhibit people from responding in a significant manner. These involve the ways in which many seek to manage the pain and suffering inherent in acute grief. One's natural reaction is to avoid as much pain as possible. Our society is sympathetic to this tendency, and in many ways it supports and encourages individuals in their efforts to avoid pain. When this happens, the grief is not resolved successfully. It is buried beneath a variety of denial defenses.

The individual who has sought to escape his own suffering must now avoid honest participation in the grief experience of his friends. Such a person is unable to relate meaningfully to the newly bereaved in their time of grief. To do so would mean that he would have to relive his own past grief. Old hurts would become fresh again and the past would dissolve into the present.

One who would comfort must *remember.* To comfort means to relive one's own grief, not to deny pain and sorrow. The mother who lost a child some years back, sitting with the mother whose child has just died, remembers. She remembers as though it were now. The cries of the bereaved are the cries issuing up from her own wounds; she feels her own sorrow. Once again she is aware of her desperate emptiness. The agonizing moments of helplessness and despair have been resurrected to live again.

Too many people are either unwilling or unable to enter into this kind of relationship. Innovative activities must be initiated within the community if the funeral is to be a dynamic part of the healing process and expressive of the kinship of sorrow. These activities should deal honestly and forthrightly with the ways of grief, educating the community in the ways of its resolution and in the crippling effects if this resolution is ignored. There is a need for people to understand and appreciate the worth of their own persons to those in acute grief. This understanding would enable them to take the initiative in grief experiences rather than holding back saying, "There's really nothing that I can do." Finally, community resources must be created which will actively support movement toward the expression of this kinship of sorrow.

But why? What right have we to ask those who have lived through their grief to reopen the wounds? Why not leave things as they are? Is it really so bad this way?

By participating in the process that brings a person from brokenness to wholeness we are taking part in one of the great moments of the human spirit.

What in life is more impersonal than death! It strikes without feeling or concern about the effects of its action. Yet, as destructive as it is, through sorrow felt and remembered we can transform this impersonal, unfair event into a moment of compassion and understanding. In the face of death, through simple gestures, the clasp of a hand, thoughtful sentences written on cards, the human spirit finds its rebirth, its dignity, its greatness.

How many centuries of human growth did it take for man to be able to achieve such an expression in the face of death? How much unrelieved despair and agony were required of him before understanding, compassion, and sympathy became parts of the human spirit? How many walked alone in unrelieved loneliness before there came the touch of understanding from another?

In opening our own wounds we deal with more than hurt and pain. We deal with the greatness of the human spirit. The kinship of sorrow can make the funeral an experience of hope and meaning; without it, the funeral represents little more than a passing event with no impact on the lives which are shattered by grief.

Tomorrow — Yesterday's Legacy

John J. Curran

It is our human nature that allows us to view our future as an unbroken procession of tomorrows leading to eternity. It is difficult for us to accept the fact that all tomorrows do not belong to us, that we will not be allowed to share them with our loved ones ad infinitum. Consequently, when death intervenes, there follows an awesome separation and the stark realization that some plans, hopes, and dreams will never be fulfilled.

I am convinced that when a life ends, those whose lives have been inter-mingled and entwined with it must experience a rebirth. The process of accept-ing the loss sets in motion an unbelievably complex and intricate program of mental retrieval that can result in a continuous, play-by-play re-presentation of the countless past experiences of togetherness in an amazingly colorful kaleido-scopic fashion.

Now the challenge is presented! To preserve the beauty, the tenderness and the strengths that came from such togetherness—and to hold aloft the treasures that had been wrought for all the world to see. It is somewhat like seizing the shield of a comrade who has fallen in battle and continuing with a determination that refuses to die.

Herein, I believe, lies the secret for still fighting the good fight, for continu-ing to live a life filled with promise that assures self-fulfillment. I have walked in the shadows of the Valley of Death and I have been profoundly affected.

I have been blessed over the years with many friendships and over the last quarter of a century as a funeral director I have been privileged to sit in the center of many private family groups following their loss of a loved one. Often, I had shared an intimate friendship with the deceased. Therefore, it has always been an inexhaustible source of strength and renewal for me to listen to the family members expressing their innermost feelings and emotions. If at those times I had closed my eyes, I could honestly believe that I was again listening to the one who had died.

What they were repeating, to my joy, were expressions of those hidden qualities and strengths that I had recognized and had loved and admired, and now these further extensions of those gifts revealed to me a repository of great beauty. I sensed each time that none of the members of that family would ever again be alone. Hidden away in deep recesses they were probably not even aware of were memories of courage, honor, truth, love, and beauty—enough to last all their lives.

Once, a wise clergyman related to me what he had told one of his parishioners who was contemplating remarriage after the death of his spouse but who was concerned about the possible reactions of his relatives and friends. He was concerned that they might feel that he was not showing the proper respect. The minister's answer, which I'm sure was prompted from Heaven, was, "What you contemplate doing is an expression of the highest regard and love that can be manifested. What you are proclaiming for everyone to know is that the love and devotion your wife gave to you was so all-encompassing and magnificent that you can never again live alone in peace and serenity."

This is the rebirth I speak of that can kindle new fires in life. Added to all that a person was before his loss is a new dimension given by sorrow, a new compassion sorely needed by our world today, and a new sense of purpose inspired by the legacy of yesterday's joys.

Some Thoughts on Grief

Joseph L. McCracken

As a practicing funeral director, I often witness the pain people suffer in acute grief. I am also very cognizant of the difficulties in communicating with persons experiencing such trauma. In one situation, a father and two of his children were killed in a train-and-car crash. Our firm was retained to assist the family of the deceased. When I arrived at the family residence for my first visit with the widow, I found her withdrawn, hysterical, and belligerent. She refused to see me and told her son she would not talk with any funeral director. I realized she was in great shock and suffering the pain of severe acute grief. I also felt that she knew a confrontation with any funeral director would be her first acceptance of the reality of this tragedy.

Denial of death is a characteristic of American culture, perhaps because of the affluence and productivity of our society. We can keep people alive with organs from other humans, control birth and death in many ways, put men on the moon, and enable them to live in outer space, but we cannot conquer death. We can produce it and delay it, but we cannot stop it.

History records the saga of man's continuing defiance of death. So far as we know, people have always engaged in physical activities that carry great risk to their lives. Today, this situation is communicated by media stories of a younger generation involved with high-powered racing cars, drugs, or an "antiestablishment" life style. However, even as death is defied, many questions are asked about it, particularly by this same younger generation. In response, schools at various levels have incorporated courses on death and human reactions to it. Yet,

21

some faculties and administrations are so "hung up" on the subject of death and fear it so greatly that they refuse to consider including educational programs of this nature in their curriculum.

I recently asked a senior high school administrator for permission to show his students an educational film produced by the National Funeral Directors Association. My request was prompted in part by my knowledge of the grief many students in the school were experiencing because of the recent death by drowning of three of their classmates. I also knew that many of the students had never before been so closely associated with death.

The school official was hesitant so I suggested that he review the film. Instead, he assigned two faculty members to see it and then reported to me that these teachers didn't think that the student body was ready for such a program. At my insistence, the administrator himself agreed to view the film, following which he granted permission to have it shown at a general assembly. As I had expected, the students viewed it with interest and empathy.

We know that few people want to die. We also know that too many act as if they believed that if death is ignored, it will go away. Yet it has been well documented that improperly handled grief can cause catastrophic emotional and physical disturbances. In my opinion, funeral directors have an obligation to assist people in understanding not only what grief is, but also some of the ways they can work through this pain. Through appropriate education, people can be taught what to expect in grief and how to cope with it. Such education cannot start too early. A television show, entitled "In My Memory," was developed for preschool and slightly older children to help them understand the problems of separation and loss which divorce, death, and even moving bring into life. Most funeral directors are aware of the urgent need for this understanding by people of all ages.

A funeral director, Forest G. Wikoff, Jr., has written: "As for myself, a member of this caretaking profession which serves the living, while caring for the dead, I obtain a large measure of personal satisfaction in the knowledge that the individuals served by us are thereby aided in the process of making healthy adjustments for the future. I hope they have gained a fuller understanding of the dignity and worth of human life, and have found value in the tribute to that life through the funeral service" (1969).

REFERENCE

Wikoff, F. G. A funeral director talks about the funeral. In "But Not to Lose," A. H. Kutscher (Ed.). New York: Frederick Fell (1969).

Acute Grief, Disposal, Funerals and Consequences

Roy Vaughn Nichols

INTRODUCTION

The purpose of this paper is to demonstrate the disruptive potential of grief by briefly citing from the literature a few of the many studies which report that grief can destroy; to demonstrate the nature of the disposal movement in America by analyzing a collection of memorial society literature and by describing the direct cremation movement in California; and to demonstrate the incompatibility of acute grief and disposal.

While the paper as a whole may appear to be an indictment against disposal and an absolution of the funeral director, that is not quite so because all is not well for the funeral director either. Therefore, the closing portion of this paper will offer some suggestions for bridging the chasm which exists between the traditional funeral profession and the disposal movement. The kind of death referred to throughout the paper is untimely death, and I would caution that the anticipated death following long illness not be confused with untimely death. Lastly, I should admit that the thoughts herein are an outpouring of my own experiences as a funeral director who has contracted for several years with a memorial society while conducting a traditional funeral home.

I

Contemporary American society denies death. So many knowledgeable writers have expressed this viewpoint that it hardly seems necessary to document it. American society has been labeled as death-denying, death-defying, death-

23

frightened, and death-misunderstanding; further, it has been said that the American view of death is absurd and insane. America now has the world's first death-free generation, meaning that it is now possible for a child to grow into adulthood in the United States and not experience a personal or emotional death at any time in his minority. At first glance this may seem to be advantageous; in the longer term it proves to be a disadvantage because it conflicts with and eventually collides with reality. Sound exposure and experiences at a younger age help establish a stable pattern of coping for later experiences.

In most parts of the world, aging, illness, and death are daily experiences of living which are shared by all members of the family and community, from the very young to the very old. Aging, illness, and death are seldom daily experiences of living in contemporary America. The uniqueness of America in this regard is accompanied by many trends, such as a strong youth culture which sets certain moral and ethical standards and is copied by an older population; a trend to use devices to conceal aging; a trend toward retirement cities and retirement geographical regions; a trend toward senior citizen clubs, centers, and buildings; a trend toward geriatric wards in hospitals; a trend toward having nursing homes to care for old people; a trend in the clothing industry to assist in the denial of aging; a trend in the mass media system to portray death as tragic, horrible, unlawful, and unwanted; a trend toward euphemistic language which detours around reality; a trend toward the cryonic suspension of bodies rather than decay; a trend in the medical profession to thwart death with great heroic efforts; a trend for hospitals to deny that death occurs, as when cadaver stretchers appear on the ward as laundry carts to convey the dead to the morgue concealed below a tray of neatly folded and stacked linens. Death in contemporary America, contrary to most other parts of the world and also in opposition to earlier America, can be summarized as being less child-centered, less family-centered, less home-centered, less love-centered, less community-centered, and more institution-centered and more stranger-centered. Death is now the stranger in the night.

It is safe to assume that people grieve over significant personal loss of any kind—especially death loss. The influence of death is more than biological and involves a psychosocial role for those who have a love attachment to the person who died. It is the slow and intensely painful breaking of those love-ties, coupled with a broad range of emotions, both wanted and unwanted, that constitutes the mourning process. Most writers seem to agree that it is very difficult to experience a comfortable adjustment to significant loss in much less than a year, and some seem to indicate a time span of closer to two years.

A final premise, that people need people, should also be acceptable. Man, a gregarious animal, seems to prefer to live in the company of other men. Historically, man seems to have always wanted to share both happiness and sadness with others and has sought to support his fellow men in like circumstances.

Switzer (1) discusses six needs of the bereaved. These are:
1. Release of negative emotions
2. Affirmation of oneself
3. Breaking of libidinal ties
4. Resurrection of the deceased within the self of the bereaved
5. Renewal of relationships with others
6. Rediscovery of meaning.

In similar manner, Irion (2) has also outlined six needs that are present in the bereavement state:
1. To confront and to accept the reality of the loss
2. To learn to live with the memories of the deceased by converting the relationship of presence to a relationship of memory
3. To express real and authentic feelings
4. To gain insight into new, strange, and unexpected feelings that accompany loss
5. To receive public support
6. To relate the experience to a context of meaning.

Irion (3) also suggests that grieving must be done both on the intellectual level and on the emotional level. Intellectual grief can come readily, the mind admitting that the death is real. Emotional admission and acceptance are more difficult, coming more slowly, marked by spontaneous regression—sudden surges of intense distress triggered by old and familiar scenes, settings, or expressions; by sensing the presence of the deceased, yearning for reunion, or hearing the voice of the deceased in dreams; by sleeplessness, restlessness, irritability, and so on.

The wide chasm between intellectual acceptance and emotional acceptance rang true clearly to me some time ago as I walked about the home of a widow who had undergone psychiatric care, had lost her job, and whose weight had dropped to the nineties since her husband had died eighteen months earlier. Everything was in place—his clothes, pipe, tobacco, razor. His picture was in every room in the house. His favorite color was dominant: blue car, blue carpeting, and Sarah was wearing a blue dress. I asked her, "Sarah, when are you going to let Karl die?" Her reply, "I don't want him to die." "But he's dead," I said. "Yes," she acknowledged, "but I don't want him to die."

The power of grief is risky in terms of the physical health of the bereaved. Following the death of a significantly loved or valued person, illness and death become dangerous possibilities; the incidence of various diseases and death increases several times for the bereaved according to several studies. An increase in illness, both physical and psychosomatic, and an increase in hospitalization were reported by Parkes and Brown (4) in a study of young Boston widows and widowers. Carr and Schoenberg (5) cite nineteen separate studies which link grief with physical diseases such as cancer, tuberculosis, ulcerative colitis, burning mouth, asthma, obesity, thyrotoxicosis, rheumatoid arthritis, congestive heart failure, leukemia, lymphoma, and diabetes mellitus. Rees and Lutkins (6) reported that during the first year of bereavement, 12.2 percent of widowed people died as compared with 1.2 percent in the control group. They also found a relationship between the place where a person dies and the subsequent mortality of the bereaved. The mortality risk of close relatives during the first year of bereavement is twice as great if the death had occurred some place other than at home. Perhaps the experience of active personal participation on the part of a family caring for a dying patient at home has some bearing on the ultimate physical health of the bereaved. In summary, it appears to be a logical conclusion that grief can predispose the survivors to disease.

The power of grief to be further disruptive is reflected in the psychological and emotional well-being of the bereaved. The potentially maladaptive outcome of grief has been described by numerous writers who warn of the possibility of the bereaved manifesting asocial or antisocial behavior which inhibits their ability to live compatibly with other persons. Parkes (7), in his study of bereaved psychiatric patients, suggests that ambivalence contributes to pathologic reactions. While the evidence is not as clear as one would wish, he was impressed by the frequency with which mixed feelings of hostility and affection towards the dead person served to contribute to psychiatric disorder in the bereaved.

As a funeral director, I have observed many persons struggling at the time of the death experience to conceal feelings and to "be strong." Partly because there is a sense of embarrassment at the expressing of real feelings and partly from a mistaken notion that expressing sorrow is a weakness, there is an effort by the griever, at the expense of immense psychic energy, to repress emotions that are thought to be negative. In our exuberance and diligent attempt to achieve "the good life" in fulfillment of the American dream, we have lost sight of the fact that sadness and its expression are integral parts of human experience and that there are appropriate ways to express sadness which are just as acceptable in human behavior as the expressing of happiness.

Human beings are vested in emotion. A full range of emotions gives life balance. That balance is perverted when we deny the existence and/or experience of sorrow. It is unnatural to share happiness with someone and not share sadness. Some try to intellectualize grief. Why don't they also try to intellectualize happiness and not laugh? Because happiness is a pleasant, wanted, "positive" emotion and sadness is an unpleasant, unwanted, "negative" emotion. We want joy; we don't want grief. We seek happiness; we deny sadness. We would do well to accept the fact that both are legitimate human responses to experience and both deserve full acceptance and expression.

Apparently what many people do not realize is that when emotions are repressed, they do not go away, but continue to live and fester within the self and eventually force an expression in some manner. Unresolved grief will fre-

quently manifest itself in a destructive way in the grieved person through irritability, hostility, chronic sadness, rejection of others, and even physical illness as shown above. In a study of 50 families with schizophrenic members and
25 families with at least one neurotic member, Paul and Grosser (8) reported
that all of these families had one feature in common: maladaptive response to
object loss. Switzer (9) concludes that successful working through of the anxiety
of grief at the appropriate time is very important in contributing to the later
stability of the closest possible personal relationships, those within the family.

The desire for reunion with a lost loved one was the predominant factor in
motivating an attempt at suicide, reported Moss and Hamilton (10) in a study of
50 patients. In the control group of potentially suicidal persons only 40 percent
had suffered the loss of an emotionally significant person, compared with 95 percent of the experimental group. Suicide may be an attempt at reunion with the
dead person, not simply a road to death.

Finally, some interesting work has been reported indicating that extreme
delinquent behavior in juveniles may be, in part, the result of pathological mourning. Shoor and Speed (11) found that the death of a significant family member
was the common denominator in a group of fourteen adolescents in a juvenile
probation department in California. When they had achieved a mourning process
in some of the juveniles, the delinquent behavior decreased. Gorer (12) concluded
in his study of bereaved persons in Britain that when youth are either refused the
right to mourn or don't do so because of social stigma, they are more apt to exhibit hostile and aggressive behavior which may manifest itself in acts of violence, vandalism, and so on.

Suppressed and submerged sadness will exhibit itself. Beautiful people
don't just happen. Emotions ventilate themselves either honestly or dishonestly,
either naturally or unnaturally, either positively or negatively, either progressively
or regressively, either appropriately or inappropriately. The expense of emotional denial and suppression is in terms of physical health, mental health, com-
patability with others, and comfort with the self. Emotions are dynamic, not
static, and they deserve an honest and honorable place in our lives.

II

The following segment of this paper analyzes some memorial-society
literature and contracts and a description of the "direct-cremation" movement.
The first task is to define the term "disposal movement." Another term, "direct
cremation," is the more prevalent term on the western coast of the United States.
The intent of the direct-cremation movement is to remove the dead human body
from the place of death to a crematory where the body is incinerated as soon as
the permits can be secured from the Board of Health. It is the essence of both
the disposal movement and the direct cremation movement that no one sees the

body, that it not be viewed, that it is not available for funeral purposes, and that the final disposition is done in private by professionals who have assumed the task. Direct burial and direct donation to a medical school are not implied in the term "direct cremation." Therefore, throughout this paper I prefer to use the more inclusive term "disposal movement" as meaning all three—that is, direct cremation, direct burial, and direct donation.

Memorial-society literature was gathered through telephone and mail requests from memorial societies located in Chicago, Cleveland, New York, Paramus (New Jersey), the Bay Area of San Francisco and Berkeley, Orlando, San Diego, and the Canadian province of British Columbia. The literature from the Cleveland Memorial Society is the most informative in terms of the relationship between the memorial society, the individual, and the funeral director because this funeral director has been a contract funeral director with the Cleveland Memorial Society for about seven years.

While the 25 pieces of memorial-society literature would have served the purpose of this paper better if they had been bound into an appendix for inspection purposes, much of the literature is protected by copyright. Therefore, it is possible only to document the source of the quotations. There is little flexibility in the arrangements made to observe the death, and nowhere is there recognition that the type of death encountered might affect the nature of the observance of the death. It must be presumed, in the absence of interpretation in this area, that the service is intended for all deaths with no variation. There is no provision for a child who is killed in the street, compared with an elderly person who has been senile for ten years; for a suicidal or homicidal death, compared with a stroke or heart attack; no differentiation between natural and unnatural death, welcome and unwelcome death, sudden and expected death, peaceful and catastrophic death.

Seven propositions will be demonstrated in the analysis of the memorial-society literature. They are:

1. The literature uses a heavily weighted economic yardstick in appraising the value of funeral service.
2. The literature portrays the funeral director as basically untrustworthy.
3. The literature states that the body is to be avoided.
4. The literature suggests that the ritual services are not necessary.
5. The literature encourages preplanning of the destiny of one's own body.
6. The literature offers very little recognition of grief.
7. The literature instructs that the ritual service, if held, address itself to concepts which are difficult for the person in acute grief to relate to early in grief.

A pamphlet from the Continental Association of Funeral and Memorial Societies, Inc., the parent national organization for the various memorial societies in the United States, lists 109 individual funeral and memorial societies as members of the Continental Association (13). The question-and-answer format of the text contains 26 items, ten of which refer to the economics of the funeral. This is characteristic of the literature. Inspection of the literature reveals that of the twenty-five pieces of literature, 24 of them speak directly (and often sharply and scandalously) to the cost of funerals. Expressions such as

... that you don't have to pay a small fortune to have a dignified funeral.(14)

... in most instances these elaborate rites simply impose additional hardship and cost on the survivors.(15)

... elaborate and expensive funeral arrangements are neither necessary or desirable ways of expressing respect for the dead.(16)

To avoid unwanted funeral expense ...(17)

When in doubt the tendency is to "do the right thing" by making lavish and unnecessary expenditures for funeral arrangements, particularly when subjected to subtle pressures from the funeral director who is being *so* sympathetic and professional about everything.(18)

Such statements are widespread in the literature. It is apparent that the primary arguments used to convince people that they should join the memorial society are economic. The memorial-society literature clearly states that funerals are too costly to be justifiable, thus implying that the principal measure of the value of funeralization is economic. Virtually unused in the literature are the other three yardsticks—the sociological, the psychological, and the philosophic (sometimes referred to as religious) yardsticks. To use a heavily weighted economic yardstick as a value-measuring device to the exclusion of the other three is to prejudice the readers of the literature.

Many of the expressions in the literature generally portray funeral directors as being untrustworthy and cunning and indicate the need for protection from the sly businessman. For example:

You don't have to choose a casket or negotiate for a funeral.(19)

Now and then pseudo memorial societies are set up as "fronts" for funeral directors.(20)

At the same time they do have high overhead and do prefer to sell their "best" merchandise.(21)

[This] memorial association in effect acts as your collective bargaining agent in dealing with funeral directors.(22)

... do not altogether blame the National Association of Funeral Directors if it takes a dim view of Memorial Societies.(23)

It has been the experience of this funeral director, who contracts with the Cleveland Memorial Society, that some of the families I have worked with have met me with a hostile untrusting attitude which has inhibited what could have been a better and more helpful relationship. The kind of expressions above surely do not favor good relationships between funeral directors and clients.

The memorial-society literature is explicit in its direction that the body should not be viewed and should not be present at the service:

> . . . service held with a closed casket, better yet, in the form of a memorial after the body has been removed. . . .(24)
>
> There is no viewing of the remains, and no funeral service with the body present.(25)
>
> The body may not be viewed after the mortician has taken it. (26)
>
> There shall be no embalming or viewing by relatives or friends. . . .(27)

While many funeral directors have built arguments in favor of the viewing of dead human bodies for purposes of reality-testing, most of these have been interpreted as being invalid because of a vested interest funeral directors have in having bodies available for viewing. Funeral directors could cite experience after experience of the positive nature of viewing. Few, however, could approach the candidness and clinical experience of Dr. Elisabeth Kübler-Ross, who makes a very strong case for viewing in the hospital setting (28). In a dialogue with an emergency-room nurse, Dr. Kübler-Ross devotes the final twenty minutes of a cassette tape entitled "Sudden Death" to the emergency-room management of the family in the sudden-death circumstance. Excerpts from the discussion follow:

> Nurse: Do you think that we should encourage relatives to see the body before they leave the hospital?
>
> Dr. Kübler-Ross: Yes. . . . These families should probably be encouraged to see and touch the body. . . . They need very much to be in verbal and tactile communication with the deceased. Many people who have not been allowed or perhaps even didn't want to see the body have had troubles afterwards facing the reality of the thing. . . . leave the face uncovered if it is not too mutilated. . . . family should then be informed about the disfigurement and prepared that they may face a horrible appearance.
>
> Nurse: We have the tendency to protect the family and discourage seeing the body when it is mutilated.
>
> Dr. Kübler-Ross: But you have to understand that you are not really protecting the family. We do this for our own needs.

These remarks by Dr. Kübler-Ross are in reference to viewing the body at the hospital. I am certain that no direct transfer of the validity of these remarks can be made to apply to the "cosmetically treated, sleeplike, lifelike body resting peacefully in an elaborate expensive casket," as Dr. Kübler-Ross told to me personally in a two-hour conversation.

The point is, however, that viewing appears to be very important in some death circumstances. However, the memorial-society literature makes no exception for those certain deaths or those certain people. The directive is clear and concise—there shall be no viewing.

If viewing is helpful for the family, could it not also be helpful for friends? If viewing is helpful in the hospital setting, could it not also be helpful in the funeral-home setting—if proper precaution is taken by the funeral director not to make death look so "pretty" or so "sleeplike" as to confuse the reality-testing? Could not viewing on a cot be helpful? Without the alleged "trapping" of an ornate casket? Is that where the objection is?

Memorial-society literature discourages by suggestion a ritual service of any kind. The following are excerpts:

... giving instructions therein for the final care of his body and for a memorial service if desired. . . .(29)

TYPE I service (cremation, prior to any Memorial Service). . . .(30)

TYPE II service (Burial, prior to any Memorial Service). . . .(31)

Some members prefer to dispense with the memorial service.(32)

... private burial before the memorial service, if any. . . .(33)

If a Memorial Service is to be held. . . .(34)

Some persons prefer to have no memorial service. If this is your wish, write the word "none" in the items 1 and 2 above.(35)

It seems clear from the literature that not only is the funeral with the body present undesirable according to the memorial-society concept, but also a memorial service without the body present isn't at all necessary. To clarify a point, this funeral director-writer is referring not to the welcome death of a senile old lady, but rather to the kind of death which carries with it much shock, denial, and numbness and which slams into someone's life in a tragic and horrifying manner. An Alfred Hitchcock type ending to the life of a significant loved person would in my understanding seem much too swift for the grief-needs of survivors. I would be wary of a person who displays a sudden disinterest in a body, now dead, when just minutes or hours ago the person had long-abiding and deep love-ties to the loved one who had resided in that body.

Every memorial society with which I have become familiar, either through personal contact or by reading the literature, holds out as one of its purposes the opportunity to preplan one's own funeral and to control the disposition of one's own body. The following excerpts are from the literature.

... permanent registry for your wishes to be made available at the time of your death.(36)

... people are choosing every day, well in advance and without the emotional strain of recent bereavement, the funeral and memorial arrangements they prefer.(37)

At the time of the death of a member, the funeral director designated
by the deceased is contacted directly and he assumes responsibility
for carrying out the arrangements as specified on the instruction
sheets in his files. (38)

The Society advocates preplanning and aids those who wish to be
assured of dignified, inexpensive funeral arrangements. (39)

ADVANCE PLANNING cannot be over-emphasized since it avoids
burdensome detail at a time of emotional distress, and also grants
the individual the privilege of planning his own funeral. The person
planning his own funeral is usually less inclined to stage an elaborate
affair. . . . (40)

IF . . . you want to exercise control over the manner and content of
your last rites by thoughtful planning in advance . . . (41)

The funeral is for whom? For the dead? I have been a funeral director over
ten years and I have yet to see a body that needs a funeral. Only living people
need funerals. Of what difference should it make to any of us what happens to
our bodies? We speak of respect and honor for the dead, but I prefer to think in
terms of respect for and support of the grief-needs of the living. No person should
ever manipulate and control the destiny of his mortal remains at death unless
there is no one who loves him. True, we live on in deeds, in memories, in ideas,
in love left behind; but our wishes should die with us. The disposition of the dead
body should be a decision made by the survivors; if disposal meets the needs of
those who survive, then and only then is disposal appropriate. One of the greatest
injustices the memorial society serves is the struggle/conflict of the widow who
insists that she will do what her dead husband has arranged, in spite of what she
feels or needs or in spite of what seems to be sound advice.

The concept of preplanning is admirable when it is flexible and permissible.
It is appropriate to discuss all the alternatives and implications and to voice our
desires. But to place ironclad written directives without knowledge of the circumstances of death, needs, feelings, and desires of survivors provides the possibility of enormous emotional conflict between "doing what I want to do" and
"doing what he always said I must do."

In my experience, the best funeral arrangements are made at the time the
feelings are being felt, at the time of the death itself. None of us knows when he
will die; where he will be; how old he will be; or the nature of the death—sudden,
slow, wearing, welcome, painful, accidental. No foreknowledge of the status of
one's family involvement at the time of death is available, nor of the status of
community involvement or the strength or weakness of our love-ties. Waiting
until the death to make arrangements has two pitfalls:

1. Ostentation—which can be avoided by having a trustworthy funeral
   director or having someone along to think with you.
2. Avoidance—the tendency to abbreviate the death observance sharply

and thus attempt a pseudo-solution to the problem.

If the death is imminent because of old age or terminal disease, then the answers to the above questions can be anticipated and prearrangements can begin to take appropriate form.

Because death cannot be rehearsed, prearrangements cannot be appropriate except when made in a very general and flexible manner. To try to be explicit in securing prearrangements is to be ignorant of the varying grief-needs that prevail with each different death.

One ingredient is noticeably almost totally lacking in all the memorial-society literature—proposals for the treatment of grief and the related emotions. It is almost as if grief and emotions and memorial services and funerals and bodies are unrelated. An inspection of the literature reveals a partial or single sentence here and there in a brief reference to grief. Seldom is as much as a single paragraph devoted to the topic of grief. Several sources do state that "grief should be dignified."

When grief is acute, when death is sudden, when the event is unwanted, grief knows no dignity; it is raw, naked, and cruel, and it tears one's dignity to shreds. To try to maintain dignity or to even propose that it should be possible to remain dignified under intense distress is to deny oneself the right to grieve, to insulate oneself against honesty, and to set oneself up for later possible maladaptive responses. This will be demonstrated later.

Only one piece of the literature, from the Memorial Society Association of Canada, speaks of grief, and it is almost entirely an anecdotal portrayal of grief(42). There are several "for examples" given, but there is little actual discussion of grief or instruction on how to grieve. In comparison to other literature that is available, it is probably of lesser value.

Lastly, the memorial-society literature encourages memorial services, when observed, to embrace deeper meanings and enduring values and to emphasize the quality of life. Following are excerpts:

... emphasize the deeper meaning of the occasion ...(43)

... stressing the enduring values of the life which has passed ...(44)

In a funeral the center of attention is the dead body; the emphasis is on death. In a memorial service the center of concern is the personality of the individual who has died, and the emphasis is on life.(45)

... stress the ongoing qualities of the person's life rather than his death.(46)

... emphasis on a more spiritual level.(47)

... with emphasis on the life of the departed one ... is favored ... (48)

... can be an occasion for stressing the enduring significance of the life that has passed, bringing comfort, fellowship, and inspiration to the survivors.(49)

The implication is that if the body is present at the service (a funeral), it is deathlike. If the body is not present, the service can be lifelike. Does the body remind one of death? Is this an attempt to neutralize death by concentrating on life? So frequently I have read in the many books dealing with death, grief, and bereavement that one cannot fully understand and appreciate life until he first understands and appreciates death. To know death is to know life. To accept death is to accept life. To understand death is to understand life.

From my experience as a funeral director, I am certain that no one in deep acute grief—at the time of the funeral or memorial service—is ready to concentrate on life, enduring values, deeper meanings, and ongoing qualities. It takes weeks, even months, of difficult grief work to focus on these concepts. In acute deep grief at the time of the funeral or memorial service, the mind is numbed, insensitive, or denying the whole affair as a bad dream, or fixated on death so intently that it cannot waiver from that fixation. To alter the natural response of the mind, heart, and emotion, to cast a pseudo-dignity, an artificial calmness over the event, is to tamper with nature's grief timetable and to unduly delay the grief reaction. I know from deep and close experience with grieved people that you might as well speak to the here and now and to the hurt because that is where the grieved person is. There will be time enough later to speak of deeper meanings and ongoing qualities—if the contact with the grieved person is an ongoing one. Perhaps the need to speak of nebulous concepts at the time of the service serves the needs of the officiant, the funeral director, or the memorial society because it is realized that the relationship with the grieved will end at that point and there will be no ongoing relationship.

Let me speak briefly of my relationship with the Cleveland Memorial Society and its families. Except for those few who are involved in the operation and function of the Society, the thousands who have contracted with the Cleveland Memorial Society have been merely mail contacts with the society and exist only as cards in the file. The same is true for my firm, as a contracting funeral firm with the Cleveland Memorial Society. When death occurs, the family calls our firm directly and we perform the indicated function. The Cleveland Memorial Society office becomes aware of the death only after we have completed our work and mailed the file card to the memorial-society office. I am unaware of followup services, if any, to the families on the part of the Cleveland Memorial Society. To my knowledge the same is true of memorial societies throughout the United States.

Summarily, according to the memorial-society literature, death presents one basic need: to dispose of the body swiftly, simply, and economically. The memorial societies do that and virtually no more.

As an extension of the memorial-society concept of body disposal, California now has the "direct cremation" movement. The Telophase Society was founded in February 1971 in San Diego by Dr. Thomas B. Weber, an Atomic

Energy Commission Fellow, a nuclear scientist and biophysicist, who has done postdoctoral work in law and business management(50). In a tape-recorded interview, Weber said that his interest in a Telophase Society type of disposal service was stimulated by his membership in the San Diego Memorial Society, when he realized that the memorial society had the basic liability of not being able to perform all the task and had to be dependent upon a mortuary to complete its plans(51).

After studying the funeral industry, Weber further stated, he found that here was an industry that grossed over three billion dollars annually and yet had remained essentially unchanged since the turn of the century. The opportunity was there to be in the vanguard and hopefully to upgrade an industry. He consequently founded the Telophase Society(52).

What is unique about Telophase that differentiates it from the memorial society movement? First, it is a profitmaking business venture, whereas the memorial societies are largely voluntary, nonprofit organizations. Telophase has the incentive to expand and grow because it is an effort in private business, and it has employed some astute businessmen to guide its growth. There are indications of plans to go nationwide, perhaps through a franchise arrangement.

Second, Telophase is operating outside any public health and sanitation licensing laws in California on the logic that it does not direct funerals, and therefore it does not need licensed funeral directors; neither does it embalm bodies, and therefore it does not need licensed embalmers. Telophase is presently free to remove dead bodies from the place of death, transport them under no legal safeguard for public health, and cremate the bodies as soon as the cremation permits can be secured from the proper authorities. This is contrary to the intent and purpose of the public health and sanitation basis of licensure of funeral directors and embalmers.

Telophase is expanding and experiencing success in its service option. *The Death Report* recently reported:

> Telophase Society, one of the several up-and-coming direct cremation services, is already expanding outside San Diego. According to President Tom Weber, the first associate office, centrally located in the Los Angeles area of North Hollywood, is now handling five bodies per month. . . .
> Telophase, San Diego, handles approximately forty-five bodies per month. Another associate office will open in Long Beach within sixty to ninety days, to be followed by three more offices within the next six months. Tom projects that the Los Angeles area offices will handle one hundred bodies each month by the end of 1974 and four hundred bodies a month within two and one-half years. Assembly Bill 1828, which has already been radically amended to reduce control by the funeral industry over direct cremation services, is presently the only major impediment at the state level.(53)

Since Telophase has demonstrated that present health regulations regarding the disposal of dead human bodies are unenforceable, other similar businesses are springing up. The San Diego Union(54) and the Los Angeles Times(55) carry classified advertisements from several disposal businesses (Cypress View; Dial-A-Mation; California Mortuary Service, Inc.; The Neptune Society; West Coast Cremation Service; and Sea-Mation Society), all of which have come into existence within recent months. The advertised prices range from $187.70 to $250.00, and several advertise "direct cremation, no undertaker involvement." The St. Petersburg (Florida) Times(56) printed a half-page lead story about National Cremation Society which has offices in two counties and will soon open offices in two more counties in Florida. The story offered encouragement to the public to avail itself of the service.

Some interesting parallels can be drawn between the English society and the American society. The disposal rate in England is much higher than in America. Stephens has described how the English society has moved from a land of rustic village scenes and crowded market squares.

> It was a community that hailed every birth into their midst. When the wedding bells rang, they danced and drank their ale together and when the bell tolled they found their unity in tears!(57)

The industrial revolution promised wealth and fame which materialized for only a few. Stephens relates that for the rest and for England as a whole, industrialization and urbanization brought dehumanization, loneliness, frustration, a breach in communication, and insufficient sociological forethought.

> In strict terms, the community no longer exists and these families who are thrown together in a tower block at the whim of an official in County Hall no longer feel morally obliged to care for the neighbour about whom they know so little. With the demolition of terraced houses and back to back slums a spirit of care and concern has been exorcized which even the most astute of sociologists will find very difficult to recover. Perhaps the price of progress has been too great, and for the material wealth, we have sacrificed too easily and too willingly those bonds which hitherto have held us together as both a community and a family. And it is in our surrendering of these bonds that we have lost the ability to cope effectively with stress situations—notably grief.(58)

Anthropologist G. Gorer holds that the lack of interpersonal concern and the public denial of mourning is responsible for the great increase in public callousness in England. Nowhere is the absence of an accepted social ritual more noticeable than in the first contacts between a mourner and his neighbors, acquaintances, or workmates after a bereavement(59).

Personal and public denial of death as a daily and integral part of life, the decline of the role of the funeral as a way for people to help other people, the rejection of the significance and importance of appropriate and timely grieving, even the attempt to have "dignified, lifelike" memorial services with emphasis on deeper meanings and enduring qualities in place of gut-level emotional experiences—all of these are characteristic of both English and American society. Further, the notion that grief and sadness and the admission of emotional and psychological "hurt" are symptomatic of weakness, selfishness, and self-indulgence pervades both societies and promises to grow even more rapidly with the advancement of the disposal movement. Gorer's statement on public callousness in England will become true of America. Such attitudes are encouraged by the disposal movement because the compounding effect of the denial of one's own grief by remaining silent about death is to become ever more reluctant to express oneself to others in their grief.

That America is a rapidly changing and fast-moving society is certain. Toffler(60) speaks of the overstimulated individual, the odds against love, Monday-to-Friday friends, weekend defectors, fun specialists, and style setters. Packard(61) describes America in terms such as company gypsies, three-shift towns, spillover cities, modern nomads, transients, loosely rooted people, high mobiles, and community demoralization. Feifel holds that death has become a "wall" rather than a "door." Death is seen as loss of identity and extinction because of the waning of traditional belief in personal immortality and the potential for redemption. Further undercutting our capacity to integrate personal death is the impoverishment of the communal relationships which girdle death in a technologically dominated society, with its increasing fragmentation of the family, growing impersonality, and deritualization of grief and mourning practices. In a society that emphasizes the future, the prospect of no future at all is an abomination. Hence, death invites our hostility and denial, and expression of grief is slighted(62).

The western seaboard is an example of an area of rapid change in the United States. It is estimated that 75 percent of the people of San Diego, the birthplace of Telophase, are not natives of San Diego. Multigenerational family structures within are few. Regular church attendance is at 9.5 percent. In October 1973, the classified advertisement section in the *San Diego Union* carried in adjacent columns within an inch of each other ads for direct-cremation services, divorce services, and escort services(63)—instant death, instant divorce, and instant sex—all escapes from stress. Further, at a recent workshop on grief for San Diego area clergymen, Dr. John Ruskin Clark, head of the San Diego Memorial Society, stated that of the approximately 350 families that use the San Diego Memorial Society Plan annually, probably less than 20 percent have a service of any kind. Stated Dr. Clark:

> In any case, I find this a rather alarming occasion of what I suppose
> I could call the secularistic trend in our society. I find it alarming be-

cause I believe that ministering to grief, that commemoration of the dead at the funeral service or memorial service are vital to the psychic health, the spiritual health of human beings.(64)

As previously stated, the disposal movement is strongest in California, there are 109 memorial societies in the Continental Association, and the direct cremation movement is currently doing business without regulatory laws regarding public health. I am certain that the furor over the cost of funerals, plus increasing public callousness, plus the denial of death, plus the disposal movement will bring only increased aberrant behavior and further disruption of care and concern for the self and for others in grief.

Ritualized and prescribed social behavioral patterns offer stability to individual behavior. Whether it be in routine daily rituals such as bedtime rituals, work rituals, or play rituals or in crisis rituals such as births, first communions, baptisms, marriages, or deaths the element of sanctioned repetition in expected behavior offers security to the self. This is particularly true when the security to one's sense of stability has been threatened. Anthropologist Margaret Mead states:

Highly stylized activities . . . are an essential part of the whole . . . Improvisation is possible because it can be done within a known and valued frame . . . Ritual, a repetition of recognized forms of expression, cannot be relegated to the past—to antiquity, to barbarism, or to the life of early man. Ritual is an exceedingly important part of all culture . . . we Americans believe that *ritual* is a bad word . . . *Ritualistic* means empty, formal, soulless, when applied as an adjective. And our odd definition of ritual as bad prompts an intolerance of all repetition . . . One ability that man lacks . . . is the ability to invent continually something entirely new. Real innovation is rare and inexpressibly precious, set as it always is within a rich and productive legacy from the past, or a shared view of the present or the future. And if the greatly original artist has to create the kind of tradition on which other artists are able to draw, too much energy goes into creating such forms. Endless (and inevitably mediocre) innovation is far more stereotyped than traditional form . . . A good ritual is very much like a natural language. The important thing about a natural language . . . is that it has been spoken for a very long time by very many kinds of people . . . It has become a language that everyone can speak and everyone can learn, a language that carries overtones of very old meanings and the possibilities of new meanings. I think we can describe ritual in exactly the same way. It must be old, otherwise it is not polished. It must be old, otherwise it cannot reflect the play of many men's imaginations. It must be old, otherwise it will not be fully available to everyone born within that tradition. Yet it also must be alive and fresh, open to new vision and changed vision . . . The essence of ritual is the ability of the known form to reinvoke past emotion, to bind the individual to his own past experience, and to bring the members of the group together in a shared experience . . . (65)

An attempt at delayed grief or avoidance is beginning to emerge from the literature as one of the primary causes of atypical grief. Gorer reports from his study that of those considered unlimited mourners, seven of the nine had arranged for cremations and had not given any formal or ritual elaboration to the disposal of the body. Gorer is "inclined to see a connection between this inability to get over grief and the absence of any ritual either individual or social, lay or religious, to guide them and the people they came in contact with"(66).

Parkes was able to group the widows in his study to exhibit three patterns of expression. One group became severely disturbed within a week of bereavement and remained disturbed throughout the first two months, but by the third month was only mildly disturbed. The second group showed moderate emotion the first week and severe disturbance the second week, but recovered more rapidly than the others. The third group showed little or no emotion during the first week of bereavement, succeeding in avoiding their grief; by the fourth week most were moderately disturbed, and at three months all were moderately or severely disturbed. The last group did not avoid emotion, they only postponed it; improvement was seen subsequent to the third month, but the anniversary of the death posed greater problems than for the previous two groups. The third group of widows also complained of more physical problems—headaches, insomnia, and so on. Thirteen months later only one widow of the third group was rated as having made a good adjustment; the rest all had psychological symptoms of some kind(67). Parkes summarizes the third group:

> In sum, here were a group of unstable young women who were unprepared for bereavement, members of a society of a generation, which has largely abandoned both the formal expression of mourning and belief in the efficacy of ritual. They came from families which either actively discouraged the open expression of negative feelings or were so widely dispersed that they conveyed no expectations at all. Urgent life tasks and the conviction that one must not "break down" in front of children also seem to have contributed to cause these widows to restrain expression of their grief.(68)

One of the indicators that the reaction to bereavement may take a pathological course is a delay in the onset of grief of more than two weeks(69). Parkes refers to the two-week period in several places in his text. He further states that the two features of intense separation anxiety and strong but only partially successful attempts to avoid grieving were evident in all the forms of atypical grief which he has found(70).

Peretz states that one of the basic defenses against unpleasantness is repression. It is an unconscious riddance phenomenon. A bereaved person may say that the wish or the feeling exists but that he is not responsible for it and that it does not belong to him. The bereaved may express his feeling as an idea, but isolates its emotional content. While the person will acknowledge missing the deceased, he expresses this in an aloof and unemotional manner. Another mechanism may be that of denying the reality or possibility of loss. The person who needs to deny that a loss has occurred maintains his denial by avoiding scenes and settings that remind him of the lost object . . ."(71).

The point seems to be clear. Grief is a condition which can be cleansing and beautifying or it can be devastating and destructive. Mismanaged grief jeopardizes physical health, mental health, and social behavior. It is also clear that American society is changing and is beginning to embrace all of the component trends which will encourage its members to reach out for immediate disposal of the dead. The denial of death is heightening. The traditional funeral is expensive and largely misunderstood. The disposal movement allows avoidance and an escape from stress. It is my fear that as a result of these factors the prognosis is poor in terms of the way Americans will observe deaths and the consequent aberrant behavior caused by maladaptive grief.

III

The rest of this paper will be devoted to suggestions—first to the funeral service profession, second to the disposal movement, and third to both groups together.

I would suggest to the funeral director that not every death situation *needs* all that the traditional funeral service has to offer. There are some deaths for which the immediate disposal of the body with or without subsequent ritual service would satisfy all of the needs of the survivors. A service at the gravesite or the omission of the visitation may be appropriate. Furthermore, there is a minority of people who can sustain a significant personal death loss, have no ritual or people involvement, face adjustment, and recover quite well—all on their own. These people have sufficient internal resources to restructure their lives without outside guidance and without an outpouring of public concern. Funeral directors must learn to recognize these situations and appreciate their appropriateness.

Funeral directors would serve people more effectively if they understood that the funeral service, while functioning within the framework of a business endeavor, is closely aligned to professional practice because it is influencing and giving direction to the physical, mental, and emotional well-being of individual people and of a whole society. Consequently, the amount of attention given to the business management of the practice should be held to providing reasonable budgeting and the simple techniques of maintaining appropriate income to meet budgetary needs and return on investment, while the emphasis on education, interest, and approach must be the principal professional responsibility of the practice.

Funeral directors must allow their minds to be open to alternative ways of "peopleizing," which may or may not include traditional merchandising. The basic purpose of the funeral is therapeutic, and the risk of losing the goodness and rightness of the funeral is too great a price to pay for inflexibility and rigidity with regard to merchandise. As in any professional practice, appropriate fees can be realized for services rendered.

I would first suggest to the disposal movement that the basic form of the funeral is good and therapeutic. Having evolved long before any profit motive was attached, the involvements of people, flowers, undressed graves, the presence of viewable bodies, time spans longer than an hour or two, food, periods of visitation, and ritual services were all born out of expressed needs; the functions were performed by family, neighbors, and friends in an outpouring of community love and concern. The evolution of the basic form as a response to expressed need is what makes the funeral right and helpful. Dr. Weber of the Telophase Society was distressed because the funeral industry "had remained essentially unchanged since the turn of the century"; perhaps he has not considered that even though times, values, societies, and social systems do change, the basic psychic nature of man does not change. Therefore, perhaps the basic form of the funeral should not change either. While my intent is to say that the funeral is all right, it is not my intent to say that the funeral director is necessarily all right.

Second, one hears frequent references to the funeral as being morbid, pagan, and barbaric. World history reveals that death observances in other cultures in other ages since written records began have always involved people, bodies, and rituals. If contemporary American funerals are morbid, pagan, and barbaric, then man's death observances have been morbid, pagan, and barbaric throughout history. I want to suggest that rather than man being morbid, pagan, and barbaric for so long, perhaps it may be the attitude of the American mind instead that is morbid, pagan, and barbaric and that this attitude may be an exhibit of social anxiety and denial of death.

Third, I would suggest that aside from an economic value, the memorial society offers no sound reason as to why viewing bodies, involvement with people, and going to gravesites are not psychologically helpful; yet memorial societies imply these have no value. I have the strong suspicion that for the families I have worked with through the memorial society, it was frequently anxiety and avoidance that caused them to join the memorial society, not economics. I would conclude from this that for many, the memorial society has provided an escape mechanism, an evasion of stress. The memorial society needs to recognize this and begin to work on attitudes rather than funerals.

Consequently, I would propose that if viewing bodies, having people in-

volvement, and looking at naked undressed graves are helpful, perhaps the memorial society would do well to seek funeral directors who will provide the therapeutic services without merchandise. Many funeral directors would recognize the
value of this.

In that way, the memorial society movement will not add to an already de-
prived social climate, but learn how to take from the system that which is good
and let the American people benefit from the system. The old adage "Don't
throw the baby out with the bath" has great merit.

Finally, some suggestions to both the disposal movements and the funeral
service industry. Dr. Kübler-Ross has suggested that honesty is the best approach
in relationships with dying people(72). Might honesty also be the best approach
for the about-to-be-bereaved and the bereaved? Both the funeral service profession and the disposal movement could be more open and frank about what the
group is offering to grieved persons. Both groups facilitate denial in some ways.
Both groups misrepresent elements of their function. Both groups are prone to
utter sweet nothings about nebulous concepts rather than speak directly and
factually to the problem.

It would be well to think less in terms of respect for the dead and more in
terms of respect for the living. The memorial society offers respect for the wishes
of the dead in its concept of prearrangements. It seems to make little difference
what the living want or need. I know that this sounds disrespectful to the dead;
I am also aware that most people will do what the dead wanted, rather than do
what they want or need, because it sounds right and is expedient, and that is
being disrespectful to the living. The funeral service profession tends to focus on
the dead body as the principal concern of the occasion, rather than on the living
people.

In an effort to ease the sting of death, the funeral service profession has
negated almost the entire function of family, friends, and community in caring
for the details of the death observance. The memorial society allows no one to
function except in the barest necessary manner. Both are inappropriate. In the
days when people cared for their elderly, their sick, their dying, and their dead
in the context of home and family, people understood the propriety and natural-
ness of death. Without that level of participation, in today's role of spectatorship,
is it any wonder only a few understand death? As in the game of football, one
can be a spectator in the stands and pretend the game is basketball, or get lost in
his thoughts, or watch only the cheerleaders, or be sidetracked passing hotdogs
down the line. But if one is playing the game of football, feeling the pain of every
blow, in all likelihood the game will be recognized as football. If our health-care
delivery system permitted families to care for the dying in the institution and if
our funeral service system permitted daughters to comb mother's hair and families
to dress the body, encourage family participation in the ritual service, use the family
station wagon as the hearse, with everybody filling the grave (I am intrigued by

the number who avail themselves of the opportunity for such involvement when offered), there would be less denial. We need to handle, pursue, and work with death so that we know it is death and not sleep or something else our defense mechanisms permit us to believe. With a basic trust and understanding in the process and its ultimate outcome, a high level of involvement, of distress, of coping, of disturbance will be found worthwhile, and the griever will not disengage.

There is frequently a vast difference between what the grieved want and what the grieved need. The memorial society encourages people to have what they want, in spite of what they need. Funeral directors are similarly inclined. For the good of the bereaved, somehow we need to appraise each death circumstance for the factors which bear upon that one death only, and then structure a death observance which will be appropriate for that death, regardless of what the family did the last time they encountered a death.

A general guideline which seems valid is: The more unwanted and untimely the death, the more ceremony and ritual is needed to ease and gentle the grieved into reality. It is better to have too much observance than not enough. The ambivalence of acceptance and denial existing simultaneously in the same person further jeopardizes the welfare of the person. It has been my frequent experience to observe a person vacillate between denial/rejection and acceptance, all during the funeral activity. That both strong avoidance and calm acceptance can oscillate between surface and submergence is crucial. The critical question is, which condition will prevail? Absence of or brevity of the death observance in cases of untimely death permits the avoidance and denial defenses to prevail and override the acceptance process. A 20-minute memorial service with the receiving line afterwards is scarcely enough to call the bluff on denial and rejection.

Both funeral directors and the disposal movement must be less concerned with "what are you going to do with the body?" and more concerned with "what are you going to do with the concepts of death when death occurs?" Avoidance of grief and delayed grief are the outcome of arrangements which focus on the body.

Finally, I would suggest that the funeral be considered an investment rather than an expenditure. The funeral is an investment in the survivors' physical health, mental stability, and social behavior because, being about the only thing which happens in those first two critical weeks, the funeral will tend to get the grief work started at the appropriate time. Without the funeral, the grief work may be delayed beyond the critical two-week time period, and the risk of maladjustment heightens.

That death is the most upsetting and stressful of all life's experiences was concluded by Paykel, Prusoff, and Uhlenhuth(73). In their study of 61 stressful life events, the respondents ranked the 61 events in order of stressfulness. The top four were:

1. "Death of a child";
2. "Death of a spouse";
3. "Jail sentence"; and
4. "Death of a close family member (parent, sibling)."

Death of a close friend, the only other death-related life event listed, was ranked sixteenth, also high in the ranking. It is significant that three of the top four involved death, which makes the management of death extremely important in terms of future physical, mental, and social health.

The message comes through stronger and stronger from the literature: face the fact, admit the hurt, cry, and do it publicly.

Could the absence of involved social ritual in the disposal movement mean lack of meaning or feeling or lack of understanding of the purpose and possibility of ritual? I believe the disposal movement attempts a kind of nondefinition of death, an absence, a neutralizing, a blank wall, a nondescript event which has no meaning, no importance.

It would seem that Mead had exactly the chasm between the funeral service profession and the disposal movement in mind when she wrote,

> Two dangers are inherent in ritual. One is when the ritual is too rich and the highly elaborate symbolism too old to be appropriate to contemporary life. When this happens, one finds people who are overwhelmed, detached, alienated, and apathetic. Then again, where the individual's imagination, or the imagination of a whole group, is capable of expression that is denied by the poverty of a symbolic system, one may find glossolalia—speaking in tongues, abandoning the structure of conventional speech—and states of mind that resemble schizophrenia. In fact, where the individual has no way of setting his vision, his hope, or his need within any kind of boundaries, within the framework of any formal symbolic presentation, one is likely to find the most varied forms of aberrant behavior. (74)

We find the disposal movement overwhelmed, detached, alienated, and apathetic towards the funeral, probably because the funeral may be too rich and highly elaborated. We see the disposal movement speaking in ways that encourage abandoning the structure of convention. The grief literature indicates that without the framework of formal symbolic presentation, varied forms of aberrant behavior will result. The social tranquilization and muted expression which the disposal movement brings about in the expression of grief will be detrimental.

The death experience should not be fragmented. The body, the precipitator of the event, the common denominator of all deaths, is necessary. To take away the body is to remove the stimulus, the physical element. It is to rob the experience of one of its ingredients, to rob the whole of one of its parts. Abstractions are much more difficult to make "real," and to visualize death as only a concept or an abstraction is to make reality exceedingly more difficult to recognize. Unfortunately, the funeral service profession has placed too much emphasis on the body, and the reaction to that is the extreme of not dealing with the body at all. The overreaction seems to imply that to get rid of the body is to get rid of the problem. But the whole consists of family, friends, neighbors, community, ritual, celebration, grief, body, food, crying, laughter, joy. That is the whole, and to not permit the whole is to deny a complete and proper expression.

The experience of death is critical and the potential destructive nature of acute grief makes the events preceding and succeeding death vital to the well-being of the grieved person. Caregiving professionals who are involved in death must encourage appropriate and timely grieving, particularly to get the grief work well started within the crucial two-week period. That makes the responsibility of the funeral director and the disposal movement very important, and it is past time for the two groups to mediate their differences and join together in one common effort to help in the resolution of grief. It can be done.

NOTES

1. Switzer, D. K. "The Dynamics of Grief." Nashville: Abingdon Press (1970), pp. 195-207.
2. Irion, P. E. Bereavement and the process of mourning. (A tape recording available from the Center for Death Education and Research, University of Minnesota, Minneapolis, Minnesota 55455.)
3. Irion, P. E. The pastoral role in the resolution of grief. (A paper read at a national invitational conference entitled "Grief—Its Recognition and Resolution.") The Pennsylvania State University, University Park, Pennsylvania (Nov. 13-15, 1973).
4. Parkes, C. M., and R. J. Brown. Health after Bereavement. Psychosomatic Medicine, XXXIV: 5 (September-October 1972).
5. Carr, A. C., and B. Schoenberg. Object loss and symptom formation. In "Loss and Grief: Psychological Management in Medical Practice," B. Schoenberg, A. C. Carr, D. Peretz, and A. H. Kutscher (Eds.). New York: Columbia University Press (1970).
6. Rees, D. W., and S. Lutkins. Mortality of bereavement. British Medical Journal, 4 (1967), pp. 13-16.
7. Parkes, C. M. "Bereavement Studies of Grief in Adult Life." New York: International Universities Press Inc. (1972), p. 134.
8. Paul, N. L., and G. H. Grosser. Operational mourning. Community Mental Health Journal, I (1965), p. 340.
9. Switzer, op. cit., p. 189.
10. Moss, L., and D. Hamilton. The psychotherapy of the suicidal patient. American Journal of Psychiatry, CXII (1956), pp. 814-15.
11. Shoor, M., and M. H. Speed. Death, delinquency, and the mourning process. Psychiatry Quarterly, 36 (1963), pp. 540-558.
12. Gorer, G. "Death, Grief, and Mourning." London: The Cresset Press (1965), pp. 114-115.
13. "Funeral and Memorial Societies," a pamphlet distributed by the Continental Association of Funeral and Memorial Societies, Inc., 1828 L Street, N.W., Washington, D.C. 20036.
14. "How to Beat the High Cost of Dying," a pamphlet distributed by the Memorial Society Association of Canada, Suite 410, 207 West Hastings St., Vancouver, British Columbia.

15. Quoted from an informational brochure entitled "Bay Area Funeral Society," P. O. Box 264, Berkeley, California 94701.
16. Quoted from an informational brochure entitled "San Diego Memorial Society," 3656 Eugene Place, San Diego, California 92116.
17. Quoted from a registration and planning form distributed by the Chicago Memorial Association, 59 East Van Buren Street, Chicago, Illinois 60605.
18. "Are We Being Unpleasant?," a pamphlet distributed by the Chicago Memorial Association, 59 East Van Buren Street, Chicago, Illinois 60605.
19. "Funeral and Memorial Societies," op. cit.
20. Ibid.
21. Ibid.
22. Quoted from a form letter by Richard James Stevens, President, Chicago Memorial Association, 59 East Van Buren Street, Chicago, Illinois 60605.
23. Quoted from an informational brochure entitled "The Orange County Memorial Society," c/o Andrew Meyer, President, 2121 Mt. Vernon Street, Orlando, Florida 32803.
24. "Funeral and Memorial Societies," op. cit.
25. Quoted from a letter written by the San Diego Memorial Society, 3656 Eugene Place, San Diego, California 92116, which is given to members of the society and details specific instructions and costs when death occurs.
26. San Diego Memorial Society brochure, op. cit. (Ref. 16).
27. Quoted from an undated bulletin to its members by the Cleveland Memorial Society, 21600 Shaker Blvd., Cleveland, Ohio.
28. Statement by Dr. Elisabeth Kübler-Ross in the tape "Sudden Death," part of a cassette tape series entitled "Coping With Death and Dying." Ross Medical Assoc., 1825 Sylvan Court, Flossmoor, Illinois 60422.
29. San Diego Memorial Society brochure, op. cit. (Ref. 16).
30. Quoted from a membership application form from the Central Memorial Society, 156 Forest Ave., Paramus, New Jersey 07652.
31. Ibid.
32. Quoted from an informational brochure distributed by the Cleveland Memorial Society, 21600 Shaker Blvd., Cleveland, Ohio.
33. Quoted from the "Request for Funeral Arrangements" form of the Cleveland Memorial Society, 21600 Shaker Blvd., Cleveland, Ohio.
34. Ibid.
35. Ibid.
36. "Are We Being Unpleasant?," op. cit.
37. "Daddy Won't Talk to Me . . . A True Story," a pamphlet distributed by the Bay Area Funeral Society, P.O. Box 264, Berkeley, California 94701.
38. "Bay Area Funeral Society," op. cit. (Ref. 15).
39. Quoted from an informational brochure distributed by the Community Funeral Society, 40 East 35th Street, New York, New York 10016.
40. "The Orange County Memorial Society," op. cit. (Ref. 23).
41. Central Memorial Society application form, op. cit. (Ref. 30).
42. Sable, M. "The Positive Role of Grief," a pamphlet available from the Memorial Society Association of Canada, Suite 410, 207 West Hastings Street, Vancouver, British Columbia.
43. "Funeral and Memorial Societies," op. cit.
44. Ibid.
45. Ibid.
46. Ibid.
47. San Diego Memorial Society brochure, op. cit. (Ref. 16).

48. "The Orange County Memorial Society," op. cit. (Ref. 23).
49. Central Memorial Society application form, op. cit. (Ref. 30).
50. Weber, B. The alternative. The Death Report, 1:2, pp. 4-5.
51. Statement by Dr. Thomas B. Weber in a personal interview with William Goveia of Funeral Management Services of Springfield, Illinois, October 1973 in San Diego.
52. Ibid.
53. The Death Report, 1:5, p. 3.
54. San Diego Union, Oct. 21, 1973, Section I, p. 1.
55. Los Angeles Times, Oct. 29, 1973. Part 2, p. 2.
56. St. Petersburg Times, Oct. 21, 1973, Section B, p. 1.
57. Stephens, S. E. Grief in the family context. A paper read at a national invitational conference entitled "Grief—Its Recognition and Resolution." The Pennsylvania State University, University Park, Pennsylvania, Nov. 13-15, 1973.
58. Ibid., pp. 5-6.
59. Gorer, op. cit.
60. Toffler, A. "Future Shock." New York: Random House (1970).
61. Packard, Vance. "A Nation of Strangers." New York: David McKay Company Inc. (1972).
62. Feifel, Herman. Attitudes toward death: a psychological perspective. Journal of Consulting and Clinical Psychology, 33 (1969), pp. 292-295.
63. San Diego Union, op. cit.
64. Clark, John Ruskin. Statement made at a workshop "Ministering to Grief." First United Methodist Church, San Diego, California. October 1973.
65. Mead, Margaret. "Twentieth Century Faith, Hope and Survival." New York: Harper & Row (1972), pp. 124-127.
66. Gorer, op. cit., pp. 81-83.
67. Parkes, op. cit., pp. 138-140.
68. Ibid.
69. Parkes, op. cit., p. 117.
70. Parkes, op. cit., p. 112.
71. Peretz, op. cit., pp. 10-12.
72. Kübler-Ross, Elisabeth. "On Death and Dying." New York: The Macmillan Co. (1969).
73. Paykel, Eugene S., Brigitte A. Prusoff, and E. H. Uhlenhuth. Scaling of life events. Archives of General Psychiatry, Vol. 25 (October 1971), pp. 340-347.
74. Mead, op. cit., p. 129.

Fighting Preconceived Notions

Susan Trachtenberg

I have often been asked why a young person would devote so much time to an extensive look into death. The answer is not entirely clear, but it is not, I am sure, attributable to any one single experience. It seems to me that my interest was triggered by several traumatic events in our family, as well as the bewilderment I felt at the contrast between my own naive acceptance of death and what appeared to be the "mature, adult" ways of coping. Aside from that, I naturally wondered what I would feel if I learned that I were dying. To be alive, to exist—and then all of a sudden not to be anymore. It seemed strange that people were so scared of dying and yet refused to talk about it. They expected death, but when confronted with it, they couldn't handle it. It was as if they thought that they were immortal, and so were their loved ones. In trying to analyze my interest, I have seriously reviewed not only losses which affected me significantly, but also my thoughts on death. Children are extremely impressionable and yet I see how I attempted to resist society's general perception of death while still being highly influenced by it. This paper is intended, therefore, to lend an insight into this problem and to give some picture of a young person's thoughts on death. I am 17 years old as I write this.

The earliest incident which I recall was the death of my father's father. It affected me profoundly because he was the first important figure I lost and because I saw how close it came to destroying my father. I don't know how much of this episode I truly recall and how much of it seems to be a memory while actually it was told to me; I was only 3 years old. I have seen pictures of my tention I craved: out of a sense of exasperation and helplessness my mother exploded. She asked me how I could be so selfish and insensitive and didn't I realize that when she and my brother went off every day it was not for their pleasure;

father which were taken at that time. He was like a transformed man; he had a heavy black beard and a steely faraway look in his eyes. He appeared beaten yet hard. Looking at those pictures always made me sad, but it also made me angry. I would wonder what right I had to be angry but the man in the pictures did not seem like my daddy. So I would quickly skip over the pages in the album which contained these snapshots.

It was a time of tremendous strain on my parents' marriage. My father was unreachable in his grief, and it seemed to my mother that all of a sudden she had lost a beloved father-in-law and that her husband was gone as well. This always struck me as being tremendously contradictory to what I had been taught by my parents. Our philosophy was to stick together during hard times; supposedly, if we helped each other along, we would all come through, perhaps a little battered, but whole. And then I would be mad at myself for having so little "understanding"—after all, what did I know of death, a little girl so afraid of separation, a child who needed to check her closets and leave her door open at bedtime. If I couldn't separate for a few hours, what would I do if I had to separate for a lifetime?

These questions were very real, as was my anxiety over separation, my fear of abandonment. They led me to fantasize about what I would do if both my parents were to die in a plane or car crash. Where would I go, who would take care of me? Equally compelling was the anger—why the hell can't they take two separate flights? It almost seemed to me as if they were making a statement, were saying to me that life without the partner was not worth living and that this consideration surpassed their concern for me. Which, I suppose, meant to me that, since they were all-powerful, their dying would mean that they did not care what happened to me, they didn't want to be with me, they were mad at me, they didn't love me. And I reacted: so go ahead, die, see if I care! The vicious cycle had started—the anger, the guilt, the anger, the guilt. Because, of course, the child, too, feels a little omnipotent . . . might not her anger, too, be killing?

Death, especially that of a loved one, is a harsh reality for children to learn to cope with, and the death of a sibling is particularly an outrage. When I was 6 years old, my brother became very ill. For quite a while it seemed as if he were going to die. In retrospect, there appears to be no way that I could have failed to realize the seriousness of the situation; yet, conveniently, I did. I don't remember very much about that time, something which is, of course, significant in itself. But I do recall wanting to be a very good, nice girl. It seemed to me that I was graciously running endless errands for my mother and brother. I wanted to show them how concerned I was, how much I cared. But no matter how good I was, how much I tried, it didn't seem to be appreciated.

Of course, now I see that again my behavior was expressing tremendous anger; I was convinced that my parents loved my brother better. I accused them repeatedly of this until I succeeded in producing the scene that gave me the at-they were going to the doctor. She asked me whether it was possible that I did not understand how sick my brother was. I will never forget the terrible feeling of shock and disbelief I felt at that moment, not to mention the immense shame. After that it seemed inappropriate for me to go about my own affairs without even a feeling of guilt and sorrow. From that moment on, I recognized all the things I had not previously allowed myself to comprehend. And yet, my behavior was far from angelic. I refused to go to school or learn how to read. And as far as God was concerned, I decided that he was far from benevolent if he allowed such a thing to happen to a child. Well, my brother lived, but in my mind this period of my life is closely associated with death; certainly, three years later when I found that I had the same disease, I felt great concern for my continuing existence.

Several years later I lost an uncle whom I had loved very much. After my parents received the news they simply sat on the couch, stunned. I remember walking into the room and knowing that someone had died. At last I dared to ask—and after some fumbling attempt at preparation, I was told. I wanted to know what had happened and they said that he had "just died." But how, when, where? I wanted to know all the details. Most of all, I wanted to attend the funeral. I was told that I could not. I pleaded with my parents; I loved him too, I also wanted to grieve for him, I wanted to be with his wife and children on this day—to no avail. My mother told me not to be a sensation-seeker and that I should be grateful that I could get out of it; she wished she could. She told me not to be morbid, that there would be plenty of times in my life when I would be required to go to a funeral and that I did not know what I was being spared. I felt very hurt; I thought that she was putting me down; I wasn't important enough, or old enough, to truly grieve for him. I wanted her to understand that I was not being sensationalistic or morbid but that I felt an inner need to participate, to share my sadness. It seemed to me that comfort and consolation had to result from this sharing. I felt that if I attended the funeral the reality of his death would be reinforced in my mind and this would help me to come to terms with it. Today, writing this, the thought occurs to me how many "I wants" this death evoked in me. A reaffirmation of life over death?

When I was 14 years old, I decided that in order to define death one must define life. This hypothesis was the result of having observed an aunt battle hopelessly for life; it took six months for her to die. During that time, I did a lot of thinking. When she was admitted to the hospital, the doctors did not expect her to live very long; yet, the days passed and she went from one crisis to the next. The only thing that seemed to keep her breathing was her will, her hope that something unforeseen might occur, that she might have a remission and live a bit longer. However, one day she could no longer sustain any hope; she told us that now she was ready. I was particularly struck that there seemed to be no despair; there was only finality. She went into a coma shortly thereafter and was dead within 24 hours.

Many things resulted from this experience, including my thoughts on what is today a much disputed subject—euthanasia. When I say this, I am referring to indirect euthanasia—permitting death rather than inducing it. I knew that one should always have a reverence for life; yet I could not help thinking that if we are powerless to restore some modicum of comfort, of "life," to a patient, then how can it be considered beneficial to that patient to cheat her of peace? But my aunt was far from being a vegetable. In between medical crises she was in full command of her senses; throughout her illness she wrote us lucid, beautiful letters. And after all, isn't it consciousness which is the essence of life for a human being? She did not really complain, but her emotional state was apparent. In one of her letters she wrote: "Between fever attacks I feel as if I've been through a wringer. What a nasty business—when and how will it end?" She told us how she dreaded the weekends because no one was ever around. And I saw what a lonely business death is. And I wondered why we should suffer when there is another door open to us, and I wondered whether this was compassion.

Yet, I felt a little guilty for having these thoughts and I never, ever, told anyone that I had had them. After all, the adults never gave up hope—did they? And most of all, she seemed to fight so hard, so why was I defeatist, who was I to give up?

After she died, I was struck by a few other observations. When we spoke of her it was with sadness, and what we said was never negative. All of a sudden she was almost saintly; we failed to be mad at her for destroying her children or for the aggressive way in which she used to demand our attention. I could not figure out whether this attitude toward her was because she was dead and, of course, one should never say anything bad about the dead, or because we respected the tremendous courage with which she faced her death and thus remembered her favorably. No doubt, as in most such cases, it was a combination of the two. The other thing which became very clear to me was how much my parents had tried to protect me. First I could not visit her in the hospital—too much for the child—and then, when I finally did, how I was prepared for the "shock"! After seeing her I was expected to be exhausted because of the "tremendous emotional toll," and yet, guiltily, I was not tired in the least; I really felt that I must be extremely callous. It was hard to take since I naturally did not yet understand that my parents were projecting their own conflicts and anxieties concerning death onto me.

All of these experiences, however, did not touch me as deeply as did the death of my beautiful cousin Steven; he died ten days before his twenty-third birthday. And we were not even surprised when the news that his motorcycle had slammed into a telephone pole reached us—we had been expecting him to kill himself for years. Had I? "That boy is killing himself!" was such a shopworn phrase used in connection with the drugs, the trouble with the police, flunking out of school, and the previous three accidents. But had I really believed it?

Such a brilliant and sensitive person, he had everything to live for.

Somehow I had always felt that the adults must be wrong. Because, during the whole time when no one in the family heard from him, he wrote to me. I always had faith in him; I was sure he would straighten himself out. But then the last time I saw him, I could not deceive myself any longer—he was different, strange; the lies poured out of him—oh God, how easily. Yet he was still the same—the kind, gentle boy I had grown up loving. I believe that the grief I felt at the moment I realized that he was living a suicidal existence outweighed the grief I felt on learning of his death. I wanted to cry out to him, to tell him not to repudiate the help we offered, to tell him that he was worth saving. How much I wanted him to understand that! I wanted to run to him, to shake him; how could he alienate himself from us, from me, when we loved him so much. And I wanted to ask him how he could possibly dread life so much. But when he was ready to leave, we simply hugged, long and hard, and I said, "Stevie, please, please come back." And he promised that he would.

I never could understand how he could allow death to tempt him. After having been acutely ill for six years and constantly living with the knowledge that an exacerbation could always occur, I found it incomprehensible that Steven did not share my reverence for life.

His death was very difficult for me to accept; he had been my hero for too long. But what made it even worse was the desolate feeling of waste which this death evoked. My brother was working at a kibbutz at the time, a kibbutz right under the Golan Heights; he experienced the same emotion, perhaps more profoundly even than we did. We had a letter from him in which he said that every day as he looked up at the Golan Heights from the banana fields in which he worked he wished that Steven's life could have been traded for one of the lives lost taking those precious foothills. Then, at least, he said, there would have been some sense to the sacrifice.

For a long time after Steven died I thought a great deal about suicide, but to this day I cannot fathom it. Even intellectually I can barely tolerate the thought, nor can I condone it. It still seems incredible to me that there are people who do not celebrate each new morning. And so, it is with anger as well as much sorrow that I remember Stevie.

Three months later, in the fall of 1972, I was offered the opportunity to do an independent-study project. It was not difficult for me to choose a topic. But when I actually sat down and tried to make a start, it was a different thing. Where could I begin and what would I include in my study? My parents could not help me—it made them too uncomfortable that I was studying death. In fact, they tried to dissuade me: "Don't you think it is a little morbid? I am afraid that you'll get terribly depressed. Wouldn't you get just as much out of studying something else?" And how could I tell them that their attitude was exactly why I had to learn about the realities of death and dying in today's society? And so I started. simply by reading—reading and thinking.

I became so involved in this study that I inquired into the possibility of teaching a course on it in my senior year at school. After initial objections, this proposal was accepted and I spent a summer choosing the materials and writing a curriculum.

The course has since been taught and seems to have been a great success. I did feel, however, that in many ways my students were too young. Though, had they been older, they might have already been influenced completely by society's concept of death. As it was, many of their attitudes were stereotyped. I was also disappointed that so much class time was used to rehash what had been read; I had hoped that more of the students would use their reading materials as a springboard to do some serious thinking of their own. And those students who did give this extra effort were often very romantic in their ideas. Perhaps, however, when I say that they were too young, I am confusing this excuse with a simple lack of motivation, insight, or inclination; probably a problem teachers always encounter. In any case I still feel that it is crucial to make information on death and dying available in secondary schools. And while the students' initial reaction to the subject matter varied of course, in time, I noticed a considerable "loosening up." After a while, the kids seemed to be able to express just about any opinion without feeling that they should censor it or preface it with some kind of a defense. And it was because they developed this ability and because a free dialogue was stimulated that I, too, came to feel that the course had been successful.

One of the things which I have often been asked since I started my study is whether I now feel better able to cope with death, especially with thoughts of my own death. I presume, theorize as I might, that if my own life were actually threatened, that I would react as would anyone else: denial, anger, fear, depression, isolation, hope, and finally, I pray, acceptance. I think that it is true that to view ourselves as anything but immortal is almost too much for our conscious minds to grasp. It is simply too painful to think of having to terminate every single relationship ever established. And, I think that my own inability to accept death is probably one of the reasons that I want to be a doctor, a counterphobic defense against all this sickness and death, a reaction to my earlier fears.

As far as other peoples' deaths are concerned, I hope that I would now be able to react in a manner that would be helpful to them and their families without being destructive of myself. I hope that my studies have enabled me, while still feeling pain and grief, to better cope with the guilt-shame-and-anger syndrome. If so, if I can help myself, I feel sure that I can be effective in aiding others.

To be born mortal is, by definition, to be destined to die. There must, therefore, be a way of rationally facing this most elemental adjunct to living—dying. A way beyond the extremes of blind faith or complete escapism. A way to help human beings to end their lives in dignity, to help their survivors to go on living, uncrippled, able to overcome their healing sorrow.

Planning for the Inescapable

Robert E. Delany

Practicing law for 37 years has convinced me that many steps should be taken to change our attitudes toward death. My feelings are reinforced by my background as a member of a funeral-directing family. I have long deplored the refusal by the average American to acknowledge the need for recognition of this inescapable event and for making plans for it; I have always counseled that an indifferent attitude induces dire consequences for beloved and quite often helpless survivors.

As a young boy on the fringes of the funeral business conducted first by my grandfather and then by my father, I observed avoidable tragedy caused by the failure of a deceased to consider what he owed his wife and children. What made this observation more pointed was overhearing the occasional comment, "It's a terrible loss, but he did some planning and we have some idea on how we can take care of things."

The differences cited above did not occur because of any genius, but merely because of a willingness on the part of the deceased to discuss his responsibilities with some competent and knowledgeable person: his banker, his lawyer, his accountant, a business associate, a fellow-employee, or a friend with common sense and a willingness to help. Eventually these discussions will persuade most people to consult a lawyer and consider the making of a will. Such action begins an estate-planning operation.

It is not the function of this paper to stress the need for recognition of the inescapability of death. Rather, my focus is on the need for estate planning with the hope that this, in and of itself, will encourage people to consider the broader aspects of death, principally because of the difficulties caused survivors by the deceased's failure to do some estate planning.

Why should a person plan his estate? A primary reason is that it forces him to examine his assets and his responsibilities and to take a look at himself. I well remember one man who shocked me by saying at a will signing that he was going to have to cut down on his drinking. When I asked him what brought that subject up he said this will had made him realize that he should do some long-range planning; that his play days were over; that he was getting his kicks from observing his growing family; that he owed them something for the gratification they were giving him; that one way in which he could repay them was by avoiding self-indulgence.

More commonly, a person has a will prepared because of a desire to get his affairs in order and to make sure that the individuals for whom the testator is responsible (including those he brought into life) are protected until they are capable of independent operation.

An example of what can happen by reason of a refusal to face up to death, is the case of the man who finally divorced his alcoholic wife (a nymphomaniac to boot); she refused to accept custody of their three young children, leaving that responsibility to him. He died unexpectedly at age 41 of a cerebral injury. His insurance, including the group insurance of his firm and a profit-sharing plan which made up the bulk of his assets, named the divorced wife as the beneficiary. He had failed to follow the advice of his lawyer, his accountant, and the firm personnel officer to do some estate planning. His three young children are suffering from the result of his refusal to exercise foresight.

Another case involved a man who was very devoted to his paralyzed wife, who required constant care at great expense. This man opened two bank accounts, each joint with two business associates, which provided for the survivor to take all. The three men were killed as a result of an automobile crash in which they were all involved. The devoted husband died immediately and the other two survived him, dying several hours later in the hospital. Investigation revealed that he had wanted some responsible friends to be able to draw cash in an emergency; further, he was of the belief that having his bank accounts in this joint form exempted them from estate tax; and further ensured that the two friends would use the proceeds of the bank accounts for the care of his wife after his death.

It was acknowledged that the two business associates would have spent the proceeds of the accounts on the wife, but their own estates were little more than adequate to take care of their own families. And no one in any of the families was in a position to sacrifice for anyone else.

The deceased's tax assumption was not correct; joint bank accounts are included in and presumed to be part of the estate of the first one of the joint tenants who dies. This presumption can be overcome, but the proof is not always easy.

Another common problem resulting from a refusal to plan the estate is illustrated by the damage done to friends who have lived with and cared for a deceased for many years. Time after time an invalid who has no close relatives expresses the intention of leaving a substantial amount of his estate to someone who has been extremely good to him. When he dies, it is discovered that he failed to make a will. All too often, the entire estate is distributed to nephews and nieces whom the deceased either disliked or didn't know. The loyal friend and confidant receives nothing.

Estate planning is not difficult, at least not for the client. One aspect which does require effort is a determination of the assets of one's estate. And many people are worth considerably more dead than alive. In one estate, administered by me, the testator's income was so small that he was eligible for tax relief on the real property he owned. Yet at death, his gross estate evaluation warranted the payment of a federal estate tax.

Questionnaires are available at banks, title insurance companies, and even funeral establishments which are completely self-explanatory and can be of great aid in determining the need for planning one's estate. The thrust of these forms is that a single document should list the items, value, size, and location of one's major assets and personal data. These would include the following: bank accounts, both checking and savings; stocks, bonds, and annuities; pension and profit-sharing plans; insurance policies; business interests; real estate; safe deposit box; information on family, previous marriages, and so on; social security numbers of family members; location of will; hospital and medical policies; liability policies; income tax returns; gift tax returns; and military records.

Once the entire story is revealed to a lawyer skilled in estate planning (and quite often an insurance man and personnel officer of a business firm will become involved), the preparation can begin of a will or living trust or similar document of positive value. It protects one's loved ones; it also can result in considerable tax savings for the survivors if the instrument is properly drawn.

Such a document can also provide for an estate representative who is skilled in administration. It is not always in the best interests of the family to automatically select the closest relative as the executor of one's estate.

A continuity in administration is also provided which protects not only a spouse but also children and grandchildren. Particularly, it can make protective provisions for relatives who require unusual assistance, such as retardates, emotionally disturbed or physically handicapped heirs, and so forth.

Proper care can avoid the situation where, unexpectedly, minor children become vested owners of property of an intestate (one who dies without leaving a will) and are required to participate in decisions on disposition or other actions concerning the property. In such cases permission of courts must be sought, legal representatives appointed, and other complicated actions taken, all of which cost needless sums of money and cause damaging delay.

There are many other factors which could be cited as valid reasons for estate planning. But again it is stressed that this paper is not written as a thesis on that subject. The principal advice given here is given to convince the average person that he damages those he loves when he refuses to plan for death, the inescapable event; that the planning is not difficult; and that his memory will be cherished by those he protected rather than neglected.

Public Health Considerations with Regard to the Funeral

Jerome F. Fredrick

Deutsch first formulated the basic principle for the clinical treatment of grief in 1937: the process of mourning as a reaction to the *real* loss of a loved person must be carried to completion (Deutsch, 1937). Commenting 30 years later upon the value of the funeral as part of the process of mourning and its neglect by more and more elements in our society, Paul (1967) stated, "Such ceremonies have been lost to us through secularization, urbanization, and a smug reliance on rationality, and we have discovered no viable substitute."

Recognition of the reality of the loss referred to by Deutsch depends to a large extent on the focus of the funeral—the dead body, or what Jackson (1971) has called "the effigy." Parkes (1965) and Lindemann (1944) both collected data which revealed the direct relationship between unresolved grief and various degrees of disability.

One must look at the collection of emotions classified as "grief" as the symptomatology of a very real disease in the individual (Engel, 1961). In their pioneering study on the mortality of bereavement, Rees and Lutkins (1967) extended the notion of the "disability" aspect of grief by showing that within one year of bereavement 4.76 percent of close relatives died, as compared with only 0.68 percent of a control, or nonbereaved, group. It was further found that the bereaved relatives who died were on the average younger than their relatives who predeceased them. Certainly these statistics show grief to have a negative effect on longevity.

Some of the basic physiological changes associated with grief can be appreciated if one views grief as a stress on the organism (Fredrick, 1971). The pituitary responds rather selectively to stress by the secretion of ACTH, with the consequent stimulation of corticosteroid production (Selye, 1963). Whatever the mechanism for the increased production of corticosteroids, whether via the pituitary-adrenal axis or through the increased output of those hormones needed to maintain microcirculatory homeostasis as a result of the increased rate of induced histamine synthesis in nonspecific stress observed by Schayer (1964), the end-result is the same: *a rise above "normal" in the level of corticosteroids in the stressed individual.*

Very recently, Hofer et al. (1972) observed a marked positive correlation between high levels of urinary 17-ketosteroids and the severity of grief in parents whose children had recently died of leukemia.

There is ample evidence that alterations in the levels of corticosteroids have dramatic effects upon the immune-response of individuals. For example, Kinsell and Jahn (1955) have shown that one of the most profound and predictable effects of administration of cortisone-like steroids is that of inhibition of the inflammatory reaction. These authors found the inflammatory reaction to be a necessary part of the immune machinery and that its inhibition caused an otherwise localized infection to become disseminated, with the resultant death of the organism. In this respect, Lurie's (1960) observation that cortisone deprives the mononuclear phagocyte cells in the lungs of their capacity to inhibit the multiplication of tuberculosis bacilli in their cytoplasm, thereby markedly lowering the resistance of animals to human tuberculosis bacilli, serves as a specific example. The direct relationship of emotional factors, particularly stressful situations, to susceptibility to tuberculosis infections in animals was studied by Tobach and Block (1955). The size of the inoculum was the same for all animals used, and all other factors, such as heredity, diet, and environment, were rigorously controlled. Stressful factors, when introduced, were found to influence directly the susceptibility to infection with the tuberculosis inoculum.

In general, the findings of Nicol and coworkers (1956, 1957) that one of the physiological disturbances that increased susceptibility to infection through an effect on the activity of the reticuloendothelial system (such as the macrophagocytes) was injection of cortisone emphasize the importance of corticosteroids in suppressing the immune mechanism of the individual. This is also echoed in the statement by Reiser (1966) that "stress-responsive adrenal hormones may be immunosuppressive and that the CNS may even directly influence the reticuloendothelial system which is intimately related to immunologic function."

Indeed, the suppression of immune mechanisms extends beyond those involved with bacteria and beyond those responsible for protection against pathogenic organisms.

Since 1950, there has been an increase in the incidence of infections with the "innocuous" or opportunistic fungus Aspergillis flavus directly related to corticosteroid usage (Louria, 1962). This increase in aspergillosis probably occurs via the mechanism described by Merkow et al. (1968). When cortisone-treated mice were exposed to aerosols of viable spores of the fungus, it was found that these animals exhibited a diminished lysosomal response in forming phagocytic vacuoles as compared with control animals. Therefore, the immune mechanism appears to be suppressed against fungi as well as against bacteria and, more ominously, against so-called innocuous fungi as well.

Of great interest, because of the possible implication of oncological viruses in the malignant process, are the reports of Muslin et al. (1966) and Greene (1966) concerning the direct loss (through death) of a relative immediately preceding the appearance of malignant breast lesions in females and of leukemia and lymphoma, respectively. Their findings have been summed up in the observation by Grinker (1966) that if long-continued anxiety can produce a premature-aging syndrome with its alterations in adrenal, gonadal, and hepatic functions, it might be presumed that certain long-standing emotional changes may be significant in the development of carcinoma. Indeed, Hallett et al. (1951) and Ormsby et al. (1951) have shown that in cases of the disease herpetic keratitis, caused by the common herpes simplex virus, corticosteroids markedly increased the viremia.

If the emotional stresses induced by separation or the loss experience (or grief) can stimulate the overproduction of corticosteroids which interfere with the immune-response in bacterial and fungal diseases, then the possibility of a diminished immune-response to viral diseases particularly, including oncological viruses, must be taken into account.

The indications are, therefore, that the grief-stressed individual, possibly because his corticosteroid load is greater than normal, is in a precarious state with regard to his immune mechanism. Such a person is probably much more susceptible to infections of bacterial, fungal, or viral origins than the nonbereaved individual. Of importance is the fact that this susceptibility may extend over long periods of time (Rees and Lutkins, 1967) depending upon the resolution of the grief and the return of corticosteroid levels to normal (Hofer et al., 1972).

Since the focus of the funeral, so important for the positive resolution of grief, is the "effigy," or the dead body, it is incumbent upon those involved in preparing the effigy to assure that the remains do not also function negatively: as a possible source of contagion and infection for the bereaved relatives.

The biomedical literature is replete with documentation of the transmission of infection from unembalmed human remains by two main routes—direct contact and airborne contagion (Weilbaecher and Moss, 1938; Reid, 1957; Purrman, 1964; Hedvall, 1940; Alderson, 1931; Sulkin and Pike, 1951; Sloan, 1942).

There seems to be ample evidence that the unembalmed dead body may be contagious and that pathogenic bacteria continue to develop and multiply in dead tissues (Balbi, 1931; Rose and Hockett, 1971). There are also indications that immediately after death the virulence of microorganisms increases, especially that of the tuberculosis bacillus (Popper, 1932) and of streptococcus and staphylococcus (Toschkoff, 1965). The recent study by Rose and Hockett (1971) showed that bacteria rapidly moved from their initial sites in the body immediately following death. These findings have been recently confirmed in a study performed on fresh cadavers at George Washington University Medical School.

In this preliminary study, using commercially available embalming chemicals, it was found that within two hours of the completion of embalming there were dramatic decreases in the bacterial counts in the lungs, heart, colon, bladder, and so on. On the average these decreases were greater than 90 percent, and in some cases, exceeded 99 percent of the initial count prior to embalming (Snell, 1973).

This decrease in bacterial count was also evidenced in the orifices of the dead body. The oral cavity, the nasal cavity, and the anus of embalmed cadavers all showed dramatic reductions in the bacterial flora as compared with unembalmed control cadavers. This is particularly important because these orifices can serve as portals for the dissemination of infectious materials to the immediate environment.

In a recent communication, the Defense Department (1973) in consultation with public health experts stipulated that as a public health measure an embalmed body must show no less than a 60-70 percent decrease of the pre-embalming microbial density. It seems logical to expect that a greater than 90 percent decrease in these densities should greatly aid in preventing the dissemination of infectious material from human remains.

Therefore, since grief imposes a definitive stress on the individual and results in the over-secretion of corticosteroids through the probable mediation of the pituitary-adrenal axis, and since these hormones tend to suppress the immune-response of the individual, such an individual during the period of acute grief would probably be in a most precarious state with regard to susceptibility to infection with known pathogens and, more insidiously, with opportunistic innocuous microorganisms as well. Since the funeral is all-important for the resolution of grief, and since the focus of the funeral is the dead body, any contact with the remains by the bereaved must avoid the possibility of transmission of infectious materials from the body.

It would seem of paramount importance that the dead body (the effigy), so important in the psychological confrontation with reality of the bereaved, be as free of contagion as possible. Hence, extreme care must be exercised in the preparation of the remains. Certainly, from both a moral and a public health standpoint the thorough disinfection of the remains should be attended to as an obligation by the professional embalmer.

REFERENCES

Alderson, H. E., Archives of Dermatology and Syphilology, 24:98 (1931).
Balbi, E., Pathologica, 23:351 (1931).
Defense Department, United States Army Natick Laboratories, AMXRE-CSQ (Feb. 6, 1973).
Deutsch, H., Psychoanalytic Quarterly, 6:22 (1937).
Engel, G., Psychosomatic Medicine, 23:18 (1961).
Fredrick, J. F., Omega, 2:71 (1971).
Greene, W. A., Annals of the New York Academy of Sciences, 125:794 (1966).
Grinker, R., Annals of the New York Academy of Sciences, 125:876 (1966).
Hallett, J. W., Leopold, I. H., and Vogel, A. W., American Medical Association Archives of Opthalmology, 46:33 (1951).
Hedvall, E., American Review of Tuberculosis, 41:770 (1940).
Hofer, M. A., Wolff, C. T., Friedman, S. B., and Mason, J. W., Psychosomatic Medicine, 34:492 (1972).
Jackson, E., Dececo Magazine, 63 (3):4 (1971).
Kinsell, L., and Jahn, J., Annals of the New York Academy of Sciences, 61:397 (1955).
Lindemann, E., American Journal of Psychiatry, 101:141 (1944).
Louria, D. B., Annals of the New York Academy of Sciences, 98:617 (1962).
Lurie, M. B., Annals of the New York Academy of Sciences, 88:83 (1960).
Merkow, L., Prado, M., Epstein, S. E., Verney, E., and Sedransky, H., Science, 160:79 (1968).
Muslin, H. L., Gyrafas, K., and Pieper, W., Annals of the New York Academy of Sciences, 125:802 (1966).
Nicol, T., and Bilbey, D. L. J., Nature, 179:1137 (1957).
Nicol, T., Snell, R. S., and Bilbey, D. L. J., British Medical Journal (Oct. 6, 1956), p. 800.
Ormsby, H. L., Dempster, G., and Van Rooyen, C. E., American Journal of Opthalmology, 34:60 (1951).
Parkes, C. M., British Journal of Medical Psychology, 38:1 (1965).
Paul, N. L., Perspectives in Biology and Medicine, 11:153 (1967).
Popper, H., Virchow Archivo für Pathologische Anatomi und Physiologie und für Klinical Medicine, 285:789 (1932).
Purrman, W., Deutsche Gesundheit, 19:2389 (1964).
Rees, W. D., and Lutkins, S. G., British Medical Journal, 4:13 (1967).
Reid, D. D., British Medical Journal (July 1957), p. 10.
Reiser, M., Annals of the New York Academy of Sciences, 125:1028 (1966).
Rose, G. W., and Hockett, R. N., Health Laboratory Sciences, 8:75 (1971).
Schayer, R. W., Annals of the New York Academy of Sciences, 116:891 (1964).
Selye, H., in "Life and Disease," D. J. Ingle (Ed.). New York: Basic Books (1963).
Sloan, R. A., New York State Journal of Medicine, 42:133 (1942).
Snell, F. D., "The Antimicrobial Activity of Embalming Chemicals and Topical Disinfectants on the Microbial Flora of Human Remains." (Mar. 19, 1973) (Embalming Chemical Manufacturers Association).
Sulkin, E. S., and Pike, R. M., American Journal of Public Health, 41:769 (1951).
Tobach, E., and Block, H., Advances in Tuberculosis Research, 6:62 (1955).
Weilbaecher, J. O., and Moss, E. S., Journal of Laboratory and Clinical Medicine, 24:34 (1938).

PSYCHOSOCIAL ASPECTS OF THE FUNERAL

The Funeral Director and Bereavement

Paula J. Clayton

The psychiatric, sociologic, psychologic, and lay worlds have recently been deluged by books about dying, death, and bereavement. The general public has been exposed to large public funerals because of three assassinations and the deaths of three ex-presidents. Talks on the bereaved and bereavement are requested by physicians, resident physicians in training, medical students, college students, high school students, nurses, women's clubs, lawyers (estate planning), funeral directors, memorial societies, and so forth. Death, dying, and bereavement have become part of the public domain. It can no longer be asserted that death instead of sex has become pornographic (Gorer, 1965), a taboo subject, in the 20th century. Where does the funeral director fit into the complex phenomena of bereavement?

It seems that each person who works with or studies the bereaved develops his own language concerning stages of bereavement. This author has designated the stages of grief as numbness, depression, and recovery. These stages correspond to the stages that Dr. Phyllis Silverman (1966) applied to the crisis—namely, impact, during which the widow seems to be dazed; recoil, when her awareness of what has happened is reawakened; and recovery, that is, acceptance of the fact of widowhood and a willingness to look for new relationships and new roles. It is in the first stage of numbness or impact that the funeral director serves.

*This paper was supported in part by U.S.P.H.S. Grants MH-13002, MH-14635, and MH-21027.

Research has shed some light on the symptoms and feelings men and women experience in the immediate bereavement period. In a recent study, 109 randomly selected widows and widowers were seen approximately one month after the death, again at four months, and then again at 13 months after the death. The interviews were started by asking the bereaved individual to describe the husband's or wife's terminal illness. After this question, a systematic interview was used and the same questions were posed to every man and woman in the study. Toward the end of each opening interview, the investigator asked, "Who has been the most helpful since the death?" In addition to this question, a list of people was presented to be graded in regard to whether they were helpful, not helpful, not involved, or disappointing.

It was found that children were the most helpful in the immediate bereavement period. There were 132 "not helpful" or "disappointed" responses. These referred to the physician in 25 percent of the subjects, to the in-laws in 22 percent, to sisters and brothers in 20 percent, to neighbors in 19 percent, and to close friends in 12 percent. Less than 10 percent of the subjects found the minister, parents, children, the lawyer, or the funeral director not helpful or disappointing, in descending order. In fact, only one person said that the funeral director was not helpful or disappointing, and this happened to be someone who was a distant relative of the funeral director and perhaps expected some special treatment which he did not receive. A few, and by far a minority, said only, "He did his job." Most listed the funeral director as helpful. Since the interviews were not restricted in any way, there was ample opportunity for the respondents to complain about the events surrounding the funeral. There were no complaints about the financial burden, the feeling of being pressured, and so on. However, there were complaints about physicians, in-laws, siblings, neighbors, and close friends.

In a somewhat similar study in Boston, 40 widows were interviewed more than one year after the deaths of their spouses (Maddison and Walker, 1967). On the basis of their health in the year after bereavement, 20 women were rated as having good outcomes and 20 as having bad outcomes in the bereavement period. Of these 40, 19 (48 percent) rated their clergyman as indifferent and only 18 (45 percent) found him to be helpful. (The report of the study did not mention, however, how this rating was related to the individuals' involvement in church. It is also interesting to note that the respondent's rating of the clergyman as helpful or not helpful did not make any difference in the outcome at one year.) In contrast to the rating of the clergyman, 33 of the Boston women (83 percent) considered the funeral director to have been helpful. Despite the "Jessica Mitford image," when randomly selected widows and widowers are interviewed, the services given by the funeral director are viewed as beneficial. In the author's experience, almost everyone who has systematically worked with the bereaved has positive feelings about the funeral director and his expertise in fulfilling the bereaved's needs.

Why is this so? Obviously, the standard services provided are in part the answer. In addition, ancillary services, such as notifying the social security office of the demise of the subscriber and initiating all financial benefits, are helpful. Also, from the above-described study conducted by the author and another study, it appears that early in bereavement the widowed have great difficulty making decisions and the aid of the funeral director in this regard has great value. Concrete suggestions offered concerning immediate plans are viewed as appropriate and helpful. Perhaps this is why in the study from Boston, the clergyman did not have good ratings. It would appear that the widow also wants him to be decisive, to tell her whether the memorial service should be held in the chapel of the funeral home or in the church, to help her select the hymns, and to plan the service in detail. An indecisive clergyman or someone who leaves decisions up to the widowed is not being helpful. Because of this indecisiveness, the period of acute grief would present fewer problems if most of the details of the burial were worked out prior to the death. However, only 19 percent of the widows and widowers in the author's study had even talked about dying with their spouses and no one had made concrete plans.

However, decisions about the future should be avoided in the early bereavement period. The widow should be advised to make no changes, not to sell her house, not to move, but to wait and see. In the months following, experience has shown that she will begin to rely more and more on her own abilities to make decisions and will be less receptive to outside suggestions.

There are certain symptoms common in early widowhood and a few that appear with less frequency. Most widows and widowers feel sad, lose weight, don't sleep well, and cry a great deal (even more than depressed patients who see a psychiatrist). Crying is the normal, natural thing to do, if the family will allow it. The bereaved also feel anxious and physically ill, with tightness in the chest, difficulty breathing, and palpitations. They may feel and express guilt, usually over things that were neglected during the terminal illness. Several investigators have felt that hostility was a normal component of bereavement. Although funeral directors may encounter hostility in the bereaved, this author believes that such hostility is probably a part of the personality of the person expressing it and should not be taken personally by the funeral director, the physician, the minister, or whoever is involved with the person. This idea is supported by various research studies. In two separate studies of bereavement, it has been found that two people expressed hostility early in bereavement and both of these people were angry at the doctor or the hospital personnel. At follow-up interviews, both of these subjects still felt angry but the anger had switched to someone else. For instance, the woman was now angry at her in-laws who she felt were neglecting her. The man was angry because he felt that his employers had not treated him fairly on the job at the time of his daughter's death. Researchers (Friedman, et al., 1963) who worked with parents of leukemic children have reported similar findings. Several fathers expressed anger at them when the child's illness was diagnosed. As the researchers got to know these fathers better through the course of the illness, during hospitalizations and treatment of the leukemic child, it was found that these men could be diagnosed as having "paranoid personalities," that is, they were angry about a number of different things in life and they frequently thought or felt that people mistreated them.

Finally, there are two symptoms which are not common in the bereavement period. Most bereaved do not feel that they are losing their minds (a fear frequently expressed by psychiatrically depressed patients) and most do not think or talk of suicide (another common symptom of the psychiatrically depressed patient). Many of them say, "I wish I were dead" or "I wish God had taken me with him," but they do not actually think of taking their own lives. If thoughts of suicide or the fear of losing one's mind are openly expressed, it is not inappropriate for medical help to be suggested. This can be done either to the bereaved or to his relatives simply by saying, "You (or the person involved when talking to a relative) seem(s) to be very low; perhaps you should talk to your doctor about this." The author is suggesting that the referral be to the family physician. Bereavement seldom precipitates psychiatric illness; therefore, the bereaved may seek counsel from the funeral director, the clergyman, the family physician, neighbors, friends, and relatives.

REFERENCES

Friedman, S., P. Chodoff, J. Mason, and D. Hamburg. Behavioral observations on parents anticipating the death of a child. Pediatrics, 32:610 (1963).

Gorer, G. "Death, Grief, and Mourning." New York: Doubleday and Company, Inc. (1965).

Maddison, D., and W. L. Walker. Factors affecting the outcome of conjugal bereavement. British Journal of Psychiatry, 113:1057 (1967).

Silverman, P. R. "Services for the Widowed During the Period of Bereavement, Social Work Practice." New York: Columbia University Press (1966).

The Social Meaning of the Funeral to the Elderly

Patricia P. Hannaford

Ceremonies represent the values of a society and continually reinforce its norms. Each major social stage of a person's life is formalized by rituals which provide social recognition for the individual and which also provide continuity for society as every generation celebrates the long-established ceremonies and rituals (Firth, 1951). The gathering together of members of the community or members of the kinship group for a ceremony provides stability and solidarity by reminding the people involved of their membership in the group and reinforcing society's values and goals (Bocock, 1970). Moreover, Toffler (1970) suggests that rituals "cushion . . . against the fragmentive impact of super industrialism."

The study of ceremonies and rituals usually is approached in one of two ways. First, a ceremony is important to the individual because it socially recognizes the person as he passes to another social stage in his life (Maddox, 1968; Merton, 1949; Bossard and Boll, 1950; Stein, 1960). For example, a bar mitzvah celebrates maturity, and a wedding celebrates the beginning of family life. Second, a ceremony serves the community by providing an opportunity to assemble and to perform a traditional ritual (Firth, 1961; Parsons, 1951; Merton, 1949; Lynd, 1929). For example, the ritual of a Christian baptism involves reciting and repeating vows which all baptized Christians have previously professed.

There has been little discussion concerning members of the community as individuals whose reactions to a ceremony may differ from that of the group. Depending upon their individual personalities, they may bring to or gather from a ceremony several different emotions or satisfactions. Specifically, different age

71

strata may experience different reactions to the same ceremony. This paper points out the relative exclusiveness of funerals and the importance of the funeral, as a ceremony, to elderly people.

Ceremonies, although serving similar purposes, vary in their rituals and performances. There are separate and distinct rituals for each stage of life, and although these may be similar, they vary with each individual personality. Consequently, some prefer religious ceremonies whereas others prefer secular ones. However, some ceremonies are traditionally religious. For example, baptisms, confirmations, bar mitzvahs, some weddings, and some funerals are generally conducted in churches and/or include religious rituals. Usually these ceremonies celebrate the more significant events of one's life. Of lesser importance are secular ceremonies, such as birthday and anniversary celebrations. These seldom include formalized rituals but function mainly as social occasions. Other ceremonies, such as academic graduations and nontraditional weddings and funerals, fall between the religious and the secular. They usually have a form of ritual but it may not be religious in nature.

Ceremonial functions, other than funerals, are attended by invitation only, and usually invitations are issued to kinship members and peers. Peers play an important role in the life-style of an individual (Coleman, 1961; Lazarsfeld and Katz, 1955). Career plans, aspirations, and the daily interests of cohorts have a great effect upon an individual and his interests. Consequently, as the youth develops into a young adult, peers constitute a large part of the friendship-and-influence circle. Thus, this cohort and peer group is included in the observance of ceremonies performed for the individual.

If an individual attends ceremonies for his peers and family only, and if he has more friends than kin, it appears that the ceremonies he attends, in most cases, would be for friends. His friends, moreover, would be celebrating similar ceremonies during the same age periods. As a result of this, distinct age segments attend ceremonies in differing proportions at specific periods of their lives. For example, young children attend more birthday parties than those in other age groups. Similarly, most people are married between the ages of 20 and 30. Thus, attendance at weddings would be more frequent between those ages. Similarly, baptisms for friends' children would occur within a few years of the baptisms for the individual's children. Funerals are the only ceremonies not celebrated extensively by young people. Younger age groups attend fewer funerals because there are fewer deaths in that age group. This is partially a result of the decline of infant and child mortality and the effectiveness of medical control over diseases of the middle years (Pine, 1971). In fact, the death rate for ages 1-25 has been reduced by 83 percent since 1920, and the rate for ages 26-65 has been reduced by 40 percent (U.S. Bureau of the Census, 1973). Because of this, death, for the most part, becomes concentrated in the elderly years, and elderly people attend more funerals.

The following chart is constructed from 1968-69 population statistics issued by the U.S. Bureau of the Census. Using the crude birth rate by age of mother, the crude all-marriage rate by age of bride and of groom, and the crude death rate, these figures are plotted on a graph representing the chronological age of an individual.

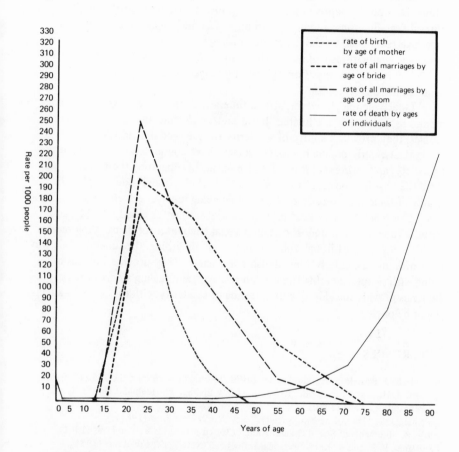

The chart presents the rates for three ceremonies over an individual's lifetime. First, the rate of marriage by age for both bride and groom reaches a peak between 17 and 35. Similarly, the rate of birth by age of mother (which correlates with the age of the mothers at baby baptisms) is highest between ages 20 and 30. Finally, the death rate by age of individual is such that deaths, and consequently, funerals are infrequent until after age 60.

There are ceremonies which are not easily plotted on a graph and which are also interesting to investigate. Birthday parties are often difficult to define by age.

For young children, the "party" may include cake, ice cream, gifts, and games; for teenagers, it may be a "party" with food and music; for young marrieds, it may be a dinner party; and in some senior-citizen centers, it may include a recognizing "birthday song" and a cake shared with several others.

However, most ceremonies are celebrated by or for adolescents or young adults. Beyond the baptisms and weddings mentioned earlier, there are bar mitzvahs, graduations, and housewarmings. The median age of a "new home" mortgage taker is 30.8 (U.S. Dept. of Housing and Urban Development, 1968). Moreover, graduations from high school and college usually occur at about 18 and 22 years, respectively. Consequently, younger people are frequently in attendance at these ceremonies.

Elderly people, however, attend funerals. There are few "younger" ceremonies to which they are invited. But even though funerals are unhappy ceremonies, they provide a source of solidarity for the aged individuals.

Most elderly people in modern society have completed their contribution to society, and retirement is an effective means of separating these elderly people from the ongoing society. This exclusion from "functional" society plus the deaths of their peers results in older people being lonely.

Ceremonies of any kind provide a social setting for elderly people, and because funerals are the most common social encounter for many, they serve a positive function. Although solemn, and often disturbing, the funeral is one way of reinforcing the elderly's membership in society. They provide a means of being with people, greeting friends and relatives, and feeling a part of society. Funerals provide the elderly with a feeling of solidarity with the society—a feeling of belonging.

REFERENCES

Bocock, R. J. Ritual: civic and religious. British Journal of Sociology, 21:285 (1970).

Bossard, J. H. S. and E. S. Boll. "Ritual in Family Living." Philadelphia: University of Pennsylvania Press (1950).

Coleman, J. S. "The Adolescent Society." New York: Free Press (1961).

Firth, R. "Elements of Social Organization." (3rd ed.). Boston: Beacon Press (1961).

Lazarsfeld, P. F. and K. Katz. "Personal Influence." New York: Free Press (1955).

Lynd, R. S. and H. M. Lynd. "Middletown." New York: Harcourt, Brace (1929).

Maddox, G. L. Retirement as a social event in the United States. In B. L. Neugarten (Ed.), "Middle Age and Aging: A Reader in Social Psychology." Chicago: University of Chicago Press (1968).

Merton, R. K. "Social Theory and Social Structure." New York: Free Press (1949).

Parsons, T. "The Social System." New York: Free Press (1951).

Pine, V. R. Social organization and death. Omega, 3:149 (1971).

Stein, M. R. "The Eclipse of Community." New York: Harper and Row (1960).

Toffler, A. "Future Shock." New York: Random House (1970).

U.S. Bureau of the Census. "Statistical Abstracts of the United States" (94th ed.). Washington, D. C.: U.S. Government Printing Office (1973).

U.S. Department of Housing and Urban Development. "HUD Statistical Yearbook." Washington, D. C.: U.S. Government Printing Office (1968).

Grief Therapy for the Bereaved

Willadean W. Turner

Grief stems from the fact that every person who dies has been an entity in himself and every death provokes specific reactions in specific individuals. The subconscious activities of the bereaved are directly affected by this fact, and reactions vary according to individual emotional responses. Man is to a great extent unpredictable when under emotional or physical stress. Because of this, those who are bereaved should be provided with an outlet during the emotional crisis, as well as a certain amount of grief therapy.

Bereavement is a most common cause of family disintegration. Any member of a family may be involved. While all families are eventually disrupted by bereavement, death rates have decreased due to the advancement of medicine and health practices (Jackson, 1953).

During the mourning period, the bereaved person remembers the deceased as he was when he lived (Irion, 1954). He reminisces about any or all affiliations he had with the deceased. As painful as it is for him to face the reality of his bereavement, in grieving he can reveal his true feelings. Grief reactions expressed through tears, conversation, and the recollection of experiences shared with the deceased help ease the pain of grief. Any mention or thought of the deceased usually activates tears. This is a normal reaction.

Religious persons frequently use religious symbols in seeking help in grief. Symbols may take the form of an altar, a cross, a crucifix, or the church. The bereaved feels he must have something he can see or touch in his hour of need. In this case, the minister and the immediate family members can perform a great service to the mourner by helping him to grieve normally (Irion, 1954). While asking the questions needed for the obituary or parish records, the minister helps the person to express his feelings freely. When the minister expresses his own belief in God, he can assist the bereaved in doing likewise. In certain situations, this will help relieve some of the pressures of the mourning period.

"Organ music should have a consoling radiance" (Fos, 1969). When playing for a memorial or funeral service, the organist should produce clean, uprising sounds, as opposed to the heavy, ponderous tones which the organ is capable of making. As an organist who has played at many funerals, I try, when playing the incidental music before the service, to play a variety of pieces which tend to "say something" to each waiting individual. My greatest satisfaction during this period is to hear someone hum along with the music being played. I feel that the music then is reaching someone, and relieving some part of the emotional burden of the occasion. The choice of composition or piece played is very important. Although I never really have a planned program (which includes organ and vocal solos), I am able to determine what to play or sing as the family members enter the chapel. If they are emotionally demonstrative, I try to add nothing to upset them further. If, however, they are controlled, I become empathetic and perform what I would like to hear were I among the bereaved. Certain kinds of phrases will immediately cause people to sit up straight, to look as if they were interested in taking hold of reality, to view the future as a challenge with which they can cope. Other kinds of music can affect people who already are too excited and bring them right down, giving them great quiet and peace. Thus, music can comfort a person under the pressures of great sorrow, distress, and overwhelming odds. The musician can elevate a person or can depress him. One can do so many things with music because it is abstract, not concrete like something to be read. Music is stronger and takes a firmer hold on the emotions. The organist's touch is all-important.

The funeral director has a large role in the funeral arrangements. He is no longer limited to preparing the deceased for burial. He performs many other services, as his duties usually require his "furnishing the chapel, musicians, pall bearers, transportation, ordering flowers, making all the necessary arrangements" (Irion, 1954). The funeral director is the administrator of the greatest portion of the funeral rites and plays a large role in assisting the bereaved family.

After the funeral, relatives and friends will visit the bereaved family (Gorer, 1965). They will give a great deal of thought to initiating this first visit, what they should do, and how their efforts will affect the immediate survivors. Should they talk about the deceased? Will the mourners respond with tears? How can they offer sympathy to the family without creating a disturbing (to all) emotional display?

During the mourning period the bereaved family may stay away from public functions for a prescribed period of time. The decision of the family to express its grief publicly is optional. Whatever the family members decide does not alter the fact that their grief is real and the hurt is deep. If a person can be helped to really feel his bereavement, the pain will be moderate.

Grief is said to be a complex, or mixed, emotion. A person experiencing grief will experience times of love, hate, fear, and many other forms of emotions (Peters, 1960). The most important factor in communicating with bereaved people is not what we say, or even what we do, but what we are. Unfortunately, our communication habits are rarely related to our psychological needs. Consequently, we are the victims of a conflict between what we are and what we are expected to be. Our words and gestures frequently are not consistent with our real self, and we communicate something other than what we wish.

Life must be made meaningful for the bereaved person, and death should become of secondary importance. He must be helped to realize that grief, sorrow, and deprivation are not the ultimate things, but only incidental to the larger significance of life.

REFERENCES

Donald, W. C., II. Understanding and meeting the needs of the bereaved. Casket and Sunnyside, 85:10 (1955).

Fos, V. Organ music should have "A Consoling Radiance." American Funeral Director, 92:29 (1969).

Gorer, G. "Death, Grief and Mourning." Garden City, New York: Doubleday (1965).

Irion, P. E. "The Funeral and the Mourners." New York: Abingdon Press (1954).

Jackson, E. N. "Understanding Grief." New York: Abingdon Press (1953).

Peters, C. A. How to deal with grief. Casket and Sunnyside, 90:28 (1960).

Spriggs, A. O. "The Art and Science of Embalming." Springfield, Ohio: The Champion Company (1959).

The Psychotherapeutics of Pastoral Care

Eugene T. Dyszlewski and Daniel J. Cherico

The circumstances surrounding death have effects both varied and intense upon those involved. The delicacy and intimacy of the situation often structure and limit contacts that the dying and bereaved have with other individuals. One of the few persons whose intervention is recognized as appropriate if not necessary is the minister. Unquestionably, his involvement is theologically mandated as essential not only to his office but also to his role in the community. Yet despite its singular importance, the minister's proper intervention in the death situation is often unclear. The expectations of the dying and bereaved are at times different from the minister's role perceptions (Kutscher and Kutscher, 1972). A need to go beyond the liturgical role into a personal involvement is generally recognized, but the attempt can be thwarted by feelings of inadequacy compounded by a reluctance to wander into the realm of psychotherapy.

The minister has been assigned a central role in the funeral. The funeral service very much is in his domain. The performance of his ritual-symbolic role in the liturgy is not to be lightly regarded. Indeed, it has a major psychotherapeutically potent and palliative effect upon those experiencing grief. The formality of community prayer and public worship presided over by the clergyman, however, does tend to obscure many of the feelings of the bereaved. Nonetheless, the formal service begins rather than exhausts the possibilities of ministerial involvement at the time of the funeral.

We seem to feel that we have come a long way since the time when the pastor was physician, lawyer, and counselor, and everyone sought final certitude in theology and the authoritative voices of the ancients. However, we must not be misled into permitting certain aspects of our daily lives to be unduly usurped by "experts," and we must also not be intimidated by the sciences. The therapeutic possibilities in human relations are not in the exclusive domain of the psychotherapist. His qualities of humanness and personhood are the basis of the help he offers, but he holds no copyright on warmth, understanding, and communication.

There is available, despite the many and varied theoretical postures, fundamental research dealing with what appear to be some of the major bases of psychotherapy. These all have to do with qualities or dimensions of human relationships. Researchers and theorists designate three particularly important qualities of human relationships: (1) genuineness or authenticity; (2) nonpossessive warmth, an atmosphere of safety and trust, or, better still, love; and (3) accurate empathic understanding—being able to "be with," to appreciate the meaning of the client. These ingredients, as aspects of human encounters, underlie psychoanalytic, nondirective, eclectic, and learning-theory approaches to psychotherapy.

It perhaps becomes questionable to break up relationships into three qualities—we may just be creating three ways of saying the same thing with different nuances. However, concept and myth must be created in order to be able to analyze and communicate or we would not have both science and philosophy. We might just as easily use the biblical model of human encounters and speak in terms of "emeth" and "hesed." Nevertheless, in investigating the three-element model, behavioral science research seems to indicate its usefulness very strongly.

An analysis of the literature on therapeutic process and outcome from evidence presented in 16 studies of 2,588 therapist-client interactions spanning the spectrum of hospital-clinic, pathology-adjustment, and inpatient-outpatient situations by Truax and Mitchell (1971) states: "These studies taken together suggest that therapists or counselors who are accurately empathic, nonpossessively warm in attitude, and genuine are indeed effective. Also, these findings seem to hold with a wide variety of therapists and counselors, regardless of their training or theoretic orientation . . . ." Further, the implications this may have for psychotherapeutic training and practice include the "inherently helpful person" hypothesis as one possibility.

Bergin (1966; 1967; 1971), also analyzing therapeutic outcomes and addressing himself to the question of spontaneous recovery of untreated psychoneurotic patients, pointed out that a number of these people, rather than avoiding therapy, actually sought and obtained help from nonprofessionals (friends and relatives) and lay counselors (clergy, lawyers, and general physicians). Distressed people can discover therapeutically potent agents as they exist naturally in society.

A number of experiments and empirical investigations have been undertaken on the use of nonprofessionals as psychotherapists. Many studies have indicated that college student volunteers could work successfully with schizophrenics. Other studies have shown that chronic patients seeing college student volunteers have a much higher discharge rate than could be expected and show greater improvement than do control patients in the studies (Beck, Kantor, and Gelineau, 1963). Also Carkhuff and Truax (1965) have reported that lay group counselors have a uniform positive effect on patients compared with control patients.

In fact, evidence from individual studies and series of studies and surveys of the reported literature do not demonstrate that the trained psychotherapeutic professional, on the average, is more effective than minimally trained or untrained nonprofessionals. Furthermore, studies of nonprofessionals involved in psychotherapeutic intervention indicate their positive effectiveness. Gurin, Veroff, and Feld (1960), in a rare examination of the use and effects of trained and untrained helpers, found that more people turn for assistance to a clergyman than to any other professional. A higher percentage of those "treated" by the clergy feel the intervention was successful than do those treated by psychologists and psychiatrists.

The allied mental health professions have not ignored these data and have moved to avail themselves of this valuable resource. In fact, the decade of the 1960's brought a vast reconceptualization of mental health care. The roles and positions of the established professions were reviewed and many roles traditionally performed exclusively by professionals were relegated to persons with limited education, skill, and experience. Thus, training was discarded as a prerequisite and could occur after employment. Community agencies hired the unskilled poor from their own neighborhoods to perform functions previously in the domain of highly skilled professionals (Pearl and Reissman, 1965). This change was easily translated into the hospital context. A number of psychiatric institutions have reported using paraprofessionals in psychotherapeutic capacities (Euster, 1971; McPheeters, King, and Teare, 1972; Ellsworth, 1968).

This development, though recent, is not without precedent. Hospital psychiatry, where it existed, in the 19th century, pre-Freudian era was almost exclusively the domain of the keepers or attendants until gradually the role of the physician in the treatment of the insane began to grow. Effective hospital treatment seems to have started around 1792 when the French physician Pinel broke the chains of patients and replaced imprisonment and punishment with humane treatment and care. The heart of this approach, "moral treatment," was the quality of philanthropy, an active quality of love for mankind (Pinel, 1806).

Under the influence of the Society of Friends many hospitals, founded on these principles and following the sage instruction of biblical literature, continued this treatment model (Tuke, 1813). Mid-19th-century psychiatry, having accepted the moral-treatment philosophy, defined it fundamentally as treating patients with kindness and benevolence (Earle, 1844). The model of philanthropy (kindness) benevolence (genuineness, warmth, and empathic understanding) does not differ radically. In fact, it was later 19th-century medical psychology which first posited the "inherently helpful person" hypothesis, suggesting that the qualities of the helper are often possessed by the common people and that "Education may not always improve this power" (Bucknill and Tuke, 1879).

The foregoing analysis does not preclude the utility of training professional psychotherapists. Acknowledging that an essential feature of the therapist's involvement in the psychotherapeutic enterprise is the therapist-as-person is not to exhaust the list of important therapeutic skills. There are others which accrue through education and experience in dealing with human emotional problems. In no way should everyone set up his own clinic. The professions are necessarily reconceptualizing and restructuring the mental health care delivery system in the light of new evidence and experience; they are not tearing it down.

The "hard core data" from behavioral science research and the new posture of the psychotherapeutic professions do have implications for the clergy. The issue of whether or not the minister should attempt a personal involvement in situations in which members of his congregation are undergoing stress and emotional disturbance can be more easily answered. Though he must face the issue himself, each individual clergyman can provide tremendously helpful therapeutic assistance in situations which demand warm human encounter and concern. This requires neither a role redefinition for the clergy nor a specialized interest in psychotherapy. What becomes important is simply meeting the demands of the ministry with genuine pastoral concern for the wholeness of his people. At the time of death and the funeral, when the minister may find he is not only a central figure but one of very few people to whom the bereaved can readily turn, he assuredly can help initiate a psychotherapeutically potent and palliative human interaction.

A second implication is the need to recognize that people do want their clergymen to be involved in their lives. The clergyman more than anyone is sought in times of distress. Often he may be the only person available. A final point of interest is the fact that the clergy are effective. Confidently, then, the clergy may feel free to continue to respond to the call.

REFERENCES

Beck, J. C., D. Kantor, and V. A. Gelineau. Follow-up study of chronic psychotic patients "Treated" by college case-aid volunteers. American Journal of Psychiatry, 120:269 (1963).

Bergin, A. E. Some implications of psychotherapy research for therapeutic practice. Journal of Abnormal Psychology, 71:235 (1966).

_____. An empirical analysis of therapeutic issues. In D. Arbucle (Ed.), "Counseling and Psychotherapy: An Overview." New York: McGraw-Hill (1967).

_____. The evaluation of therapeutic outcomes. In A. E. Bergin and S. L. Garfield (Eds.), "Handbook of Psychotherapy and Behavior Change: An Empirical Analysis." New York: John Wiley and Sons (1971).

Bucknill, J. C., and D. H. Tuke. "A Manual of Psychological Medicine." Philadelphia: Lindsay and Blakiston (1879).

Carkhuff, R. R., and C. B. Traux. Lay mental health counseling: the effects of lay group counseling. Journal of Consulting Psychology, 29:426 (1965).

Earle (1844).

Ellsworth, R. B. "Nonprofessionals in Psychiatric Rehabilitation." New York: Appleton-Century-Crofts (1968).

Euster, G. L. Mental health worker—new mental hospital personnel for the seventies. Mental Hygiene, 55:283 (1971).

Gurin, G., J. Veroff, and S. Feld. "Psychotherapeutic Agents: New Roles for Nonprofessionals, Parents and Teachers." New York: Holt, Rinehart, and Winston (1960).

Kutscher, A. H., and A. H. Kutscher, Jr. Results of a survey: opinions of clergy, widows and widowers. In A. H. Kutscher and L. G. Kutscher (Eds.), "Religion and Bereavement." New York: Health Sciences Publishing Corp. (1972).

McPheeters, H. L., J. B. King, and R. J. Teare. The middle-level mental health worker: 1. his role. Hospital and Community Psychiatry, 23:329 (1972).

Pearl, A., and F. Reissman (Eds.), "New Careers for the Poor: The Non-Professional in Human Service." Glencoe, Illinois: Free Press (1965).

Pinel, P. "A Treatise on Insanity." (D. D. Davis, translator). Sheffield, England: W. Todd (1806).

Truax, C. B., and K. M. Mitchell. Research on certain therapist interpersonal skills in relation to process and outcome. In A. E. Bergin and S. L. Garfield (Eds.), "Handbook of Psychotherapy and Behavior Change: An Empirical Analysis." New York: John Wiley and Sons (1971).

Tuke, S. "Description of the Retreat, Etc." York, England (1813). Reprinted, London: Dawsons of Pall Mall (1964).

Children and the Ritual of the Mortuary
Paul R. Patterson

With the dissociation and separation of families, many children reach adult-hood without experiencing the death of a family member. A form of separation anxiety, very like that caused by the death of a loved one, is experienced by at least one out of every three children as a result of the divorce of parents. Others experience sadness and grief over the death of a pet, the loss of a friend who moves away, the prolonged hospitalization of a close relative, or over some other type of emotional and physical separation.

When the death of a close family member does occur, however, and the child is exposed to the rituals of mourning, most often including the rites of the funeral parlor, the child has his first introduction to society's attempt to assuage the fear of death, the most permanent and emotional separation.

When one considers the hundreds and thousands of dollars spent on fune-rals, it could be said that the modern Christian world's preoccupation with the rituals of death is similar to that of the ancient Egyptians with their pyramids, embalming, and funeral practices. These customs have grown from the needs of the bereaved. Although the purposes and economics of the services rendered by a mortuary have stimulated considerable criticism, it should be stressed that fune-ral directors as professionals are responding to the emotional needs and demands of the public. Suffering from separation anxiety, bereaved individuals want com-fort and need reassurance.

There has been considerable interpretation of the "therapy" of the wake, viewing parlors, and the funeral service. Undoubtedly, the needs of different

85

mourners are satisfied by our present death customs. Catholics tend to view the funeral as an instrument for prayer and the salvation of the soul. The funeral then becomes a ceremony honoring both the memory and the body of the deceased. Priests often remind those assembled to prepare for their own death. Protestants tend to view the funeral in terms of the peace and understanding it brings the survivors. Comfort for the bereaved and hope of a future life are part of their service. The Jewish faith requires a closed coffin during the funeral services; simplicity is the rule, and "promises" tend not to be given. Praise of the departed and reminders to the bereaved of the fond memories they can always cherish are the basics of the ritual.

However, as individuals, adults may use the organized "paid for" mourning rites as additional sources of comfort and reassurance: group therapy, amelioration of guilt, exhibitionism, family reunions, mitigation of resentment, anticipation of bequests, proof of love, relief of a burden, milking of sympathy, the heroics of no tears, sudden spiritual awareness, mockery of a belief in any religion, and so on.

The child, of course, is usually unaware of such underlying needs or motives. Similarly, he is usually totally unprepared for the rites in which he is being asked to participate. For most religious services, children have received instructions or clerical indoctrination. The rituals of the funeral parlor, of viewing the remains with coffin-side prayers, and of participation in the funeral exercises are never taught except as an emergency instruction. It is not difficult to imagine how strange and possibly horrifying this first experience must be.

Following a death, children are prepared rapidly by being told that they are to visit Grandpa "at the undertakers." Once there, a kind, solemn man greets them and asks to whom they wish to pay their respects. They may be told that "he is in slumber parlor B," or that he is "sleeping in that room."

When they enter the room where each adult friend and mourner is in his or her own way expressing sorrow, sympathy, or respects, most children are in complete awe of the "action" and the flowers, lights, and soft music. Nevertheless, some children may react with laughter at this point, to the consternation of the assembled adults. To understand such a reaction, adults must recall their own childhood, when any remark or gesture made by a friend during a solemn religious service seemed so very humorous. This recall will serve to explain why, as seen through the eyes of children, the moans and cries of adult mourners are "funny."

Other children often are provoked into tears by the crying and viewing of the body—to the relief of their parents, who worry if a child is not grieving as expected. At this moment, a meaningful invitation is occasionally proffered by a relative or even a member of the mortuary staff: "Would you like to kiss him goodbye?" The child is lifted to feel the cold cheek or forehead against his lips. This memory will remain with him for the rest of his life.

While adults have social and religious obligations to experience the rituals and the emotionally charged atmosphere of the funeral parlor, the young child has none except to do as he is directed by his parents. Following such an experience, many children will play "funeral" for weeks and months. Dolls are laid out in handkerchief-lined boxes and tears may result from the frightened, make-believe thought that "Mother is lying there *dead.*" The emotions felt may parallel those of the bereaved adults: anger, death wish, and then guilt.

Pediatricians are asked frequently if children should partake of the rites of the mortuary. I suspect that the funeral director also receives similar queries. We all have our biases. I recommend no direct body viewing by any child under 14, especially a nervous, sensitive one. How much better a photograph on top of the closed casket, preventing subsequent haunting thoughts or dreams that may persist for years.

A decision not to bring children under six years of age is a common recommendation that may be based on sound psychiatric judgment—sound only if the facts of the death and grief have been discussed openly with the child. Interestingly enough, at this age, a child frequently falls asleep during the service.

Attendance at a wake with an open casket is generally the first time an adolescent views a "dead person." The sight is awesome and the shock lingers for weeks or months, especially if the deceased was a classmate or a member of his peer group. This is reality! The adolescent may not have the diverse emotionally charged gains from or reactions to the mortuary experience that an adult has, but his reactions may help diminish any guilt feelings he may have suppressed.

Occasionally, a close group of adolescents may even ask to perform their own farewell—for example, an originally composed musical lament for the dead friend. The funeral director may need to interpret this sincere offering to the grieving parents. Since adults often have special Lodge or veterans' services conducted, this act should be regarded as a loving, youthful gesture performed apart from the funeral services.

With the diminishing acceptance of organized religion and the inability of many clergy to deal with the psychology of death and mourning, more people are suddenly finding themselves seeking emotional succor from secular sources. We may discover that the funeral director's professional staff should include a social worker or a trained member capable of assisting with bereavement. His or her availability may need to be extended to weeks after the death.

Most funeral directors provide a pamphlet helpful with the economics of the mortuary services, but are reluctant to offer any psychological comfort. The funeral home staff should have pamphlets prepared by sensitive clergy of the major faiths and possibly even one by an atheist. Among these should be one on how to explain death to children of different ages. These explanations should be free of psychiatric, equivocal theories (e.g., the Oedipus complex as a cause of death anxiety, which is frequently written—to the horror of pediatricians more experienced with children).

88   Paul R. Patterson

We find that the two mysteries of life which are most difficult to explain to children are how we get into this world and how we leave it, namely sex and death. The professional who has worked with grieving children should join with an organization of funeral directors to provide educational material to help everyone understand the child's normal emotional needs and his responses when confronted by death and dying.

REFERENCE

Mitford, J. "The American Way of Death." New York: Simon and Schuster (1963).

Children and Funerals

John E. Schowalter

Funerals are an accepted, institutionalized means for group mourning. They often work like group therapy, allowing the bereaved an opportunity to be supported while they express their grief. The consensual validation of the death provided by the funeral also acts to prevent the use of excessive denial. Because of the beneficial aspects of funerals for most people, they remain an important institution in our culture in spite of the financial and emotional exploitation which is often also present. While funerals seem to be useful outlets of grief for many adults, how helpful are they for children? This question, almost totally ignored in the medical literature, will be explored in this paper, and some answers will be suggested.

To explore the question of children and funerals, an understanding of child development is crucial. Experience has shown that older children usually tolerate funerals quite well, while young children often suffer bad reactions (e.g., nightmares, anxiety reactions, phobias, etc.). The moot point then is at what age or, more exactly, at what stage of development can one assume that most children will be able to tolerate a funeral?

THE CHILD'S EVOLVING CONCEPT OF DEATH AND FUNERALS

Prior to the second half of his first year, the infant is not able to delineate himself as separate from his surroundings. He cannot distinguish his parents from

*Supported by the Maternal and Child Health Division of The Health Services and Mental Health Administration of the U. S. Department of Health, Education and Welfare, The Connecticut Department of Health, and U. S. Public Health Service Grant No. 5T1MH-5442-20.

other persons. Funerals will, of course, have no direct meaning at this age, and, if the parents wish, the infant can be taken to the funeral without the expectation that the experience will cause any special harm. This is not to say that the death of a parent or close relative has no emotional impact on the infant. The impact, however, is indirect and comes through the mourning survivors' inability to provide the infant with his usual care. Attending the funeral per se will probably neither add to nor detract from this impact.

During the second year, the infant becomes a toddler. According to both psychoanalytic and Piagetian theories, he develops a stable, internalized image of his parents and, later, of other important people in his life. From this age on, the death of a loved one becomes a real loss. The central question for this paper is whether or not attending the funeral will make that loss easier or less easy to bear.

My own belief is that children should not usually be taken to funerals before the age of seven or eight and should not ever be taken routinely if the child does not want to go.

Prior to about the age of seven, the child has great difficulty differentiating between the psychological and the physical. Cause and effect are commonly based on spatial or temporal rather than logical considerations. Animism, the bestowal of human characteristics on inanimate objects and natural phenomena, and egocentrism, the assumption that others think and feel the same as oneself, are commonly manifested in children up through the preoperational stage of cognitive development, which ends about age seven. Up to this age, death is often personified as something or someone who comes and takes the victim. In the mind of the child, a dead person often acquires this ability, and this is one reason why the corpse becomes so frightening. Of course, adults' fear of the returning dead has a long history too and probably was influential originally in the development of wakes and funerals. However, until the child can grasp intellectually the meaning of a funeral, attending the event will result in an additional emotional burden for him to bear.

Optimally, every child will have the death explained to him in a manner in which he can understand. The funeral should also be explained in those terms which describe how that family views it, and the child should be encouraged to ask questions. Around the age of six, seven, or eight, children may be asked if they wish to attend the funeral. If the child has no strong feelings or does not wish to go, my inclination is to not have him attend. If the child does want to attend, this wish should be given weight. Children who want to go but are not allowed sometimes exaggerate the mystery of the funeral or conjure up fantasies of skulduggery or murder. Even when the child decides to go, it should be with the understanding that he can change his mind at any time up to or during the service. This "escape clause" is important and is not infrequently used by a child who overestimated his own emotional strength or underestimated the strangeness of some funerals. Whether a child goes to the funeral or stays home, he should be accompanied by someone who is not so involved in the death that he cannot give undivided attention to the child.

A common question adults ask themselves in planning a funeral is whether or not to have an open casket. In some cultures an open casket is a tradition, although many younger adults believe it is more honored in the breach than the observance. My own experience is that although it is often helpful to allow a child to see a person who has just died, the prepared corpse is so artificially "real" that it seems unreal. Unlike what many morticians suggest, the image seen in an open casket is not what one would wish the child to carry with him. It is not life or death, but a confusing "fake life." The trip to the cemetery and the lowering of the coffin into the ground are also experiences which often overwhelm children and even young adolescents. Here again, however, at the older age the individual should have a voice in the decision whether or not to go. Periodic visits to the grave by the child with adults who are in control of their emotions can later help with mourning by stressing the permanence of death while also providing a permanent reminder of the deceased.

CHILD-ADULT INTERACTION

Probably the most important influence on how a young child acts around the time of a death is the response of his parents. When one parent dies, the child usually loses both, since the surviving parent's mourning often renders him unable to give of himself in a way consonant with adequate parenting. This occurs, of course, at just the time when the child desires and requires an increased quantity and quality of care. Even when it is a grandparent or other relative who has died, children are usually forgotten by grieving adults. When parents are unavailable emotionally to look after the children or prepare them for the funeral, an "outside" but familiar person should be appointed specifically to fulfill this task. A pediatrician, if he is close to the family, can be excellent in this role. An additional example of how children are forgotten at times of grief is the fact that adults seldom send children sympathy cards, even children to whom they regularly send holiday or birthday cards. This is unfortunate, because mail means much to a child, and the card remains as tangible evidence of the event and of its remembrance.

Around the time of the funeral and in addition to the shock of the death, it must be expected that the child will be bewildered by the presence of many strange adults acting strangely. Even those friends and relatives whom the child knows will probably be acting in ways he has never associated with them. For example, Christian children are often confused, especially if it is an older grandparent who died, as to why the adults are crying if the dead person is now in heaven. In Sunday School they were taught that this is a joyous occasion.

Unable to comprehend the permanence of death, young children may rate adults' behavior as excessive and tell them so. Contrariwise, the child's developmental inability to mourn like an adult often disturbs relatives and family friends. They find the child's frequent hyperactivity and lack of sadness as irritating signs of insensitivity or inhumane self-centeredness. If the child is reprimanded for not acting in a way he is not able to, his confusion will only be compounded, and his behavior will probably worsen.

How the child will react if he does attend the funeral will be a function of his past experiences and his present support. Children who have been active in arranging funerals for pets or who have discovered dead animals often seem better able to experience their passive role at the funeral. If the deceased is a distant friend or relative, children are usually and understandably better able to handle the funeral than if the death is of a parent, sibling, or someone else to whom the child is very close. How often the child has attended church or temple and how comfortable he is with the services are also important considerations. Again, if unfamiliar, the strangeness will tend only to compound his confusion and to increase the likelihood that the situation will be overwhelming.

SUMMARY

Prior to the age of about seven years when the child becomes able to differentiate regularly between the psychological and the physical and to rely less on the primitive logic of animism and egocentrism, children are more often terrified than consoled by visiting funeral parlors or attending funerals. Even older children who wish to accompany the family to the funeral may be disturbed by an open casket or by being present when the coffin is lowered into the ground. Children over the age of eight or nine who want to attend the service should usually be allowed to do so. It is comforting, however, to allow an "escape clause" whereby they know they can leave at any time. Since children are usually forgotten by adults in their own grief, it is important that someone be appointed to be responsible for the children around the time of the funeral—at the service and/or at home. Adults should also be aware that a young child's mourning often shows much less sadness than a grownup's and should not be misled into criticizing the youngster or into believing that his fear and anxiety are any less real than the adult's.

A Vivid Background for Acute Grief

Margot Tallmer and Jeanette Scaros

It is easy and tempting to write in a florid manner when describing Sudden Infant Death Syndrome, whose very name is synonymous with drama. Unfortunately, the syndrome is a highly emotional event that can hardly be dealt with in ordinary, matter-of-fact descriptions; the literature, resonating to basically strong feelings, swings from indulgent sensationalism to constricted, dry verbiage. We shall attempt to maintain a middle position in reporting this condition and to confine our consideration, for the most part, to its psychological impact on the family.

Sudden Infant Death Syndrome, or as it is frequently referred to, "cot death" or "crib death," is the unexplained death of an infant in the early postnatal period (generally from one week to one year, but most often during the period from two to four months). The death is marked by no discernible forewarning, no possible prophylactic measures, and no known demonstrable explanation. The diagnosis, made through autopsy, reveals no findings which might satisfactorily otherwise explain the death. In New York City, all crib deaths are investigated. A visit to the home is made by the police and health department officials, and an autopsy is performed routinely. About 100 such cases occur there yearly, with higher incidences reported among the lower socioeconomic groups. It is conceivable that these statistics are altered as in the reporting of childhood suicides, where higher economic groups tend to suppress the evidence. Lower-income families generally do not utilize private pediatricians, who may attest to other causes of the deaths. Nevertheless, incidence is relatively high and

SIDS is the major cause of infant death after the first week of life, up until the first year. It is second, after accidents, as the reason for mortality up until the age of 15 (Bergman, 1972). These data appear constant throughout the world.

Despite much speculation, the cause of death has not been ascertained conclusively. The following have been mentioned as possibilities: cardiac arrhythmias due to an immature autonomic nervous system (Church, et al., 1967), viral infection (Ferris, et al., 1973), congenital anomaly of the parathyroids (Geertinger, 1967), predisposition to petechial hemorrhages (Ferris, et al., 1973), spinal injury (Towbin, 1968), anaphylactic reaction to aspirated cow's milk (Gunther, 1966), and renal histology (Stowens, et al., 1966). Since physicians do not know the actual reason for crib deaths, they may add to the guilt and misinformation shared by the surviving parents. Crib death is also often mistakenly associated with child abuse.

As recently as 1973, an article appeared stating that "it is rare to have an unexpected child death when the relationship between parents and family doctor is good" (British Medical Journal, 1973). Newspapers commonly report such deaths in terms of parental oversight or outright destructiveness, suggesting suffocation or choking on mucous or vomitus, despite clinical proof that smothering is not the reason for death and that the presence of mucous or food around the mouth is a post-mortem phenomenon. Concomitantly, the death often occurs immediately after a checkup at the doctor's office, an event not so unlikely statistically since babies are checked rather frequently, but the timing leads to doubts about the physician and the medication or shot that may have been administered. In such cases, both the family and the pediatrician must be reassured that the baby died of SIDS and that nothing could have prevented the tragedy. In regard to other children in the same family, it is generally accepted that SIDS is not hereditary or infectious and is not likely to afflict other offspring; that is, the chances are about one in 350 of having a child succumb to the syndrome, and this probability is constant no matter how many children one has.

The demographic data are more readily detailed than are the psychological findings, for the latter must be deduced retrospectively from clinical material or inferred from knowledge of human behavior. In an obscure way, possession of this psychological information may have led to a needless constriction of useful research—that is, many clinicians have overlooked the factual data, previously presented in this paper, and have concentrated instead on the possible unconscious determinants of crib deaths, focusing on poor impulse control, ambivalence, death wishes toward the child, and the like. We shall attempt to underline the possible malignant effects of this narrow, authoritarian, judgmental posture on the part of some mental health personnel and the lay public as well. However, before assessing these effects, we will examine some general psychodynamic principles underlying pregnancy and determine idiosyncratic features that may apply to SIDS.

Patently, childbearing has multiple symbolic meanings that vary temporally and substantively both within the woman herself and between individuals. Freud's notion of an incorporation of the missing penis, more specifically the father's penis, and then the replacement of the idea "penis" by the idea "child" (Fenichel, 1945) is at best only a partial explanation of the complete psychic picture. His idea is supplemented by present-day psychoanalysts, who suggest a reparative, restitutive motive arising from castration fear and guilt. Further elaborations attribute to the reproductive process "the direct fulfillment of the deepest and most powerful wish of the woman" (Deutsch, 1944), and ascribe pathological meanings to any explanations or motives not regarded as self-actualizing. As with all psychic acts, pregnancy is symbolically overdetermined in origin and actually may signify a number of possibilities—to wit, a solution to a conflict-ridden interpersonal situation; a duplication of a previously admired state of the mother figure; a defense against self-doubts in the area of femininity; a maneuver to satisfy deep, regressive drives; a struggle with competitive drives with the mother, sister, other relevant females, or men; or an expression of fear concerning self-worth without reproducing. Fantasies range widely and may include oral impregnation, bearing an anal child, or harboring a devouring, savage, fetal monster. As many possible combinations exist as there are potential variations in the mother's projections of self and objects onto the unborn child, with resultant strongly negative feelings, ambivalence, or positive affect. External factors, including real hindrances and burdens as well as interpersonal conflicts, impinge upon the mother, for an unborn child may represent a host of difficulties—economic strain, depletion of health reserves, professional impediments, and many other barriers. Under optimal conditions, the major portion of these conflicts are resolved during the nine-month period by means of general hormonal and metabolic processes which develop, pari passu, with increased primary and secondary narcissistic gratification and secondary ego rewards.

Parturition presents new challenges and requires the establishment of different biological and psychological responses. Faulty emotional attitudes may be reactivated and mobilized by the delivery, resulting occasionally in postpartum depression. Much more usual though is the appearance of mood changes, anxiety, confusion, and manifestations of separation anxiety. One may witness these phenomena merely by visiting a maternity ward, where passing depressions, crying spells, and the like are frequent occurrences. The birth has clearly interrupted the continuity of the mother-fetus relationship, their oneness. Some mothers, as they experience a sense of loss and a feeling of emptiness, begin to detach themselves from a baby who appears as an outside object. The consequences of this posture include guilt and anxiety, with possible depression and further withdrawal.

Other women become wary of aggressive impulses toward the infant and are afraid to be alone with such a vulnerable target for their anger. For the majority of mothers, the mother-child duality continues in somewhat altered form after the birth, a form marked by virtual exclusion of the outside psychological world, complete preoccupation with the baby, and a feeling of still being one with the child (Winnicott, 1965). This symbiotic dyad engenders change in both participants, as would any interpersonal situation. Childbearing, then, is seen as a developmental crisis requiring and responding to maturational processes and resulting in a higher level of personal integration.

Although the earliest life of the infant closely resembles intrauterine existence, variations in activity patterns among children and differences in the irritability of the nervous system, among numerous other factors, require individual adjustments by each mother, and it is usually some time before an equilibrium is established between mother and child. However, once the necessary alterations have been made and each member of the pair is responding to the other's signals and timing, the maternal figure frequently experiences herself as the final authority in respect to the child and is more aware of its needs than anyone else. She develops a kind of inner conviction that Erikson refers to as so necessary for successful child rearing—a firm belief in what she is doing. The gratification she derives from her ministrations is increased by her witnessing the development of a thriving child and leads to feelings of self-esteem and confidence. The fortunate mother has achieved her ego ideal—that is, to be a good mother—and has armed herself against fear of failure, concomitantly increasing her ability to love her child. It must be stressed that *both* parents are sustained in all their efforts by an anticipation of expected emotional rewards, the prizes received for rearing a child who will fulfill parental aspirations.

It is noteworthy that psychological literature concentrates on infant development, while slighting to a great degree the corresponding experiences of the mothering figure. Fathers fare even more poorly in this regard than mothers. If parenthood is to be considered a developmental phase, the paternal role deserves more research and attention than it has received up until now. Men share similarly in the resolution of earlier conflicts when they become fathers and must deal with reactivation of survival needs, competitive drives, identification with the wife during her pregnancy, and achieving an ego ideal—that is, the good father. In the same way that the woman projects and fantasizes, so does the male, while reliving earlier identifications and intrapsychic conflicts. Additionally, he is called upon to respond to his wife's receptive needs. Benedek (1959) believes that the father's relationship to his infant is "directed more by hope than by drive. Since the infant's perceptive system develops faster than his object relationships to 'total objects,' the infant soon begins to look, smile and coo at the father and so reactivates his 'motherliness.'" In short, parenthood as a phase of life will have many of the same features for both mothers and fathers and may lead either or both of them to a higher level of psychological maturity or to pathological results.

The potentially negative psychological sequelae to SIDS become relatively clear from the foregoing discussion. Although generalizations cannot be applied in a widespread fashion, there exist certain predictable deleterious effects that depend upon the psychic structures of the parents, socioeconomic status, the amount of support offered, the sequence of events, and the interrelationship of all these factors. Cognitively, pregnancy supports the mother's early feelings of omnipotence as the child is easily thought to be the result of her desires to have a child—that is, she has made a child. At the same time, notions of immortality are given a boost for both the mother and father. As with all primitive types of thinking, the greater the opportunity for such illogical ideas to be extinguished, the more will they be eliminated. Thus, the longer the baby survives, the more chance for reality testing to be absorbed and infantile thinking to be terminated. Time does not appear to have such a simple association with the matter of unconscious death wishes toward the infant. The potential for damage seems to be linked to the intensity of the wishes and their accessibility to consciousness. Clearly, this problem extends also to siblings who often are forced to deal with the anxiety engendered by the force of their unconscious ideas at a time when parents may be preoccupied.

We have previously suggested that varying amounts of time are necessary in the postnatal period for parents to resolve some of their own intrapsychic conflicts, including reactivations of childhood themes and the new responses required of parents; the mother, additionally, must undergo hormonal and metabolic alterations. This required period is afforded the mother during the first weeks when she is involved extensively in her new role and totally preoccupied with the newborn. If crib death occurs during this very early time, it may threaten her very sense of being, the inner core of her existence.

It is a rare new mother who is not anxious, absorbed, and uncertain after the delivery of a baby, for a good sense of herself only develops slowly as she foresees needs and satisfies demands. The maternal figure then can experience herself as one who has learned to anticipate the requirements through an identification with the baby. Many mothers proudly proclaim the ability to interpret the different meanings of the baby's crying: this kind of cry indicates hunger, this one fatigue, and the like. The mother can ascertain and predict accurately. In short, she knows her baby. It is difficult, given these circumstances, for the mother to explain to herself and others that she could have perceived no indications in her child who was only hours away from death.

The mechanics of the immediate post-death period exacerbate the confusion. Many parents are told that pneumonia and enteritis caused the fatality, and, indeed, death certificates often list these two reasons. A large number of survivors are informed that an autopsy is required by law because of the questionable nature of the death. Investigations, coroners, delayed funerals, and unknowing physicians often prevent much-needed societal support from being offered, support ordinarily proffered a grieving family. Furthermore, lack of knowledge concerning etiology augments fears for unborn or already living children.

The situation, then, is of a bewildered, grieving family unable to gain satisfactory explanations and denied the many institutionalized forms of comfort. Compounding these woes is the fact that for some unknown reason this type of death occurs disproportionately in the lower socioeconomic groups, where professional help is sought much less frequently and where there is little access to informed opinions. Members of such groups are also more apt to be beseiged by other stresses concomitant with low income and low status. (In regard to the father, he may have been quite isolated from the mother-child dyad and may react to the sudden death with a farrago of psychological responses—hostility, guilt, envy, resentment, and frustration—depending upon his own psychic structure, the infant's psychological meaning for him, and imponderables that must include external factors as well. The main point is that the death may occur before he has sufficient opportunity to interact with his child. If he has been able to recognize and satisfy some of the receptive needs of his wife, psychic stress may be mitigated. If the infant has been an extension of his being, a repository of his projections and fantasies only, the loss will be felt acutely.)

By definition, all the beneficial effects derived from anticipatory grief are denied to the survivors of SIDS and all effects must be dealt with ex post facto. Again, the age of the child will determine to some degree the extent of bereavement—that is, the longer a baby has lived, the more opportunity for physical contact with him, and the less the grief (Kannel, 1970). It may be noted here that the sex of the baby is often seen by friends and family to influence the extent of the grief. Guilt would be more violent if the gender was a source of disappointment, or sorrow increased if special satisfaction was derived from the sex of the baby. Sex seems to be merely part of the larger gestalt of parental feelings, wishes, and expectations.

Because of the points that we have mentioned, parents are urged to join a SIDS group, sponsored by the National Association for Sudden Infant Death and open to anyone concerned. We attended a meeting and witnessed the interest and concern these parents have for other couples who must face this dreadful experience without the support of a group. There was no question of their altruistic motives but there was also evidence of the need of some members to resolve their grief and mourning even a year or two after the death. This was shown in some of the case histories they have written and by personal talks. The sudden unexplained tragic demise had left an unbelievable traumatic aftereffect that must be in direct proportion to the swift, dramatic, juggernaut action of the syndrome.

This disease, by its very nature, instigates a severely traumatic period of acute grief. Psychotherapeutic considerations should involve research, the dissemination of knowledge, and proper counseling facilities for the bereaved families, particularly those programs instituted by the Sudden Infant Death Foundation. The funeral director is confronted by unique challenges under these extraordinary circumstances which, it is hoped, his education will prepare him to resolve.

REFERENCES

Benedek, T. Parenthood as a developmental phase. Journal of the American Psychoanalytic Association, 7:389 (1959).

Bergman, A. B. Sudden infant death. Nursing Outlook, 20:775 (1972).

Church, S., B. Morgan, T. Oliver, and W. Guntheroth. Cardiac arrhythmias in premature infants: an indication of autonomic immaturity. Journal of Pediatrics, 71:542 (1967).

Deutsch, H. "The Psychology of Women." New York: Grune and Stratton (1944).

Fenichel, O. "The Psychoanalytic Theory of Neurosis." New York: W. W. Norton (1945).

Ferris, J. A., W. A. Aherne, W. S. Locke, J. McQuillan, and P. S. Gardner. Sudden and unexpected deaths in infancy: histology and virology. British Medical Journal, 2:439 (1973).

Geertinger, P. Sudden, unexpected death in infancy. Pediatrics, 39:43 (1967).

Gunther, M. Cot deaths: anaphylactic reaction after intrauterine infection as another potential cause, Lancet (1966).

Kannel, J., et al. The mourning role of the parents to the death of a newborn infant. New England Journal of Medicine, 283:344 (1970).

Stowens, D., E. L. Callahan, and J. Clay. Sudden unexpected death in infancy: a new hypothesis of cause. Clinical Pediatrics, 5:243 (1966).

Towbin, A. Spinal injury related to syndrome of sudden death in infants. American Journal of Clinical Pathology, 19:562 (1968).

Winnicott, D. W. "Maturational Processes and the Facilitating Environment." New York: International Universities Press (1965).

Born Dead
Park J. White

. . . Striking from the calendar
Unborn tomorrow and dead yesterday
Omar Khayyam

Whatever the age of the departed, we who would be of real comfort to the bereaved must remember that whatever we may say, if it isn't extemporaneous, it's a speech. And as a grief-stricken friend of mine remarked upon the departure of an "official" comforter, "A speech I don't need." In a context of religious motivation, Jesus told his disciples, "Take no thought how or what ye shall speak, for it shall be given you. . . ." Even allowing for a few clumsy comforters like Job's three, *ex tempore* is still the best approach, with the probable exception of silence. (Job's "miserable comforters" kept silent for a week, after which Job, knowing that they would blame some forgotten sin for his afflictions, opened his mouth and cursed his day, and presumably his comforters. Silence, you see, can be sympathetic and tactful or bumbling and futile.)

Now, as our title indicates, we are considering the feelings of the parents and immediate family of stillborn infants. Here, the reader, like this writer, realizes at once that reactions are bound to vary with circumstances and individuals. Inasmuch as a newly delivered dead fetus has never had and never can have any but a passive role, we shall concern ourselves with only a few of the many forms of this tragedy. Here, omega erases alpha and the silence of the womb passes directly into the silence of the tomb.

101

A brief, but candid and sympathetic, look at three widely different forms of this situation should prove helpful.

THE WANTED BABY

We doctors know full well how some babies are wanted, even longed for, more than others. Perhaps the parents are older, unable until past middle age to have a baby, yearning for "fulfillment." Or perhaps they have already gone through the painful process of losing one or more children.

In considering the hoped-for but stillborn infant and his parents, it is not altogether unreasonable to assume the availability of good professional care. Good doctor-patient communication—keeping parents posted on progress, so far as possible—is obviously important.

We should remember, even take encouragement from, the fact that grief over a baby born dead simply cannot be as deep as that over an older child or adult who has loved and been loved. And there are no memories of a stillborn. This is one of many reasons why a doctor should never allow either parent to see a stillborn infant, unless, of course, a parent is foolish enough to demand it— making threats and so forth. No benefit can possibly accrue from "showing" the pathetic and, to the layman, misshapen little body.

For what it is worth, we might mention that at least two well-known philosophers, George Santayana and Job, seriously professed to envy the lot of an infant born dead. The former, when asked what he would consider to be the greatest boon the Almighty might grant him, replied without hesitation, "Lord, let me never be born at all." Santayana, remember, was once described by a colleague as "a soul ever in limbo, observing, but never involved." He once described life itself as "merely the interval between birth and death."

As for Job, whose patience took over only at intervals and whose sufferings justified his bitter complaints, his graphically put questions, addressed To Whom It May Concern, have been common knowledge for about three millennia. His "whys" are still unanswered. No wonder Job did not include his God and ours in his list of the Concerned!

"Why died I not from the womb? Why did I not give up the ghost when I came out of the belly?" (Job 3:11). Both Job and we may well bear in mind that 39 chapters later, Job's unknown biographer reports that after Job "abhorred himself" things took a turn for the better: "So Job died, being old and full of days," and blessed by wealth and beautiful children.

Now, those who have desired but lost their babies by stillbirth can usually take some comfort—if their doctors have been honest and kept them posted—in the fact that "everything possible has been done." All too often, "in a large proportion of deaths in utero, *no* valid explanation for stillbirth can be offered" (1).

To put the obvious a bit crassly, stillbirth illustrates the fact that bereavement is largely a matter of degree, with time and that responsive association known as love determining that degree.

Parents—especially mothers who have had educational and economic advantages—can be greatly helped by their doctors' guiding them into public-health activities having to do with prevention of spontaneous abortions and stillbirths. However motivated, lay folk have been and are valuable to professionals in getting at the causes of these all-too-common afflictions.

All of us need to be reminded that "by far the most common cause of neonatal mortality—accounting for one-half of all such deaths—is *prematurity*." The incidence of prematurity, based upon the criterion of a birth-weight of less than 2,500 gm (5 lbs.) varies with the race and economic status of the population. In 1958, the incidence of prematurity in the nonwhite population was 12.9 percent, as contrasted with 6.8 percent for the white population. The extent to which race and economic conditions are responsible is still a matter of debate. Blair has shown that in Aberdeen, Scotland, the incidence of prematurity is about two times greater among wives of unskilled workers than among wives of professional and managerial personnel. "The hypothesis that nutrition plays a significant etiologic role in prematurity is attractive but Thomson has searched the available literature in vain for proof" (2).

Of course those interested in reducing the stillbirth rate must also be on the lookout for maternal syphilis, diabetes, hemorrhagic disease, and other illnesses. Coping with factors like these has been and must continue to be a large order indeed.

THOSE WHO DO NOT CARE

Thank goodness for the great and more-or-less silent majority of parents who do care sincerely about having their growing fetuses approach term with every likelihood of being born alive and who make every preparation possible in the circumstances. We can't estimate the number of couples, often unmarried, often adolescent, who would welcome a stillbirth rather than a living baby, who "didn't want the baby in the first place."

Obviously, the only reasonable procedure here is prevention of conception by proper and safe means. If induced abortion before the fourth month of gestation is agreed upon by doctor and mother, on failure of contraceptive measures, so be it. Far more heat than light has been generated by this subject. We gladly abandon it as not pertinent here.

Finally, many of us, physicians, clergy, and laymen alike, have discovered that in trying to walk humbly with our God, as urged by Micah, we find ourselves also walking in the light of true science. In our deep concern for life's beginnings, especially in the 20th century, it is clear that, "full-summ'd in all our powers" (3) we must regulate conception, even as we must prevent unnecessary death. As for newly born infants, we have come that they may have life. Where this is denied, we can only, as in times past, offer families intelligent activity and sympathetic understanding.

NOTES

1. Hellman, L. M., and J. A. Pritchard. In "Obstetrics," 14th ed., J. W. Williams (Ed.). New York: Appleton-Century-Crofts (1970), p. 11.
2. Ibid., pp. 526-27.
3. Tennyson, A. The Princess. In "Complete Poetical Works," W. J. Rolfe (Ed.). Boston: Houghton-Mifflin.

The Creative Funeral

Linda M. Colvin

Perhaps it is a bit ironic that more often than not we have learned about the lives of our ancestors through their tombs. The archives of death have been the source of the history of life.

The Egyptian pyramids have provided extensive knowledge regarding the religious beliefs and class systems of that early civilization. Totem poles of Indian and Aztec civilizations, along with burial caves, have made similar contributions. The funeral rituals of any society document many elements of that same society's culture. However, although we have used such resources to study other cultures, we seem to have negated their worth in our own. Few serious works have been developed on the American funeral as a cultural ritual.

Many criticisms, indeed, have been leveled at funeral professionals, especially in regard to costs and with a particular focus on the "unethical" funeral director. Jessica Mitford in "The American Way of Death" strongly criticized the whole funeral industry, attributing "barbaric" practices to it. As a result, this book stirred up much venom and reinforced stereotyped images of funerals and those who serve as funeral directors. Whatever its negative features are, Mitford's book did question our present-day customs and promoted other concepts in funeral planning and practices, those of memorial societies and memorial services.

The memorial service does provide the family with an opportunity to creatively express grief by developing an individualized service, rather than being shuffled through a maze of standardized procedures. It is often questionable, though, how much the provider influences the consumer—that is, do advertisements influence the buyer, or the buyer the advertisements? Mitford stated that it is the funeral directors and not the general public who have created the funeral customs. In some respects, this may be a valid concept, but for the most part, I think it is not. This society and its value systems, which have reinforced an atmosphere of death denial, have had their influences on the funeral. A brief review of the semantics of the funeral industry gives credence to this thought.

We have gone from the "undertaker" to the "funeral director," from the "hearse" to the "limousine," from the "coffin" to "casket," from the "funeral home" to the "chapel," and finally, from the "corpse" to the "loved one." To say that contemporary technology had no part in this change, is to ignore the funeral as a part of American culture. During this same period, our "janitors" have become "maintenance engineers" and our "garbage collectors" are "sanitation men." This phenomenon has been part of the specialization process of American society. Furthermore, it reflects a sort of abstraction from the "gutsiness" of reality. The undertaker does undertake to take the corpse under ground. The word explains the profession. But now, as the profession has become more comprehensive to meet the complicated requirements of legislation and social custom, the title also changes.

In reviewing some widespread phenomena in today's culture, one might suspect that they would influence the funeral ceremony. Alienation as seen by Melvin Seeman, Kenneth Clarke, and other social scientists is common in our society. This is documented by the high suicide rate among our youth, the loneliness of our aged, and the need for hot-lines for people to "telephone in" their problems.

In part, these phenomena result from the rapid change from an industrial to a technocratic type of society. The high rate of mobility as described in "Future Shock" has been a serious threat to the well-being and security of other individuals. As a defense against man's greatest threat, I believe the funeral also reflects the high degree of specialization whereby the consumer hands over his responsibility to the expert. He assumes the role of a "helpless victim" who would rather be processed through comfortable customs than contribute to a creative ceremony. This may be for many reasons. The grief-stricken nuclear family separated from the familiar home base may not be able to develop that type of creativity within itself in an alien environment.

The funeral ceremony, as a cultural ritual, parallels the wedding as another such ritual. Within the past few years, many couples have actively created their own ceremony. They write their own vows and songs, have friends give the sermon, and face the congregation during the service. In previous years the priest, rabbi, or minister told the couple what to do and had them recite the vows. With the present shift toward more involvement, the ceremony becomes more meaningful to the young couple and adds a means whereby individual expression can be shared with others. That is the basis for a feeling of "community." With youth identifying with earthen goods, natural foods and handcrafted goods, we are witnessing a shift from depersonalization in technocracy to personalization. The "earth" popularity represents a quest for roots in an alienated setting.

Perhaps this is why the wedding, which is a common ceremony among the young, has taken on a new communal style. Thus, the life style matches the ceremonial rituals of that particular culture. But the funeral ritual, more commonly performed by older Americans, has not yet taken on the communal expression of the wedding ritual because it is not yet congruent to their life-style.

I believe that the funeral should and can change in this direction and that funeral directors can share in the responsibility for fostering and developing such a change.

Grief is a critical emotional state; if one does not adjust healthily to this situation, severe emotional impairment may result. As defined by Dr. Austin Kutscher, "grief is the phenomenon of human behavior in survivors which accompanies loss," and if those behavior patterns have not been developed through earlier loss situations, such as job loss, status loss, or even postpartum loss, then they cannot be expected to operate well in a death situation. Grief is a gateway to depression for many bereaved. The way to bar passage is to provide a means for creative expression of this grief so that pathological depression does not result.

This leads us to the need for a creative funeral as a means of freely expressing acute grief. There is no doubt that the funeral can serve as an occasion for doing this, but we need to make people feel that they are not being strange when they do participate actively in certain funeral arrangements. The taboo against preparing the body should be discarded. It may be a fact that most people don't want to be bothered, but there are many who would be willing to provide just that "little touch," like arranging the necklace, combing the hair, or fixing the collar as Grandma would want it to be. Here, the funeral director can encourage the closest family member to feel that there is nothing to be afraid of. The director can also encourage the family to individualize the ceremony: by having a picture of the deceased displayed, by celebrating the deceased's life through works of art or literature created by family members, and so forth. Loved ones who find speaking no great chore should be encouraged to give an eulogy for their loved one as part of the funeral service.

The ideas are limitless. It will take concerned and empathic people in the care-giving professions to develop and promulgate them. I strongly contend that the ceremony, be it a funeral or a memorial service, needs to be offered so that friends and family can express their grief through a type of communal experience.

The present traditional practices in many respects treat the bereaved as weak, helpless victims. In fact we set this up so that the strong appear to be rather stoic. So long as this persists, it is like saying to someone who is handicapped, "Here is a crutch," when he should be told, "This is how we can rehabilitate you to walk."

The creative funeral, providing a meaningful and individual expression of communal grief, is the rehabilitator, not the crutch.

THE HOUR AND THE PLACE

Acute Grief and the Funeral

Raoul L. Pinette

INTRODUCTION

As we begin to consider the complex problem of acute grief and the place or value of the funeral in its resolution, there are a few basic premises that must be acknowledged:

(1) Grief is the emotion experienced by man as a result of a loss or separation.

(2) It is impossible to determine just how much grief an individual has simply by looking at him.

(3) It is unwise and unfair to "specify" how much grief the bereaved should have.

(4) No two persons will suffer from the same intensity of grief or react in exactly the same manner to a loss.

(5) An individual acts and reacts within his own basic personal capabilities and limitations. He must not be expected to perform or display behavior that is outside of this spectrum.

(6) Grief is the strongest emotion suffered by human beings, especially in relation to the loss of a spouse.

(7) The funeral is not only an acknowledgment that a death has occurred, but also a societal proclamation that a life has been lived.

(8) The funeral can be a positive experience when it meets the needs of those who mourn.

(9) The funeral can be an occasion for personal growth.

111

EMOTIONS

Emotions are responses to stimulation and involve: (a) a mental attitude; (b) physiological stresses and changes; and (c) behavioral phenomena.

Emotions can be classified as positive or pleasant in contrast to negative (introverted) or unpleasant.

GRIEF

Grief as an emotion represents a disturbed psychological condition which can be described as disintegrative but which has the potential of acting as a stimulus to future integrations. Grief involves: (a) a disturbed relationship between the individual and the environment; (b) a diffused and hyperactive condition; (c) visceral responses (vasomotor, respiratory, gastrointestinal, glandular, and others); and (d) somatic behavior involving autonomic nervous mechanisms and centers.

To mitigate the effects of grief (emotion) on the bereaved, it would appear that the best response would be to take immediate action to accept the reality of its causative factors and seek emotional support (either social or therapeutic).

REACTIONS TO UNDESIRABLE EMOTIONS

Reactions to undesirable emotions include: (a) the individual tries to escape from the situation by avoiding it either physically or mentally; (b) the individual tries to overcome the situation; and (c) the individual attempts to derive pleasure from what is normally an unpleasant situation.

The last is usually considered to be abnormal by society if it is recognized as such. The second, if successful, obviously can help in adjusting to the situation. The first exists in many disguises and is a very common reaction.

ESCAPE MECHANISMS

Escape mechanisms include: (a) migration—the simplest mechanism of all, literally running away from the situation; (b) rationalization—searching for socially acceptable reasons to cover "loss of face" which might come from simple withdrawal; (c) projection—blaming others for misfortune; and (d) compensation—compensating for personal shortcomings in coping with emotional trauma by diligent application of energies in areas which can give success and gratification. (Such an individual is likely to label the things which he cannot do as not worth doing.)

DENIAL

We live in a youth-oriented society with strong desires to live; few of us wish to grow old or to die, and we do not want others to die either. It is normal to refuse to accept the fact of someone's death and to try to deny that the event has really happened. This denial can create a conflict between the mind and the emotions (with the mind acknowledging the fact and the emotions trying to deny it). The result of this ambivalence, if it is unresolved, can be serious mental or physical disorders or both.

COMPENSATION

There are those who have not resolved their personal anxieties as they relate to death, grief, bereavement, and the resultant funeral. By virtue of feelings of incompetence in this situation, they find it very easy to withdraw by the emotional means of denial and the physical activity of trying to get rid of death by disposing of the body as quickly as possible. Many may seek adjustment and compensation by becoming strong and verbal advocates of disposition without ceremonies or their own personal involvement.

Such approaches may produce relief as a form of response to the discomfort brought about by grief, but this relief for most individuals does not offer a satisfactory and lasting adjustment to grief itself. It often leaves the individual with the problems of adjustment to life without the person who has died, without an effective confrontation with the fact of mortality, or without acceptance of the fact that a significant death has occurred.

INTELLECTUALIZATION OR RATIONALIZATION

There are those who would like to resolve their grief by intellectualization or rationalization. We have already noted that rationalization is an escape and not a solution to the problem. If we approach the problem by intellectualization, we try to resolve it by separating it from its emotional ramifications. It is impossible for most people to achieve intellectual denial of the unpleasantness caused by the emotion, which is accompanied as well by physiological disturbances and aberrant behavioral responses.

Most who turn to intellectualization as a mechanism for resolving grief are simply at the wrong end of this spectrum. It might be possible for some to condition or insulate themselves from emotion before the fact, but once the emotion has been triggered, it must be expressed. For most people, it is too late to intellectualize it. Since our concern is acute grief, the emotion is a fact and the need for expressing it is also a fact. The problem to be concerned with is whether such expression will be constructive or destructive.

DEPTH OF EMOTIONS, EXPRESSION, AND REPRESSION

Depth of emotions, expression, and repression have serious implications for the individual suffering grief. The person with the most serious problem is the one with the capacity for deep emotions who finds it difficult to express them. Therefore, he may repress them until devastating emotional explosions result. If grief is not expressed at the time of the death, it will certainly be expressed later in a more regressive syndrome.

The bereaved need to express their grief, they need a platform to do it on, and they need a means of doing it. Dr. Paul Irion has said that the funeral offers a proper climate for the beginning of the work of mourning. Mourning is the pattern of behavior observable in an individual while he resolves the complex emotion of grief and the many other emotions that accompany it.

ATTITUDES TOWARD THE FUNERAL DIRECTOR

People approach the funeral director with various attitudes:

(a) There are those who have had experience with funerals and understand that they can fulfill the needs of the survivors. Many times they really know how the funeral can help them to express their emotions, to provide a setting for social support and direct confrontation with the fact that a death has occurred, and to assume sanitary disposition of the body. They have seen the funeral function as a first step in the resolution of grief. They approach the funeral director with respect and confidence.

(b) There are those who have not had experience with the funeral but who do have an open mind. They expect the funeral director to counsel with them. They expect him to give them the facts and the courses of action available to them so they can make their own decisions. They also approach the funeral director with respect and confidence.

(c) Dr. Jacques Choron, the late French philosopher, said that a philosophy of life cannot be mature unless it considers the prospect of eventual death of the individual and those around him. There are many people of all ages from every social and educational stratum who have not matured to the point of being willing to think of their own death and to contemplate that of others. When a death occurs, they withdraw into denial and try to "get rid of it" as quickly as possible. Many such persons seek all sorts of means of escape from confrontation with the truth. They try actively to rationalize their denial and withdrawal by deriding the funeral and the funeral director. Counseling is very difficult. The funeral director is viewed as the symbol of the death they are denying. They find him threatening and resent his person and presence.

(d) There are those who have not had experience with the funeral but have been exposed to a multitude of rationalizations, intellectualizations, pseudo-experts, and universal formulas, and who have taken a strong position against the funeral. They approach the funeral director as the symbol and merchant of death, expecting him to take advantage of them, distrusting what he says and does, and unwilling to accept his counsel.

(e) There are those who have had a bad experience with a previous death for one reason or another. Counseling these individuals may present problems.

NEGATIVE THOUGHTS

Funerals are barbaric—most barbarians viewed their dead and cared for them with ceremony. Would it be an acceptable criterion of civilization to have less respect for the dead than pagan societies did or than primitive communities have today?

Viewing is pagan—where is this thought expressed in the great books formulating religious doctrines or in the writings of those who have studied the psychological needs created by bereavement today?

Funerals and everything to do with them are morbid—this is said very often by those who have never even been to a funeral. Regarding something as morbid can be a frame of mind, an attitude; "morbid" is never a synonym for "sorrowful."

Funerals are too elaborate or too extravagant—who has the right to judge the actions of others? Those who need less elaborate funerals should have less elaborate funerals. Those whose needs call for the total funeral also have a right to have their needs fulfilled. It should be recognized that there are certain basics in a funeral to meet certain individual emotional needs just as there are basics in consuming food to meet certain physical needs.

Funerals are too expensive—some say categorically that funerals are too expensive. If one is not familiar with the positive values of a funeral, such a statement is easy to make, especially when "expensive" is not defined. If the funeral helps meet the needs of the survivors and it becomes an experience of value for them, how much is it really worth?

SOME POPULAR ESCAPE MECHANISMS

The Closed Casket. What better way is there to run away from death than to have a closed casket and not look at the dead person at all, unless one has seen the person die or viewed him in solitude? Regardless, the closed casket is a very convenient manner of withdrawing into denial. Whether the denial is conscious or subconscious is irrelevant. As long as it is allowed to persist, it could be unhealthy.

Dr. Erich Lindemann, when questioned after his many years of involvement in research on grief as to what was the most important moment for the survivors, said that it was the moment of truth when the survivors would stand in front of the open casket and look at the dead body. This visual confrontation by the survivors is the most effective manner of combating denial.

There are some who have an endless number of reasons why it is improper to look at the body. They say that it is pagan, that the embalmer makes the body look alive to conceal death. The only way of concealing death effectively is to make the person truly alive. The embalmer is obviously incapable of such a feat. The embalmer does not even try to make a body look alive, he simply tries to make it look lifelike in order to give the survivors a better image than the death mask by which to remember the deceased.

Many persons die of ravaging illness or from violence. At death their appearance is most disturbing for the survivors. First and final impressions are lasting, especially if the final one is traumatic. Unless something is done to present these survivors with a more acceptable or consoling image to remember the person by, they may be shocked by a haunting visual image. To believe that the survivors will be able to cast aside a traumatic confrontation in favor of a previous familiar image is in most instances naive.

No Visitations. There are some who feel that the period of visitations is a hardship for the survivors, an ordeal. Again, some use "no visitations" as an escape, a way to avoid the aftermath of death. But visitations give relatives and friends an opportunity to share their concern for the survivors and also to express their own grief. Appropriate conversation comes more easily there. It is axiomatic that joy shared is joy augmented, and grief shared is grief diminished. We must remember that there is nothing worse than going through a crisis alone.

There is a principle in psychology that says that for emotions to adjust properly to a nonrepetitive event, it must be accompanied by repetitive behavior. When the family stands next to an open casket and the visitors come, the conversation will center repeatedly around the deceased and the circumstances of the death. This constitutes repetitive behavior accompanying a nonrepetitive event, a death. These repetitive conversations also help to release pent-up emotions, a process known as catharsis.

Instead of visitations with the viewable body present, some recommend "no visitations" at a funeral home and that the family receive people at home. If the family separates itself from the body in this manner, relevant conversation becomes stultified. The visitors will not be prone to talk about the deceased, and the family may not get the necessary catharsis.

No service, either religious or nonreligious, should be a way of getting things over quickly. It could very well be that a short-term gain carries with it long-term negative consequences. Rites and ceremonies are like buffers against change. With the death of a loved person, the life of the closest survivor changes. It seems unwise to eliminate any buffer against such abrupt changes.

No Committal Service. There are people who do not want to go to the cemetery for the committal. They say the funeral should end at the funeral home or at the church. Committal prayers may or may not be made. There are many students of grief who believe that for those with a strong inclination toward denial, seeing the last station, the casket on the grave, may be helpful in dispelling this denial.

In the words of Paul Irion, "The committal service provides, as nothing else . . . does so graphically, a symbolic demonstration that the kind of relationship which has existed between the mourner and the deceased is now at an end."

Limited Funerals. There are some who would limit the number of cars at the funeral. They say that a long funeral procession can be a traffic hazard. What greater hazard is there than a number of cars racing separately to the cemetery, trying to be there on time, with many drivers not knowing where the cemetery is and where the grave is within the cemetery. The safest way to get the people from the services to the cemetery is in a funeral procession.

Who really has the right to dictate how many people should or should not grieve and how many should be accorded the right to express their grief through the funeral? Much has been cited about constitutional rights of expression on television and radio, in the newspapers, and in the public square. Throughout history when people have done something important, they get together, proclaim its importance, and express themselves by means of a ceremonial parade. Funerals serve as such an avenue of expression and have been throughout history the most dignified and most solemn of all ceremonial processions. The number of marches on city halls, college presidents' offices, public monuments, or what have you these days exemplifies that the social need for parades is still here, even in our own culture.

It is interesting to see how some will object to a few cars at a funeral but will not object to the hundreds of cars entering and leaving a shopping center or the thousands of cars leaving a race track or a ball game.

PERSONAL REACTIONS

Five factors that will influence one's reaction to a death are: (a) personality; (b) depth of emotions; (c) ability for emotional expression or repression; (d) structure of values; and (e) importance of deceased to survivor.

SOCIAL NEEDS

Six social needs have been documented as being constant in all cultures when death occurs: (a) social support; (b) confrontation; (c) rites and ceremonies; (d) procession; (e) sanitary disposition of the body; and (f) payment of some form.

WHAT IS A FUNERAL?

Dr. William Lamers, Jr., a psychiatrist, has defined a funeral as "an organized, purposeful, time-limited, flexible, group-centered response to death." With the studies that have been made recently we must add "with the body present" if the survivors are to derive all the benefits of the funeral.

WHAT DOES A FUNERAL DO?

A funeral must: (a) fulfill the needs of the survivors; (b) be a tribute to a life; (c) leave a recall image to assist the grief-resolution process.

We have already discussed the values of the recall image. The funeral must fulfill the particular needs of the family on this particular occasion. The funeral should be flexible. Since a person's reaction to death is influenced by a number of personal and social factors and the same person will not necessarily react in the same manner on different occasions of death, there should not be any universal formula for the funeral.

The funeral does not say, "John has died." You do not need a funeral to pronounce this as a fact. You just say it. However, the funeral does say, "John lived." It says that he lived a life so important that people have taken time out from their busy schedules to acknowledge it and to pay tribute to it. The funeral is a tribute to a life.

ELEMENTS OF A FUNERAL

What does the funeral include? The funeral has five ritualistic elements: (a) visitations or wake; (b) viewing; (c) rites and ceremonies; (d) procession; and (e) committal.

THE FUNERAL DIRECTOR

From his studies and his experiences the funeral director knows: (a) that the funeral has evolved in response to human needs and the basic social and personal needs of the bereaved; (b) that the funeral is a time-tested vehicle for the expression, recognition, and resolution of grief; (c) that there are dangers of repression or denial and possible repercussions if shortcuts are taken; (d) that there is no eraser on the pencil of the funeral—there is no second chance; (e) that the funeral as a tribute to a life must be right the first time; (f) that the funeral can be made effective as a vehicle for the expression of grief for those who tend towards emotional repression; and (g) that the funeral can be a first step towards rebuilding a sense of security.

The funeral director wishes to help the bereaved by providing the expertise, facilities, and merchandise for a funeral. He wants to share his understanding and his experience with his clients. He knows that his sincere efforts will be interpreted by some as exploitation, but he must have the courage of his convictions and counsel with the people. After the bereaved have been told of the choices available to them and of the consequences of certain requests, he must and will serve them according to their wishes.

ACTUAL EXPERIENCES WITH THE FUNERAL

A widow received great consolation from the large number of people who showed up for the visitations, the church services, and the committal services for her husband. She said that she knew how she had loved him and how wonderful he was, but she had never imagined that so many other people loved him and appreciated him that much. Had she not had the traditional funeral for her husband she would never have found out.

A mother who found her baby dead in the crib did not want to remember the horrible sight of the dead, cyanotic infant. After the funeral she was grateful that her baby could be viewed as beautiful as she had been in life and could be remembered that way.

A doctor whose wife had died of brain cancer was afraid of what he might see in the casket. He received great consolation from seeing a peaceful expression restored to her face and the traces of her suffering removed.

A woman who died of cancer of the face had not been seen for several months without a veil covering half of her face. She had lost much weight, and the husband wanted the casket kept closed. The embalmer performed his services, and the husband and his two teenage daughters were called in to view the results. One daughter said, "Thanks, Dad, for having had this done. We had forgotten how pretty mother was."

SOOTHING EFFECT OF VIEWING

Very often it can be observed that a family is agitated and nervous before the first visitation. Within a short time after the first viewing, a marked degree of calm appears. By confrontation with the fact of death and with its acceptance the work of mourning begins.

The mind has been tormented because it has accepted the death on the intellectual level while denying it on the emotional level. Visual confrontation confirms the fact that the one loved is really dead.

WHEN THE FUNERAL IS OVER

Some needs of the survivors for catharsis, for expression—personal, social, religious, or nonreligious—have been served.

The family has been helped to return to productivity because there were things to do, there were decisions to be made, there were people to meet. These activities help prevent withdrawal and internalization, which can result in an extended period of severance from normal productivity.

The importance of the life of the person they loved has been proclaimed, and tribute paid to it through the funeral.

On occasion, the funeral has offered the survivors an opportunity to purge themselves of some negative emotions, such as guilt. The question of whether there should or should not be guilt at this time when nothing helpful can be done on behalf of the deceased, whether the bereaved is or is not guilty, is irrelevant. The point is that if the survivor is stuck with a guilt complex, and if he can resolve it through the funeral (as is often the case), then he will be healthier in the future. Since we serve the living through the funeral, these are the kinds of needs to which we must also address ourselves.

WHAT HAS BEEN ACCOMPLISHED BY THE FUNERAL?

The funeral director, in most instances in cooperation with the clergy, has led the survivors by the hand over the turbulent waters of a crisis, with the funeral as a bridge, back to the mainstream of life. He can serve well as a true "crisis intervenor."

The Funeral Director's First Call

G. David Burton

The author's purpose is to describe the first stage of the grief process which is present during the first meeting of the funeral director with the bereaved family and to relate how the funeral director may guide, direct, and counsel a family at that time. What a funeral director does on the first call determines to what extent his function is fulfilled and thereby how well a family faces, accepts, and adjusts to the death of one of its members. The funeral director is performing the most important part of his professional service at this time. The family and extended family, all who care enough about the deceased or the bereaved to have an emotional response, are directly affected by the actions, advice, and counsel of the funeral director on the first call.

The funeral director's attitude is one of the most important aspects of a first call. He must have a good attitude about himself if he is going to communicate properly. He must have a feeling of confidence and a genuine concern for the family's problem. He must find his work fulfilling, be knowledgeable, and be ready to do all he can for the family he is about to serve.

There are many ways for a funeral director to evaluate his own attitude, many methods of self-analysis. People in a position to observe the director—a close friend who is a member of a family group, a clergyman, or other staff members—can be asked for their opinions regarding the impression he makes. The main thing is to develop a personal style, feel confident about it, and then use it as well as possible.

The funeral director must also understand how today's life has affected the

121

people with whom he deals. The book "Future Shock" by Alvin Toffler describes the tremendous changes in living brought about by the industrial revolution, the frenzied type of living patterns brought on by ever-increasing urbanization. Outgrowths of this living style are described in "Games People Play" by Eric Berne. (According to Newsweek magazine this is a "fascinating book. . . . These are not necessarily 'fun' games. In fact, most of them are hair raisingly neurotic rituals in which tensions are discharged and satisfactions gained, usually at the expense of others.")

Other evidences of the effect of today's life style are the zooming rate of mental illness, the increasing divorce rate, the increased need for psychiatric and psychological care, and the increase in the number of counseling centers and mental health units.

According to some sociologists, we live today in nuclear families with fewer people and highly intensified emotional involvements. Therefore, any disruption to the routine can be magnified to the extent of causing psychological stress or crisis so that coping becomes increasingly difficult. Dr. Robert Fulton (1965), in describing the American small family, says: "It is likely that the self develops strong emotional attachments to the family figures and has considerable affective investment in them."

All these stresses and intense emotional attachments are operating within the bereaved families served by the funeral director. He must understand them and be aware of their effect on the family's reaction—both during the time of acute grief and during the grieving period which follows once the immediate shock has worn off. Grief is normal and must be experienced. Inability to grieve freely may lead to an abnormal reaction, such as prolonged grief, which may eventually require therapeutic treatment.

Most funeral directors do not have to work with prolonged grief but, of course, must be sensitive to it so as to be able to recognize it in postfuneral calls in order to be sure that the proper people are aware and the right help is obtained.

On the first call, the funeral director is most likely to encounter acute grief and he will often hear remarks like the following:

"I can't believe this has happened."

"How could it happen to me?"

"If only I'd called the doctor sooner."

"I should never have let him take that new job."

"How could God do this?"

"We want to get this over as quickly as possible."

"We want the casket closed."

"We don't want calling."

"We'll have a private funeral."

"We don't want any of this funeral mumbo jumbo."

The first five responses show shock and disbelief; the remainder show the desire to be protected from pain. The funeral director must have his own style of handling these various responses. But he must be prepared at any moment to adapt because each first call is different, depending on the many circumstances and the personalities and characteristics of the individual family members. The director must be ready for any remark or question and must be able to respond to it immediately. When a penetrating question is asked, it serves little purpose to say, "There's a book on that back at the office," or, "One of my associates knows about that." On a first call, the director must be prepared in his own way to tactfully understand, guide, direct, and counsel a family.

The first call sets up a counseling situation for the funeral director. It may appear that he is carrying on a spontaneous conversation, but he is really counseling, using all his skill, study, and practice. It truly is a professional conversation.

The sensitive funeral director can handle the expressions of shock and disbelief with such comments as: "It is hard to believe"; "It takes time to understand, accept, and adjust"; or, "I understand how you feel." A genuine concern and a willingness to share the family's problem must be shown.

When confronted with such expressions as "hurry up," "closed casket," "no calling," "private funeral," and so on, the funeral director must try to preserve the family's options until such time as the family members progress out of acute grief into a stage of gradual realization and are more rational and willing to listen. One technique for preserving options is to try to identify the individual in the family group who seems to be the most composed and to explain suggestions to him or her. At other times, it may be best to try to delay decision making for several hours. This is one reason why it is best to talk with a family as soon as possible after death has occurred, regardless of the time of day, so it can be determined "where the family is" and what must be done to help.

Sometimes the family's first decisions are based on earlier remarks made by the deceased. An elderly person, suffering with an extended illness and feeling neglected because friends did not visit often, may have become hostile and said, "I don't want any calling or a funeral. If they didn't come to see me when I was alive, I don't want them to come when I'm dead." In such a case, the funeral director can explain to the family the value of the calling period—that it is an organized way of allowing friends to share in the moment and a way to give the family time to prepare emotionally for the funeral service. The director can assure the family that feelings of hostility and of being neglected are not uncommon in the elderly and ill and that those friends who were unable to make regular visits to the house or hospital most probably would want very much to attend the calling hours and/or the service to show their affection for the deceased and to provide support for the family.

Often the family members feel guilty about doing something they feel is against the deceased's wishes. For instance, a person who has lost weight and suffered disfiguration or deterioration may say to the family, "After I die, be sure to have the casket closed." The funeral director's technique ought to be to explain that the person's probable desire was really to make it easier for the rest of the family but that, in actual fact, what is easiest is to see the body. In order to adjust to death, people must realize and accept the fact of it. This applies both to the immediate family and to the extended family. Many concur that the easiest way to face the reality and accept it is to see the dead body.

A CASE HISTORY

A beautiful 57-year-old woman was found to have cancer and died six months later. During this period, she lost much weight and had underwent surgery, with the last surgical procedure being on the right side of her head and neck. A certain amount of hair had to be removed for this, but not all.

After her death, I was called to the family home and one of the first things the family told me was that the casket would have to be closed because of her appearance. After much discussion, we set a separate and private time for those who cared to come in to see her. This was done one morning at 11:00 with regular calling to start at 2:00 in the afternoon. When the family members came in, they were so relieved by the good appearance that they decided to leave the casket open during the calling period.

The body was placed in reverse position in the casket, as this side looked much better. Only one member of the family asked about the position. There were no other comments about this. (Here the importance of proper embalming, cosmetizing, and positioning should be noted. Often people think that they want a closed casket because of some unpleasant experience in the past.)

Funeral directors must remember that death produces a myriad of complex emotional responses which determine people's actions, reactions, and interactions. In all his work, and particularly during the first hours with the bereaved, the funeral director must be extremely sensitive and empathetic in order to share, care, guide, counsel, and direct the family in such a way as to make the funeral truly an "organized, purposeful, time-limited, flexible, group-centered response to death."

REFERENCES

Berne, E. "Games People Play." New York: Grove Press (1964).
Fulton, R. "Death and Identity." New York: John Wiley and Sons (1965).
Irion, P. "The Funeral—Vestige or Value?" Nashville: Abingdon Press (1966).
Toffler, A. "Future Shock." New York: Random House (1970).

The Impossible Task of the Funeral
Buell W. Dalton

It is not my purpose in this paper to analyze the funeral as we know it to-day, pointing out its weaknesses, nor even to suggest a new procedure which would more effectively meet the needs of those in grief. This is not to say that I will not analyze to a certain extent the circumstances in which the funeral is expected to function and the limitations which these circumstances impose.

One of the best and most thorough analyses of the funeral was written by Paul E. Irion (1966). I find myself in general agreement with Irion's exhaustive analysis and conclusions. However, I do not agree with him when he writes (p. 88), "But sound, objective bases need to be established for the determination of value (of the funeral). . . . Subjective opinion, bias based on personal experience, or special pleading do not constitute effective means for such evaluation."

I would contend that there is no "sound, objective" base for determining the funeral's value. If there is ever to be any evaluation of the funeral, it must of necessity be a "subjective opinion, [or] bias based on personal experience." If it were possible to determine objectively the value of the funeral, then the funeral could become a predictable commodity on every occasion and be of equal value to the casual visitor and to the deeply grieved. But this has not been the experience of those involved in funerals. Funerals differ in value one from another and from person to person according to a number of factors. Even the officiant and the funeral director, who are in position to be the most objective in their evaluation, find themselves responding subjectively in varying degrees.

Thus, the seemingly impossible task of the funeral is broadened to include

125

the preparer and conductor of the funeral. We must then conclude that the only valid evaluation of the funeral should, of necessity, be on the basis of "subjective opinion, [or] bias based on personal experience." Of course, this conclusion negates the possibility of any evaluation other than each affected individual's evaluation of the funeral in terms of his own "personal experience." The preparer and conductor of the funeral, therefore, has no bias for objective evaluation. The effectiveness of the funeral he has offered the bereaved can be measured only over the long term as he observes the degree to which the bereaved have each successfully handled his or her grief experience.

Irion (p. 89) seems to change his previous position when it comes to defining the funeral. He now says that the funeral is "multidimensional and thus requires a multidimensional definition. . . . A definition tends to lack meaning and ultimately usefulness if the perspective of the definer is not taken into account."

Granted that in the first reference the author is concerned with determining the value of the funeral while in the second reference he is seeking to lay the groundwork for a definition, it must be realized that these are not mutually exclusive exercises. Neither can be satisfactorily performed apart from the other. Therefore, the conclusion to which we are drawn is that the definition of the value of the funeral is "multidimensional and . . . tends to lack meaning and ultimately usefulness if the perspective of the definer is not taken into account"-which is, of course, a subjective evaluation.

To objectivize the evaluation of the funeral requires that one first dehumanize those for whom the funeral is arranged. The effective funeral can never be a mechanical process, for it is not its purpose to serve robots.

There are numerous funeral manuals on the market today for the minister or the conductor of the funeral, but I have yet to find one that meets the requirements of every funeral. Recognizing this weakness in available funeral service books, I considered preparing one myself. Then in my more sane moments, I realized that this is quite an impossible task. The consideration that there are some 212 million souls in the United States alone, each of whom differs from every other one, and all this multiplied by the countless ways and circumstances in which death may come, was the straw that broke the back of my ambition. I propose that the temperament of an individual, the degree of his emotional involvement with other persons, and the time and manner of his demise will each one separately and all collectively serve to determine the degree of acuteness of the grief of his survivors.

It is this grief in all of its multifaceted aspects—social, psychological, theological and emotional—that the funeral must seek to minister to. To the extent that the demands of grief are multidimensional, so must the ministration of the funeral be multidimensional. This means that the funeral must be flexible enough to meet the grief demands of both the nonreligious and the religious, of the good citizen and the bad, of the dearly loved and the detested, of the conservative and the liberal, all of whom may be present and in need of grief help at one and the same time. Grief comes in some dimension to everyone, young and old alike, not only in the experience of death, but especially then.

The impossible task of the funeral is further magnified by the understanding of grief as "acute"—meaning grief in which the onset is sudden, the severity deep, the duration short, and the recovery complete. I suppose that we think we are justified in trying to pattern even our grief to the highly mobile and fluctuating time and habits in which we live the rest of life. But I am not convinced that grief itself understands, or appreciates, or adjusts to our desired pattern—especially as to short duration and complete recovery. I have observed a more or less predictable cyclical pattern to grief. On or about the anniversary of a patient's initial grief experience there appears a recurrence of the symptoms, sometimes more severe than at first. Which, of course, means that some form of grief support must be available on an extended basis. This the funeral cannot supply.

The impossible task of the funeral in seeking to assuage acute grief is complicated still further by the increased rootlessness of modern society. There is little opportunity to establish meaningful social contacts and form friendships which can be supportive in time of grief. Dr. Elton Trueblood has aptly named ours the "cut flower civilization." The officiant called upon in the hour of death to prepare and conduct the funeral is limited in his ability to do an effective job by the fact that he probably has had no previous contact with the bereaved; he was probably called upon to serve the family by the funeral director; and when the service is concluded it is unlikely that he will ever have any further contact with them.

In spite of the impossible task and the limitations imposed upon the funeral in serving those who are grieved, man throughout his history has used some form of ceremonial to meet the deep need of his hour of grief. Nothing else has ever proven itself as effective. The fact that society is always trying something new does not in the least detract from the proven effectiveness of the funeral. We shall not argue the point that the traditional, contemporary funeral is far from fulfilling an ideal, but it is the best that we have, and until something new has proven its worth by being tested against man's need, I am sure that even though we may depart from the funeral for a while, we shall return for its comfort and strength.

Perhaps our discontent, if there is such, with the funeral is that it has not kept pace in its healing of our hurts with the rest of our scientific and technological advances. The very fact that we can think of grief as "acute"—that is, an experience to be soon done with—puts the whole scheme of life in question. Grief seems to be saying to us, "Here is an important experience of life that refuses to be hurried, for the hurrier will be the loser." To the tune of jangled nerves, ulcerated stomachs, hypertension, and heart failure our modern modes of transportation propose to hurry us through life in air-conditioned comfort at such speed that we might accomplish the tasks of two lives in one lifetime—that is, so long as our energy lasts. The story of the hare and the tortoise, or our re-call of the days of the horse and buggy, teaches us that it is far better to move with patience and arrive at our goal than to hurry up, exhaust our resources, and never arrive.

REFERENCES

Irion, P. E., "The Funeral: Vestige or Value." Nashville: The Parthenon Press (1966).

THE FUNERAL DIRECTOR'S EDUCATION

The Metamorphosis of Funeral Service Education

Dale W. Sly

Prior to 1900 embalming was taught by demonstration teams travelling throughout the country. Between 1900 and 1920 there were at least 12 embalming schools established to teach the art of embalming. In 1936 the term "mortuary science" appeared in the title of some of these embalming schools.

During this same period of time the association of state licensing agencies began to display an interest in the curriculum of the schools. In 1927 this organization adopted a topical curriculum for a six-month course. About the same time, it adopted a plan for grading colleges of embalming. About 1934 the length of the course was extended to nine months. In 1940 it became the Council of Funeral Service Examining Boards, Inc.; later the term "conference" was substituted for "council."

Also, during the early 1900's, the National Funeral Directors Association became more interested in education and appointed a three-man committee on education. In 1933 this committee proposed a joint meeting with like committees from both the Conference and school associations. The joint committee was known as the "nine-man committee," or the Joint Educational Council. In 1959, this committee was renamed The American Board of Funeral Service Education. Two years later it was incorporated.

During the early 1900's, the embalming schools and colleges were working together to make improvements in their educational programs. In 1930 many of them joined together and formed the National Association of Embalming Schools and Colleges. This organization was incorporated in 1935, and in 1942 its name was changed to the National Association of Colleges of Mortuary Science. This organization was responsible for conducting teachers institutes or course content committee meetings. These meetings were held for the instructors of the various funeral service educational institutions in order to develop, discuss, and revise the course content for each of the subjects their students were being examined on by the National Board Examination of the Conference. There was an attempt to have a teachers institute in each subject at least once every five years.

Unfortunately, during the early 1900's state laws were passed which prescribed complete college curricula for courses in embalming and funeral directing. Some laws would state the specific subjects and the total hours to be taught. These requirements were not determined by the colleges or the Conference but by one or two individuals in a given state who had good intentions but were not well informed. As a result the funeral service schools and colleges were locked into a curriculum with little opportunity to make changes as needed. Likewise, each state was preparing examinations for those students wishing to be licensed in their state. Because of a lack of uniformity in the questions and a desire for the colleges to have their students pass, every time a new topic appeared the states would add new materials to the course content. This of course led to curricula which supplied answers for state board examinations rather than ones which would be useful to future embalmers and/or funeral directors. (For a detailed discussion of the early history of funeral service education, see "The History of American Funeral Directing," by Robert W. Habenstein and William M. Lamers.)

On Oct. 20, 1956, a Regulation and Standards Committee of the Mortuary College Associations was organized by the Joint Educational Council. During the last week of January 1957 this committee prepared a preliminary draft of regulations and standards. In October of that same year the final draft was prepared and submitted for approval. This was the beginning of a four-quarter program of not less than 44 instructional weeks. The effective date for this program was July 1, 1959. The accrediting manual recommended four areas of instruction, which were:

(1) Basic Sciences—15 quarter credit hours including Anatomy and Chemistry.

(2) Public Health Sciences—18 quarter credit hours including Bacteriology, Hygiene and Public Health, and Pathology.

(3) Mortuary Arts and Sciences—15 quarter credit hours including Embalming and Restorative Art.

(4) Mortuary Administration—15 quarter credit hours including Accounting, Mortuary Law, Psychology and Funeral Principles, and Directing and Management.

Electives—9-21 quarter credit hours including either additional subjects or increased credit hours in prescribed subjects.

During the next ten years there was little or no progress made in funeral service education. Attempts were made to form a single association of educational institutions. The American Board, made up of three members from the National Funeral Directors Association, three from the Conference, and one from each of three educational organizations (National Association of Colleges of Mortuary Science, American Association of Colleges of Mortuary Science, University of Mortuary Science Educational Association), in an attempt to raise standards adopted a mandatory 30-semester-hours of "C"-average work as a prerequisite for entrance into an accredited school. Several of the larger states opposed such a requirement and requested the mortuary colleges not to comply. Recognizing the dilemma, the colleges which were members of NACMS and AACMS organized another accrediting agency known as the Council on Accreditation and made application to the U. S. Office of Education for recognition. Five of the educational institutions were removed from the list of accredited institutions by the American Board for noncompliance with the college prerequisite. This led to a legal action against the American Board by these five schools. In October 1969, after considerable discussion and actions taken by the Conference and the Executive Board of the National Funeral Directors Association, NACMS and AACMS withdrew from membership in the American Board. This action left the American Board serving as the accrediting agency for less than one-half of the educational institutions.

On Nov. 15, 1969, a meeting of concerned educators was held. This meeting was suggested and coordinated by the Chairman and Executive Secretary of the Conference. Those invited were not representing any organization but attending as concerned individuals trying to find a solution to a difficult problem. This committee recommended to the American Board the formation of a Commission of Schools and greater representation on the American Board by the funeral service educators. At the annual meeting of the American Board, held in February 1970, a resolution was adopted authorizing the formation of a Commission of Schools. About the same time, the membership requirement of the American Board was changed to give each educational institution a voice in the American Board. All schools were notified of a meeting to be held on March 14. At this meeting the representatives of the schools agreed to the idea of a Commission of Schools, provided the accreditation function of the Board was delegated to the Commission.

Assuming such delegation would be forthcoming, the educators informally organized, elected officers, and decided on the need for a Standing Committee. At the midyear meeting of the American Board, held in July of 1970, a resolution was passed giving the Commission of Schools the following functions: To prepare and certify to the American Board of Funeral Service Education criteria for accreditation; To prepare and certify to the American Board of Funeral Service Education procedures for accreditation; To receive reports of the Examiner and to certify to the Board those schools which meet such criteria and are to be accredited; and To accept the certification of the Commission and that the statement of accreditation shall be made in the name of the Board.

The Board also passed a resolution removing the one-year college prerequisite requirement.

These two resolutions enabled the Commission of Schools to be formally organized; however, there was still one more stumbling block. According to Article VI of the American Board constitution, membership on the Commission of Schools was restricted to representatives from schools which were solely accredited by the American Board. This prohibited those schools which were accredited by the Council on Accreditation from becoming members of the Commission of Schools. After much deliberation on proposals and counterproposals, a motion was passed which suspended until Dec. 31, 1970, this membership provision, provided the Council on Accreditation suspended its functions and agreed not to pursue any pending application or file any new application for recognition by the U. S. Office of Education for the same period. This motion made it possible for the Commission of Schools to be organized and include all educational institutions with funeral service education programs.

July 10, 1970, is a date to be remembered in funeral service education. Since that time, there has been great progress. In October 1970 the Commission of Schools adopted its Constitution and By-Laws, confirmed the elected officers, approved appointments to the Standing Committees, and established a list of funeral service educational institutions to be certified to the American Board. One year later the Commission adopted standard operating procedures to clarify the specific procedures to be followed.

The U. S. Office of Education was kept informed of the progress being made and on Mar. 16, 1972, Commissioner Marland granted a one-year recognition to the American Board-Commission of Schools. He recommended: the development and implementation of a self-study; appointment of lay representatives; and establishment of differential criteria at various levels of education. In May 1972 a special meeting of the Executive Committee of the American Board was held. The Committee was joined by the two members of the Secretariat who had represented the Board before the U. S. Office of Education, the chairman of the Standards and Criteria Committee of the Commission of Schools, the legal council, and the administrator of the Board. At this meeting action was taken on each of the recommendations made by Dr. Marland. A rough draft of a procedures manual and a self-study guide, prepared by the Chairman, was reviewed and delivered to the Standards and Criteria Committee of the Commission for its evaluation. In October 1972 changes were made to provide for two public (lay) members on the Commission, and differential criteria at the diploma, associate degree, and baccalaureate degree levels were approved. At this time, the chairman of the American Board pointed out that since the accreditation function was being so adequately carried on by the Commission of Schools, the Board could carry on other functions and should begin a curriculum study. Prior to this date the curriculum had been prepared by educators; the Conference was examining students on professional expectations prepared by instructors of funeral service educational institutions, and no attempt had been made to determine if this curriculum was meeting the needs of future employees in funeral service. Therefore, three committees were established. One committee was to prepare board curricular objectives and specific instructional objectives for embalming activities, a second committee was to prepare like behavioral objectives in funeral directing and funeral management activities; the third committee was to study the licensing laws of the various states as they pertain to specific subjects to be included in curricula.

In July 1973 the American Board was informed that its listing as an approved accrediting agency was extended for a period of three years. In October the curriculum study committees made their reports to the American Board. After thorough discussion and suggested revisions, these were turned over to another committee. The Phase II Curriculum Study Committee was approved and given the following responsibilities:

(1) Coordinate Phase I Committee reports and make revisions as suggested during the discussion of the reports.

(2) Test the objectives for feasibility, relevancy, and relative importance by soliciting responses (feedback) from educators, funeral directors, state licensing agencies, recent graduates, students in funeral service education, and so on.

(3) Recommend changes in licensing laws to specific states, where needed, so that curriculum changes can be made.

(4) Recommend changes in the curriculum as outlined in Section J of the Standards and Criteria Manual; after recommendations are approved by the Board, refer them to the Commission of Schools for final action and implementation.

(5) Recommend methods and procedures for developing basic syllabi which indicate the scope of material to be used by the Conference and the various state boards in preparing their examinations.

The Phase II Curriculum Study Committee met in December 1973. They completed their first assignment and prepared a statement of philosophy, broad curricular objectives, and specific instructional objectives for funeral service education. They also discussed and decided on the samples to be used in securing feedback. At the present time the Chairman of this Committee is assembling a list of names and addresses from each of the sampling groups. Arrangements are being made to have the responses tabulated and interpreted. The Phase II Curriculum Committee is hopeful that they will have a preliminary report prepared for the fall 1974 meeting of the American Board and a final report ready for the annual meeting of the Board in the spring of 1975. If this timetable is followed, teacher institutes can be held to determine the range of subject matter, based on curricular and instructional objectives, which has been deemed necessary and helpful to those engaged in the profession of funeral service. This should make it possible for new professional expectations to be certified to the Conference of Funeral Service Examining Boards, which, in turn, should bring about changes in the National Board Examinations. As stated earlier, July 10, 1970, was a date to be remembered in Funeral Service Education. Since that time considerable progress has been made in improving funeral service education. Within the next few years the educational institutions should be teaching knowledge, skills, abilities, and attitudes which are based on sound research and will better meet the needs of future embalmers and/or funeral directors.

Psychology and the Funeral Service Licensee

William F. Matthews

Socrates once said ". . . for is not philosophy the study of death?" Socrates along with other philosophers of his era and more recent times believed that death or the impending loss of a person's most treasured possession—his psyche, or soul—was the motivating factor behind the study of philosophy and its later offspring, psychology. Death has created an awareness of mental life. It has been stated that a full understanding of life cannot be had without an understanding and acceptance of death.

If this premise is accepted, and if it is understood that the task of funeral service as a profession is to serve the living, should not the funeral director, who is confronted with death almost daily, have sufficient training in psychology in order to understand death and its effects on people?

Psychology of funeral service should be included in the State and National Board Examinations provided by the Conference of Funeral Service Examining Boards and in the examinations constructed by individual state licensure agencies. Its inclusion would make mandatory increased emphasis on the study of psychology, for which there is presently only a limited coverage required in funeral service curricula accredited by the American Board of Funeral Service Education. This in no manner intends to diminish the importance of similar programs of continuing education for the practicing funeral service person.

The adoption of psychology as an educational and licensure requirement for funeral service personnel could have many advantages. Among these are: (1) it will tend to insure the future of the funeral and funeral service which many

137

believe are vital sociopsychological functions; (2) it will give funeral service personnel an opportunity to fulfill their social responsibility as citizens to secure the quality and duration of human life; and (3) it will provide the funeral service person with greater satisfaction from his chosen career.

Presently there are many criticisms of the funeral and its ability to cope effectively with the crisis of death. In many areas of the country alternate methods of dealing with death and the funeral are being used. Surely any increased use of these methods will jeopardize the funeral and the career of the funeral director.

What can be done? These challenges could either mean the extinction of funeral service or provide the stimulus to advance funeral service as a caregiving profession. The decision rests with the funeral service practitioner.

The challenges could certainly be an opportunity. What is essential is communication with people at every opportunity—formally or informally—as to the value of the funeral and how funeral service meets social, psychological, and other human needs.

A vital part of this communication is counseling. A well-known cleric said almost two decades ago, "The funeral director by his very position is a counselor—a person who assists another through a crisis in his life. This he cannot deny. The only decision possible is whether he will be an effective or an ineffective counselor."

Specifically, the funeral director should never fail to counsel and to recommend: when there are requests for no funeral or for no visitation with the body present, when questioned as to the child and death, when extreme grief reactions are recognized, or whenever his advice would be valuable. In doing these things the funeral director need in no way come into conflict with the pastoral counselor or trained psychologist.

But the ability to communicate and counsel effectively is based on an adequate education. One must understand what is meaningful in a funeral and during the period of bereavement. Such an understanding can come about only through adequate training in the behavioral sciences—a large portion of which involves psychology.

In the teaching of funeral service on the university level by this author, the question has often been asked of freshmen students: "What does the funeral director do that is valuable and meaningful for people?" This same question has also been asked of practicing funeral service personnel. Almost invariably, the replies mention supplying material things and embalming with no mention of social or psychological values.

In "The Psychology of Death," Robert Kastenbaum uses the phrase "professionals in our death systems." He sees as types of "death experts" the funeral director, the physician, the nurse, the clergyman, and the mental health specialist. Based on his interviews with and tests of funeral service personnel and students, Kastenbaum drew this conclusion: "The funeral director is most times ill-equipped to give any concrete social or psychological guidance toward a meaningful death or funeral experience due to either his lack of interest, his insufficient knowledge, his own inability to cope with death, or a combination of these three."

Though this statement is indicative of a problem area in funeral service, it is most definitely a recognition of the unique, influential position of the funeral service person. It would surely behoove those in funeral service to insure that the personnel currently practicing their profession and the new licensees have the type of education and training which will enable and encourage effective communication, interaction, and cooperation with other professionals and lay people, which in turn will provide for a valuable funeral experience, one which will perpetuate funeral service as a career.

The people of this country are confronted today with the idea of "social responsibility." It is used in relation to business, professions, government, the environment, or any area that involves people. Alvin Toffler, in "Future Shock," wrote of the "death of technocracy" and a new strategy called "social futurism." His thinking focuses on the realization that worldly problems cannot be solved solely through technological advances, but rather through a shift to a greater social and human awareness. That is, a shift from things to people.

This same philosophy must be held, in part, by those persons who have contributed in the past ten years so much research and writing on the psychology of dying, death, grief, and the funeral. Though psychology of death is not yet a fully developed discipline, there is an abundance of material for reference and study.

Concurrent with this research and writing has come an increased awareness of the role of the funeral director as a caregiving professional. Should not funeral service personnel as responsible individuals—as human beings—use this literature in their education in order that they can be better prepared to assume the new role demanded of them and fulfill their social responsibility?

In recent years there have also been intensive research and writing about human relations in the workplace—about employee motivation and satisfaction. It also is a part of the "what's good for people movement" in the country. Logical thinking seems to indicate that education in the behavioral sciences—in psychology—will enable the funeral service person, and most assuredly the new licensee, to identify and understand the real "reason-for-being" of funeral service and of himself as a professional. For those who follow psychologist Abraham Maslow's ideas, two concepts emerge: self-esteem, from knowing that a meaningful contribution to people is being made; and self-realization, through knowledge and ability attaining one's greatest potential in life.

These ideas should when applied result in greater satisfaction for the funeral service person and in a sense of pride in being a funeral director. In all probability, the new image will assist in both the recruitment and retention of quality personnel.

How much psychology should the funeral director know? The ideal knowledge level should certainly include an introductory course covering such areas as: the science of human behavior, personality development, determinants of behavior, individual differences, and the various fields of psychology. In addition, there should be some understanding of abnormal psychology, the psychology of dying, death, and grief as it relates to the adult and to the child, and finally, the psychology of the funeral.

The determination of what should be included is not difficult, but creating such a program for funeral service licensure in those 25 states, approximately, which do not require college or university studies in addition to professional studies for licensure is not a simple matter, especially since most of those states have not had a major licensure law change in well over 20 years. But do not all worthy accomplishments require notable effort?

True professionalism through education will not come without great effort, but it is absolutely essential for the future of funeral service. Surely, it will require courage, determination, perseverance, and great personal involvement. Funeral service as a caregiving profession is limited solely by the aspirations of those who populate its ranks.

Education and Mortuary Science —
Psychosocial Goals and Philosophy

Charles H. Nichols

The constant expansion of knowledge, coupled with the rapid pace of scientific and technological development in practically all fields, is forcing change at an accelerated rate. This change, in turn, is giving rise to new educational concepts. Preparatory education for almost any profession or vocation must encompass both these new discoveries and new techniques. This is as true for funeral service as it is for any other vocation.

Much that has been taught, of course, will still need to be taught. A thorough grounding in mortuary science will still be needed—including embalming, sanitation, and both personal and public hygiene, with sufficient background in the prerequisite contributory sciences such as chemistry, anatomy, pathology, and microbiology. Mortuary arts, primarily restorative art and cosmetology with related background subjects, will still be needed. There is little doubt that funeral direction will also be needed, with its emphasis upon different rites and customs encountered among the various denominational and ethnic groups of American society—probably with a new emphasis on the sociological aspects of the funeral.

But the old subjects no longer suffice for funeral service preparatory education today. Now there is need for "threshold" knowledge and counseling skills in the area of normal grief and bereavement reactions, coupled with sensitivity to abnormal reactions (for purposes of referral). This might be called bereavement counseling. Now, too, there is need to teach mortuary management, to equip the practitioner to cope successfully with the increasingly abundant and complex problems of business, management and administration.

PREPARATORY EDUCATION NOT ENOUGH

But "preparatory" education is no longer enough. Constant change requires continuing education. The concept of lifelong education is coming into its own. In the professions, for example, some states have considered legislation requiring periodic courses—not so much "refresher" sessions as they are "developmental" sessions, indoctrinating practitioners in new developments of their field, for license renewal.

All sorts of educational innovations are appearing on the current scene. There are new forms of educational organization, such as "free" universities, schools "without walls," community laboratories, TV colleges, class-practice alternations, and learning centers of various kinds. New measurement techniques are being applied, such as brain impulses versus traditional intelligence quotients, general educational development tests, and "no fail" criteria with their emphasis upon some measure of success. There are new educational forms, such as mini-courses, maximum election of subjects pursued, and independent self-learning. There are new groupings, such as interest groupings and sensitivity sessions— "head start" and "preschool" at one end and a multiplicity of adult forms at the other. There is new teaching-learning technology: computers, retrieval systems, closed-circuit television, teaching machines, educative games, and cassettes for hearing or seeing or both. There are new concepts of teacher-learner interpersonal relationships, in which the authoritarian role of the teacher is replaced by that of the learning counselor or the resource person among other learners.

But the concern of this paper is not with all these forms of educational innovation, some of which will survive while others drop by the wayside. Rather, the concern of this paper is with a philosophy of education for funeral service that is soundly based upon proper goals—both socially and psychologically attuned to modern American society.

SOCIAL EXPECTATIONS AND PSYCHOLOGICAL DEMANDS

Two questions must be considered. What social expectations—in the broadest sense—does today's society have of the funeral director? What psychological demands does society make upon him, even though these may not be at a conscious individual level?

The answers will facilitate the framing of proper goals for funeral service education. These goals, in turn, will help to shape appropriate means—the educational structure.

Actually, the two questions can be answered objectively only by society itself, but comprehensive survey procedures are beyond the scope of this paper. So an introspective procedure is being used—one man's position (which does seem appropriate for a "position" paper). The writer offers, as his best credential apart from being a professional adult educator, a quarter-century of experience at the helm of an educational program for funeral directors, the National Foundation of Funeral Service.

What are society's expectations of the funeral director? There are at least six major expectations. Society expects the funeral director competently to protect the public health, first and foremost—to provide safe limited retention and safe ultimate disposal of the dead human body. The vast majority of people further expect him to preserve human dignity in the process—the dignity of both the deceased and the bereaved—in an appropriate, sensitive, and understanding manner. He is expected to provide an opportunity—an occasion, a setting, a climate—for appropriate leavetaking, a rite of separation that is a part of nearly all cultures, whether it be religious or humanist. He is expected to make available a suitable place for these purposes—suitably staffed, furnished, and equipped in keeping with today's standards. He is expected to supply the guidance, services, and merchandise required to do these things in a fitting way. And this is most important, introducing the economic aspect: society expects the funeral director to perform these functions for everybody, rich and poor alike, as a social responsibility (not unlike the physician's, in this respect). There probably aren't many, if any, who would take issue with these half-dozen social functions.

The second question: what psychological demands? "Demands" may be a poor choice of words, for the survivors may but dimly perceive their own psychological needs. However, the work of such contemporary authors as Erich Lindemann, William M. Lamers, Edgar N. Jackson, Paul E. Irion, Joshua Liebman, Earl Grollman, Robert Fulton, and Geoffrey Gorer—to name but a few— all tend to indicate certain psychological needs of the bereaved.

"They," in the following, then, refers to bereaved persons, and the literature seems to identify at least nine psychological needs. They need to face the reality of their loss, to accept the actuality of their bereavement—for which reason many of these authorities openly recommend viewing of the body. They need to do this with a minimum of further shock or mental anguish—for which reason restorative art has a legitimate role to play, not to "prettify," but to alleviate disfigurement or emaciation. They need to give vent to their grief, for which reason they are encouraged to express as much emotion as they feel—to cry, to bemoan their loss, to voice their feelings of guilt or anger, to talk endlessly and repetitiously of the deceased. They need the sympathetic support of family, relatives, friends, and neighbors—for which reason the visitation or calling hours continue to be a fairly standard part of most funeral patterns. They need the reassurance and spiritual strength provided by their faith, if they are fortunate enough to have one—or at least the mental comfort of a philosophic or humanist point of view that gives meaning to the life and death they celebrate; for this reason the religious or other type of ritual is also an important part of the pattern. They need, or at least most appreciate at this time, a touch of beauty and grace to soften the difficult reality of separation—an esthetic touch, if you will, for which reason music, poetry, flowers, pleasant surroundings, and even fittingly designed funeral merchandise have some part to play. They need an awareness that they are not alone in their loss, that the one who has died was a significant person in the lives of others as well, others who have their own need for expression and leavetaking—for which reason the actual funeral service is most normally a public service. They need a note of finality, a sense of closing or ending of the life of the deceased, in a mortal sense—and this note has normally been psychologically sounded by the funeral procession and final committal. They need to continue what has been started through the funeral process, to complete their grief work—to mend the fabric of interpersonal relations torn by death and build new relations, to turn again to life.

IMPLICATIONS FOR EDUCATIONAL GOALS

If these, then, be society's expectations of the funeral director, what are the implications for his educational goals? He must be, first of all, a person capable of dealing intelligently, sensitively, and effectively with people, particularly those in an overwrought emotional state. Therefore, he should be able to meet them at least on their own average educational level, speaking now of liberal, general, or background education. Today, this would mean a prerequisite of at least one year of college, fast moving toward two years. Median school years completed for 1970 was 12.2 for the white population, 10.1 for the nonwhite; but the younger groups show much higher percentages of postsecondary education being completed, and the effect of this will be very apparent in a few years, where completion figures are concerned. Present requirements for funeral service education are moving in this same direction.

It would seem desirable to aim toward a two-year college prerequisite, which had already been realized in some 20 states by 1973. This makes it possible to include many of the desirable subjects in preparation for the college of mortuary science—for example, English language and literature; introductory survey courses in psychology, sociology, and business; biology; chemistry; comparative religion, art, and music; and public speaking. These would be general treatments, with specialization and applications in any one area to be given in the college of mortuary science, where they would be specifically geared to the vocational task to the extent needed.

Another fundamental goal of funeral service education would be to make the student knowledgeable in those specialized areas and competent in those specialized skills required in mortuary science and examined for by state licensing boards, such as embalming, restorative art, sanitation, and so forth. This poses an immediate question—should there be one license or separate licenses for embalmer and funeral director? It may be argued, with some reason, that two separate and distinct vocational tasks are involved. Some states have a single license, most have dual licensing. But, in practice, a majority take both licenses in the dual licensing states. Typical establishment size makes this almost necessary. It seems that single licensing will prevail in the future; few are inclined, nor do sufficient opportunities exist, just to embalm. So the argument may be academic. Essentially the same preparation seems desirable whether single or dual licensing exists—and this falls within the province of the college of mortuary science.

It follows, then, that a third goal—an extension of the second—is parallel knowledge and skill in funeral direction, as distinct from mortuary science. But this should be more narrowly conceived than presently; it does not, by nature, include psychology of grief and mortuary management. These deserve separate treatment and considerably more emphasis.

In fact, knowledge of the psychology of grief and bereavement, with related skills in crisis intervention and counseling, should constitute a fourth goal. It is my position that much which has been published on the psychology of death and dying, while valuable background for the funeral director, has little direct relevance for him. His primary concern is with the psychology of grief and bereavement—with those who survive after a death has occurred. He is concerned with them, moreover, at the point of occurrence, with a certain immediacy, "at the threshold" as someone has expressed it. Normally he does not have a prolonged period in which to deal with them in a counseling relationship; the typical funeral may span only two or three days. Neither is he a psychologist as such—and certainly not a psychiatrist; nor should he make the slightest pretense in these directions.

Alvin Toffler, in his book "Future Shock," used the term "crisis intervention." John P. Brantner, of the University of Minnesota's Department of Psychology, later referred to the funeral director as a "crisis intervenor." The earlier publications, by some of the individuals previously mentioned, dealt with grief and bereavement. These publications, it would seem, preceded the work by Kübler-Ross and others on death and dying. It is my conviction that the education of the funeral director should concentrate on the psychology of grief and other emotional reactions to the death of another. His special area should be help, guidance, and threshold counseling to the bereaved. Without laboring the point, the distinction would seem to need some emphasis and more time and attention in the colleges of mortuary science.

A fifth goal of particular concern stemming from society's expectations is knowledge and skill in mortuary management, the "business of the profession." Society's definitions of a suitable place for funerals, suitable staff, furnishings, and equipment, suitable funeral merchandise and services—except for the professional aspects of some services—are essentially business matters. They involve mortuary management and administration. They encompass all the business problems a funeral director faces—mortuary planning and financing, personnel, advertising and public relations, legal, merchandising, accounting and taxation, cost control, pricing, credit and collection, insurance, and office operation—the whole gamut of related business.

"The business of the profession," and the problems related thereto, are not unknown to medicine; they have, however, in a sense been separated and delegated to nonprofit, non-taxpaying, often subsidized hospitals where they are primarily (though not exclusively) found under the heading "hospital administration." The typical funeral director, however, has all these headaches personally, sometimes with the addition of an ambulance operation, and this business area needs and deserves expanded treatment in the college of mortuary science.

Goal six—a business consideration, but important enough to receive separate mention—is the matter of making mortuary services available to all, rich and poor alike. The colleges of mortuary science must inculcate this concept into the minds of their students, thoroughly indoctrinate them and develop a "service beyond return" type of dedication.

What is primarily involved in pricing? Again, the problem is not unknown to physicians, who vary fees or waive fees on occasion. And funeral directors, too, have their share of donated or welfare funerals; for them, it is more than a matter of personal or professional services, for they are burdened with all the costs of their mortuaries—occupancy costs, staff salaries, and automotive, operating, and administrative expenses. The only logical answer, the only possible answer it often seems, is that of graduated recovery. This means, frankly, that those who arrange more elaborate funerals and select funeral merchandise of higher quality must bear more of the expense of making such a range of selection available—in short, a somewhat larger share of the necessary recovery. This dilemma of the funeral director is at best but poorly understood.

A seventh goal, in my opinion, should be a year of integrated internship. This should be a kind of supervised practice in an approved, cooperating funeral home, but under the surveillance of the college of mortuary science and under the tutelage of a licensed practitioner. This would be akin to what is happening in teacher education, where a credit-bearing period of time is devoted to "practice teaching"—or to a medical internship. Reference has been made several times to the need for developing competence in the student, involving both specialized knowledge and skill. The knowledge, by itself, is not enough; it is only by putting that knowledge into practice that the skills can be developed—and this is where the year of internship assumes importance.

An eighth goal, hinted at in the opening comments of this paper, is that of continuing education. The proposals to this point have suggested the possibility of a four-year curriculum, which could be crowned with a B.M.S. degree—Bachelor of Mortuary Science—awarded by the college of mortuary science. Such a college could be a two-year institution, but requiring a two-year or junior-college prerequisite, including the subjects previously mentioned. It would provide the additional year of professional training in funeral service, plus the final year of supervised internship. Or, of course, it could be a four-year institution providing the entire program.

Idealistic? No. Something very much like it is already an actuality in a few states. A good many other states already have the two-year college prerequisite plus one year of mortuary college, but without the integrated internship. Still others have a one-year college prerequisite plus a year each of mortuary college and internship—so they wouldn't have far to go. Those states, roughly half, that still settle for a high-school prerequisite would have the farthest to go. But the whole educational trend is upward, so this seems a realistic pattern for the future.

Such a system could develop well-qualified, competent funeral directors—for now and possibly for the near future. But time marches on, bringing changes, improvements, and new developments; and the truly competent practitioner must remain abreast of the times. Continuing education is the answer. This must be a departure from "preparatory education" concepts. It must be an "unlearning," if you please, of the outmoded or discredited, for even knowledge changes. It must be a concentration upon the new. Molded to the time requirements of the active practitioner, it would have to be short, sharp, and carefully planned. It could be—and to some extent already is being—offered by the associations of the field, as well as by the educational institutions of funeral service. It might even become a future requirement for renewal of funeral service licenses. Most probably, it would continue the present forms of short courses, institutes, clinics, seminars, workshops, colloquia, and similar adult-education sessions. But who knows what new forms the future may hold?

Another Look at the Role
of the Funeral Director
Phyllis R. Silverman

All men die, and death is usually marked by a ritual separating the living
from those now deceased. Part of the ritual is attached to burial rites, to a
funeral. Someone must take this responsibility for the burial of the dead. The
funeral director has accepted this role. In his view of himself as a practitioner
he reflects all of our society's ambivalences about death and the ritual involved
with a funeral. One funeral director told me that he tells people whom he meets
for the first time that he sells furniture.

As a result of my work with the Widow-to-Widow program* I wondered
what experience the average individual had with the funeral director and how he
viewed the funeral?

Grief was viewed as being expressed in three stages: impact, recoil, and
recovery. Impact begins at the moment someone loved dies. The bereaved becomes dazed, seems to be in a state of shock, walking as in a dream. People report being numb and having a poor memory of what took place during this
period. This stage can last from one day to one month or sometimes longer.

The funeral is the major event of this stage. People select a funeral director
because they know him personally from his having served the family before or
because he is recommended by friends as someone who would understand how
they want things done.

*This program is conducted by the Laboratory for Community Psychiatry,
Harvard Medical School, Boston, Massachusetts.

People talk about the funeral as an occasion when they referred back to family and religious practices to help them decide what to do. Family tradition and community expectation dictated the kind of service they had. This was not something that caused them any conflict, nor was the funeral a subject of much discussion unless they were specifically questioned about it. Although, when asked about the funeral, they had a poor memory of what had gone on, they felt satisfied with the service they had received and were pleased with the help the funeral director had given them.

The effect of this dazed state on the mourner's ability to function is evident in these two comments. One widow told me:

> As I think back on it, I had to be out of my mind. Don't you think you have to be in a state of shock? How else could I pick a coffin, decide what he should be buried in, and get through the funeral?

This woman at least functioned and made these decisions herself. Another widow looked back and remembered:

> My husband's brother did everything. I couldn't do a thing. I'm the kind of person who did not like to call people or talk on the phone. I always said "tomorrow," and now it couldn't wait. Someone mentioned pensions and social security. It was like a dream. I guess I signed the papers, but I didn't know what for.

This second widow was immobilized, did nothing for herself during this period, and has only a vague memory of what happened. In her marriage, her husband made all the decisions; now his brother acted for him. A major problem is the need to keep going. Being dazed helps in getting some of the most difficult jobs done. The fact that there are things to do can be helpful as well.

This is also a time when many people are most available to help. The family comes together at least for the funeral. It is a time, in the words of another widow, when:

> There are so many people around trying to help, it gets so you don't even have to stir your own cup of coffee.

The impact period is also a time when the deceased's presence is still very real. Many women behaved during this period not as a widow but as their husband's wife, which is appropriate at this time. The legal fact of widowhood does not coincide with the social and emotional acceptance of the role on the widow's part. Therefore, the husband's wishes were respected quite often in deciding on what kind of funeral to have, and the widow behaved as he would have wanted her to; to please him was still most important to her. Several women had to face criticism from friends and family because their husbands wanted very small private funerals. They had discussed with their wives in advance that they could not bear the thought of people staring in at them.

The widows talked about several kinds of help. The most important was the funeral director's knowing what to do. One talked about how upset her mother-in-law was:

> She really got to me. All she kept worrying about was what suit he should be buried in. All I kept thinking about was who cares what he looks like, it doesn't matter anymore. The funeral director was very calm. He said I had to pick out a casket. I said I don't care what he's buried in. He was firm and got me moving. I did choose the coffin. He got me to act and I needed that. I was ready to tell everyone to go to hell—this is not where I wanted to be.

The funeral director didn't get involved in the family tensions, but helped this widow make appropriate plans and kept her focused on this real need to bury her husband, a task which she in fact could not avoid.

Several women remembered just feeling dazed and immobilized at the hospital when they learned their husbands had died. They were grateful to the funeral director, who came and took charge. They had no idea what to do next and no one in the hospital could tell them. Rarely do people rehearse what needs to be done at this time. The greatest need is for someone who can carry through with such things as removing the body and arranging for burial.* In addition, when the funeral director obtained all the vital statistics necessary to conduct a funeral, he initiated the application for social security and other benefits which would allow the family to continue as a viable economic unit. Many women couldn't remember what they were told but were glad someone had gotten the machinery moving for them. They recalled the funeral director's concern for their general well-being.

Some of this interest was expressed in extraordinary circumstances surrounding the burial. One woman's husband was buried in the wrong grave. The cemetery records were so unclear that four graves had to be opened to find her husband's body. The funeral director drove her to the cemetery, and when she would not let her grown sons act for her in identifying the casket, he stood by her as a friend to give her moral support through the ordeal.

Under less extraordinary circumstances, the women appreciated the fact that their funeral directors called to find out how they were afterwards. In one instance, the deceased had grown up with the funeral director who buried him. His widow received a call from this man every three or four weeks for several months.

---

*Many funeral directors encourage families to prearrange funerals so that at a time of need when they are bereaved and least able to function, the family's wishes will be respected.

He said I hope you don't mind, but I am going to call you until I know you are your old self again. I [the widow] thought this was pretty darn nice, and I think if I had any suggestions for funeral directors—if they just tell people or make one return call and say is there anything you feel that we have overlooked, or anything we can do?

These women saw the funeral director as their friend and as someone whose advice they appreciated and trusted. The funeral, as they looked back on it, was a necessary ordeal; they thought it important to do the "right thing" for their husband, and they felt they had made the right decisions at the time.

They also thought it just as well that they were in shock because otherwise they could not have gotten through it. Many of them resented efforts to tranquilize or sedate them. This they saw as interfering with their ability to function, and they wanted to do the best they could under the circumstances. One woman suggested that the drugs made it easier for the rest of the family who then did not have to experience her disconnected, restless behavior.

In summary, the funeral director served the family at a time when they were least able to serve themselves, most in need of sympathetic guidance, and least likely to recall what went on. The family was grateful for his guidance and his experience, for the fact that he knew what to do. He accepted as his responsibility the burial of the dead in a manner which was respectful of the deceased and of the needs of the bereaved family.

Unfortunately, the data do not permit me to comment on the function of ritual in this process. My impression is that the funeral served as a first step in helping women accept their loss; it is the first public acknowledgment of the fact that they are now widows not wives. The ritual and tradition of the funeral seem to provide a respectful farewell to the deceased and a separation between him and the living. This is one step in the process of accepting the finality of death and the need to go on living.

There is no outcry against the lack of aid provided by family physicians or clergymen at the time of a death. Our data indicate that funeral directors are more helpful than either of these professionals, both of whom are also involved at the time of a death. Why is the funeral director so maligned? Fulton (1965) has suggested that this may in part reflect the ambivalent attitudes toward death of those who criticize. He has discriminated between two aspects of the role— the sacred, which has to do with religious prescriptions about burial, and the profane, which has to do with the dirty work of society. Hughes (1958) has pointed out that it falls to the funeral director to help conceal society's mistakes with the trappings that dress up a funeral.

Few people give testimonials to the funeral director. He serves them at a time when they are often unable to relate to what is happening to them, when they often cannot recall exactly what took place unless they are encouraged to recall the events of this period. He is a natural caregiver, then, to families at the time of acute grief. Only when the burial is complete can the family really begin to mourn. This is the first step in the process.

Those of us who are interested in the psychological implications of mourning and its effects on the subsequent adjustment of the bereaved must understand the role of those caregivers in the community, what they can do in the normal course of events, and we must see if we can assist in making this role more effective in preventing emotional breakdown. I do not believe that "grief work" begins until after the funeral is over. I think that help is most needed when friends and family return to their own homes, when the bereaved are less dazed and at some level are at least marginally aware of themselves as widowed. This occurs sometimes only months after the death. I see a critical role here for the funeral director. He can be a link in bringing other services to the bereaved when they are needed. As a natural caregiver on the scene, he has many opportunities to observe the various difficulties the surviving family faces in moving from one state of grief to another and in accommodating to the loss.

I have talked to the widows we served. Initially, they were all suspicious about what "widow-to-widow" meant. Was this a cover for a monument salesman or a real estate agent looking to capitalize on their bereavement? Some felt it was an awful thing to refer to them as widows (they were not yet ready to see themselves in this role) (Silverman, 1972) and this made them hesitant. They suggested that if the funeral director had mentioned the program they would have been more receptive. They did not think it possible for the funeral director to continue to be helpful for an extended period of time, nor that he could be all things to all people:

> If he called, not at the funeral—because at the time of the wake and
> the funeral who listens, but I think like a month later—he could call
> to see if there is anything he could do and he could mention this
> [the Widow-to-Widow program] —maybe then when you wrote,
> we'd have known about you.

The funeral director also is a link to governmental agencies and other groups providing allowances for which he serves as a referring agent and which he helps in the preparation of forms and the provision of data. Are there other agencies and services with which he should be working as well? There are very few services available to help people accommodate to grief.

In some communities the funeral director is helping to develop programs such as widowed-to-widowed efforts where no service exists. He is using his resources to become the catalyst for organizing services.

A recent example of how such a process can work with a problem other than widowhood is in relation to sudden infant death. The National Foundation for Sudden Infant Death wants to be able to reach every bereaved parent to help during this difficult time. They are a group of parents who have coped with their grief and want to help others now.

Such deaths occur in three out of every 1,000 live births, but Sudden Infant Death is rarely listed on the death certificate as a cause of death. The funeral director is one of the few people who knows of these parents, and the members of the Foundation are eager to work out ways of receiving referrals to a local chapter so that it can be of assistance to the bereaved families.

These organizations have broad implications for the bereaved's mental and physical health. In a family in which a "crib death" has occurred women often have trouble conceiving, and have a high rate of miscarriages; sometimes because the reasons for the death are misunderstood, parents can face criminal charges of neglect.

The funeral director, if he expresses his interest in these extended problems, may break through the sense of isolation the bereaved often feel after the funeral and serve a true preventive role by putting them in touch with others who may be most helpful. There seems to be a readiness to accept such assistance from the funeral director when he has served the family well and gained their trust.

REFERENCES

Fulton, R., "Death and Identity." New York: Wiley (1965).
Hughes, E. V., "Men and Their Work." Glencoe, Ill.: The Free Press (1958).
Silverman, P., Widowhood and preventive intervention. Family Coordinator, 21 (January 1972

The Funeral Director as Grief Counselor

Walter K. Thorsell

"We know what we are, but know not what we may be."

Shakespeare in "Hamlet" appears to be speaking directly to the funeral director in America.

The funeral profession in America grew out of several vocations: cabinet-making, livery services, laying-out-of-the-dead, upholstering, and so on. It was then labeled "undertaking" and became totally centered around service. It meets human needs at the time of bereavement. We care for the dead while meeting the needs of those who mourn.

We are a viable profession; we have changed with the years because of cultural pressures. No longer do we see swallow-tailed jackets, heavily draped funeral parlors, door badges, or ostrich plumes on hearses, which characterized the 19th-century undertaker. The disappearance of these embellishments reflected far more important but less apparent changes which have eliminated older patterns. Our people have gathered in the cities. Our government has become centralized. We move our homes from place to distant place, and we live at an ever faster pace. So the funeral profession has had to continually change to meet the needs of society.

Today, the pressure for change in the character of funeral service is mounting. The explosion of literature and research in the related areas of death, dying, grief, and mourning demands additional change. Americans have welcomed changes in all areas of life. Such a backdrop makes it hard to retain existing patterns of living. Change is the order of the day. We funeral directors are not exempt.

If we are to fulfill our fundamental purpose of meeting the needs of families who have experienced a death, we must alter the nature of our services. More time must be spent in meeting the total needs of the client. In refocusing our attention we should not preclude those essential activities which we have refined, like providing physical facilities, embalming, restoration of the deceased, assisting the bereaved through the maze of government benefits and regulations, and assisting clients with warm dignified concern. We must expand our role to include yet another service.

I believe the professional activity which is lacking is counseling, with the adoption of its practices, tools, attitudes, and beliefs. We have tried to grow professionally but have failed to see the widespread acceptance of the role of counseling in society. Professional counseling has appeared in almost every life activity—marital, legal, vocational, educational, medical, psychological, and even sales. We are surrounded by counselors. To a limited extent, we find them in funeral service.

It is unfortunate that so many funeral professionals are reluctant to become interested in counseling, reluctant to investigate its nature and procedures. A profession should adopt the procedures which would enable it to more effectively and fully serve its clientele. Such efforts would change the image of our work and do away with much of the negativeness associated with dying, death, the funeral, and us.

What counseling areas should we consider? I believe we should counsel at least in matters of grief, mourning behavior, adjustment to loss, reorientation following loss, religious orientation to death, finances, and funeral etiquette. If I were to refer to these as psychological, sociological, theological, financial, and legal counseling, we could anticipate objections from attorneys, psychologists, clergy, and others. Further, many of us would say we are not trained to fill these roles. I would submit that no professional in our society has as much contact with the bereaved as we do. No one shares in the life-affecting decisions in the way we do. Who else is in a position to assist with adjustment problems faced by the bereaved? We are, ipso facto, counselors in death, dying, bereavement, mourning, and funeralization. We don't have to usurp other professional roles, but we must have a working relationship with other professions and a working knowledge of counseling procedure. Perhaps most important, we should acquire an awareness of our limitations. We should know when we are infringing on another professional.

Where and when could funeral service counseling take place? Everywhere, all the time. Effective counseling before bereavement could diminish the negativeness we see at the arrangements conference. We should seek out opportunities to communicate to potential clients our insights gained through serving others.

Certainly counseling should be used at the time of bereavement. During the arrangements conference, visitation period, the ride in the cortege, and similar unstructured moments we should counsel. Consider the post-funeral period. In the critical 30-to-90-day period following bereavement, the survivor is most vulnerable to inappropriate responses to death. We have ignored this. We have assumed that our help is no longer needed. We have focused on preparation for our next client. We have quit halfway through. Building on the relationship which started during the period of the funeral, a series of planned counseling calls on the client could aid the bereaved significantly. A byproduct of good will should be anticipated. Understanding the pressures on and the adjustment of the bereaved should form the foundation of counseling activity during reorientation.

How ready are we for an expanded role, one which would include counseling? As of this writing, I see a reluctance to pursue counseling. We fear the unknown nature of counseling. We shy away from retraining in new areas. We want to see what will develop next. We ask ourselves how this will affect our operation and personnel. In short, we find reasons why we should not pursue counseling.

However, an expanded role will be sought by those seeking competitive advantage, by those attuned to changes in society, and by those aware of the expectations of a sophisticated citizenry. To those of us who have not lost sight of our original goals, an expanded counseling role will be considered a necessary and logical extension of our existing role.

What limitations are there for the practitioner who wants to qualify himself for the expanded role? One objection I hear lies in the time available to us. Time is a limiting factor because of limited contact during the period of the funeral. The press of traditional functions also limits our time. Another factor is the interest of the practitioner in counseling. Given a grudging acceptance of an expanded role, many will not accept the role on an emotional level. This reduces counseling to a perfunctory exercise. Another deterrent is the necessary retraining. Learning the skills, techniques, attitudes, and procedures of counseling is best done in an academic setting. I cannot imagine that a large number of us would give up job time to gain additional education. A revision of funeral service education curricula would permit an increase in the number trained. This suggests that only a long-term solution is available.

In summary, I would make these observations:

(1) Changes have affected funeral service as much as any other segment of society.

(2) There is evidence that there are those among us who would welcome an expanded role which would embrace counseling as a necessary function in every establishment attempting to offer a complete range of services.

(3) For institutional survival, funeral service must become more receptive to change in our society.

(4) An expanded role for the funeral service practitioner would be of significant value to the bereaved. This would be most apparent in the reduction of

anxiety and maintenance of a reality-oriented personality.

(5) If it were possible to reduce counseling procedures, principles, techniques, and skills to a formula, there would be immediate acceptance by the profession. It is true that a considerable investment must be made by those interested in becoming effective counselors. Yet for those who are willing, the dividends will more than offset the original investment.

Shakespeare said it best: "We know not what we may be."

HE FUNERAL HOME: A COMMUNITY RESOURCE

Thanatology and Its Promise

Samuel Klagsbrun

In the field of thanatology I think that we are in too many instances working in isolation from one another: we work in separate communities, separate
hospitals, sometimes separate homes; often there is no affiliation with a major
institution. In addition, sometimes differences in disciplines further increase the
isolation. As a psychiatrist, I have felt alienated from my other medical col-
leagues because they think (and I think they think) I speak a different language,
but I really don't. I can imagine that funeral directors find themselves in a similar
position in relation to the medical profession, particularly in their work at the
time of the funeral and during the period of bereavement.

We must all grasp at any opportunity to communicate with each other, to
get back into touch with people from other disciplines, to remove ourselves
from our respective isolation wards. Therefore, I would like to suggest that we
think not only in terms of analyzing what we do at the time of the funeral, but
also to try to think about analyzing what we all ought to do prior to funerals
and after funerals and whether we can make the moment of the funeral a pivotal
point in the management and care of families who have lost someone.

We should all strive to expand services—individually and collectively. Perhaps we can make the funeral home a center for bereavement or a center for
help; without doubt, in so doing we will have altered its function considerably
and changed the ideas of people about funeral homes.

For example, I can envision inviting clergymen, lawyers, psychiatrists,
internists, social workers, and many others in the community to participate in

the "building" which has been labeled "funeral home." And I can envision re-making it into the community or neighborhood center for continuing help to be-reaved families. I do not know whether this is altogether a new view; rather, probably, it is something which has already been accomplished in one degree or another in many areas. In any case, the funeral home is a logical place for people to gather to adjust to loss after the loss has been experienced, or maybe even as a place for therapy when loss is anticipated, before it has actually been experienced.

The question of how such facilities or resources are to be made available poses many problems, but the thought of this added assistance in dealing with loss and grief is provocative.

Thanatology has to do with life and with adjustments to problems in life. Thanatology can best serve when it concerns itself with a future rather than with a past; with such an approach we will not deny the event of death but will be able to use it adaptively and hopefully grow from that point.

The Funeral Home as a Center of Grief Activitv

Terrance M. Copeland

In these case histories, I shall attempt to discuss the total funeral and what physical and psychological help the families received during their time of sorrow. Each case involved a sudden death with a resulting deep shock and grief. In each instance, the funeral home served as a neutral territory for the release of the pain and sorrow of the grief process and the beginning of decision-making in terms of the funeral arrangements.

An important factor in each instance was the therapeutic value of seeing the deceased loved one and facing the reality of his death.

All deaths are tragic deaths. In a sudden death by accident, suicide, or homicide, the shock factor is much greater than that present following death caused by a devastating or lingering illness. Sometimes death is a welcome friend for those who cannot recover and feel themselves to be a burden.

When death comes suddenly, the family and friends have no time to adjust— the fact of death is suddenly there and final. The case histories described here involve sudden tragic deaths: one by accident, two suicides, and one from an overdose of heroin.

THEORETICAL PERSPECTIVES: MATERIAL AND METHODS

In my 12 years in the funeral profession, I have arranged or helped arrange over 2,000 funerals. These four cases come from the past few years when I managed a funeral home in upstate New York. Since the town is small, the relatives and close friends were interviewed at the time of death and for some time after.

163

Their thoughts, along with the records we must keep, are the background for this report.

Each of these families had a religious service or time set aside in which prayers or poems could be recited. The caskets were left open—all the families and friends were able to confirm for themselves that the person was truly dead.

As each deceased person had left his mark in some way, each person present during the calling hours or the funeral felt a loss and sorrow over the passing but were able to have an acceptable image for recalling the deceased.

From a pamphlet prepared by the National Funeral Directors Association entitled "With the Body Present," I especially noted the section headed "Expression":

> In many crises, such as economic distress, poor health, divorce or domestic difficulties, we seek to comfort those involved. In most instances, opportunities present themselves for such expression days, weeks, and even months later.
> Death is different. Time is an immediate factor. Many find it difficult to express themselves. They may talk about every other subject but the purpose of why they are making a sympathy or condolence call. The presence of the body during the visitation or wake provides an immediate and proper climate for mourning. With the body present, it is natural to talk about the deceased.
> If tears are shed, they flow less self-consciously for both the survivors and those who call. If there is a religious service, the body present and viewed before the ceremony helps the sorrows of one become the sorrows of all. Of course, there is pain, but it is a hurt that helps to heal.

CASE 1

On a dark, rainy night, an eight-year-old boy had come into town with his grandmother and mother to pick up a brother and sister from a piano lesson. He went across the busy street to the piano teacher's home where he sat down for a few minutes until they had finished. Around 8:15, they left and went down to the curb where traffic was heavy and slow. The youngster, thinking he had a break in the line, ran into the street. A light truck came by at the same time. The left front fender of the truck struck with such impact that the boy was catapulted into the air like a missile before he dropped to the side of the street. The four people very close to the boy saw the entire sequence of events. His mother held him close to her as he was dying and prayed for God to save him. A local doctor arrived, but the child had died. The police called the county coroner and he in turn called our funeral home to come to the scene to remove the body to the county morgue.

By the time we reached the place of the accident, the father and grandfather were there also. As very little could be said, we asked if there were anything that we could do for them at that time. Their only request was for their clergyman to come to talk to them, which he did after we called him. The coroner completed his investigation and we took the child to the county morgue.

The next day, we met at the funeral home. The mother and father were concerned with having a rewarding funeral service for their son. The personnel of the funeral home had known this family for many years as close friends, making this an especially difficult case.

In spite of the overwhelming shock and sorrow of the moment, plans had to be made for the coordination of the funeral and burial. This necessitated helping the family decide when and where the funeral and burial would take place. The family's clergyman and the cemetery officials had to be called to arrange for both. It was also necessary to obtain statistical information for the death certificate which we would obtain later from the coroner with his signature and the pathologist's report as to the cause of death. This death certificate then had to be presented to the town clerk, who issues a burial permit, which must be given to the cemetery officials at the time of burial.

The parents expressed a wish for the casket to be open, and they inquired as to whether this was possible. As a funeral director, I knew that this family would best be served if the casket were open and replied that we would try our best. Upon completion of our work, they would be able to come in and decide for themselves.

(A professional note: the embalming and preparation were most difficult. The boy's entire face was very badly damaged and his limbs were badly broken. The embalming was carried out with great care, and the damaged tissue received extensive dermasurgery. Numerous chemicals and surface restorers were combined with time and patience to enable us to complete our work.)

We received our reward when the mother and father came to the funeral home for their first look. They were met at the door and accompanied into the room where the casket was. We told them in very few words that we felt they would be pleased and left them alone. After a few minutes, they came to us and told us of their decision to leave the casket open.

All morning long, the funeral home had received calls from members of the community—teachers from the boy's school, boy scouts, classmates, and others—asking what they could do, all wanting something positive to do. Many flowers also arrived. During the morning, the grandfather made a statement to the effect that this was too hard and perhaps they should have had a private funeral service.

During the calling hours that day, an especially large number of people came to call. We noted specifically the various age levels. In the early afternoon hours, the friends of the grandparents arrived, offered their help, and reminisced about the past with the grandparents. Around three o'clock, the age level dropped to the boy's age group—the Boy Scouts, the Little League team, classmates—all stopped to talk to the parents and the brother and sister.

The family returned for calling hours that evening and again the age group changed. The parents of the children who had come in the afternoon were there, as were other children who had waited to come with their parents. There were friends and there were acquaintances who had purchased fruit from the family's farm store. All in all, this would have to be classified as a community funeral, with the people of the community feeling that they had helped in a small way.

At the closing hour, the grandfather put into words what we had endeavored to accomplish: that although the pain was still there, the callers had reinforced what he already knew—his grandson had been loved and would not be forgotten. This helped ease his sorrow.

The funeral was to be held at 11 A.M., in the oldest church in our community. The parents, having come in earlier to say their final goodbyes, returned with the whole family. The pallbearers included the president of the Little League, the boy's baseball coach complete with baseball hat, and the Boy Scout leader in full uniform. Our procession to the church was escorted by our village and town police departments.

At the church, which was filled to capacity, the minister gave a brief service which included a review of the boy's life, his church activities, his work on the farm, his interest in sports. Following the service, we returned the casket to the hearse. To our surprise, most of the people who had attended the service wanted to come to the cemetery.

At the graveside, the commital prayers were brief, leaving all with a feeling of warmth, glad that they had been a small part of this funeral service for a boy who had reached only the age of eight but who had moved so many to make a positive action.

To be honest, it was not just our arrangements or the family's positive response to them but the response of a truly community funeral and the moral and psychological support given by the community that helped this family get through the ordeal of the death and burial of a beloved child.

CASE 2

Two young men, brothers from Ethiopia, were in this country to attend school, one boy in high school and the other in our local college. It had cost the family a large sum of money to send both boys here for schooling. For reasons known only to himself, the younger boy put a tie around his neck and hanged himself in the resort hotel where he worked.

The older brother, already in a state of shock over this sudden death and having no previous experience in arranging a funeral, had the additional and difficult task of making the arrangements to send his brother's body back to Addis

Ababa for burial in the family cemetery plot. Plans for and coordination of trans-atlantic transfers of deceased persons are complicated. We had to notify the Ethiopian Embassy at the United Nations and find out if there were any specific public health laws to be observed. We found that there are none in Ethiopia so we followed the international public health laws prescribed for shipment of a deceased person. Then there were calls to airlines to arrange a flight without delay, since it is the custom in Ethiopia to have religious services and burial as soon as possible. Also, of course, there were the details of obtaining statistical information for the death certificate, getting the coroner's signature and patholog-ist's report on this certificate, and presenting it to the town clerk for a burial permit which, in this instance, was also a shipping permit.

The brother wanted to participate in as many of the arrangements as he could. After the above procedures were attended to, he asked if he might be called when his brother's body was ready. A casket was selected expressly for the purpose of shipping, the embalming and dressing were completed, and the body was placed in the casket. When the brother was called, he asked if it would be proper to ask some of his college friends to come in with him to see his brother. About ten young men arrived, looked at the boy, and said some prayers in their language.

Early the next morning, the same ten young men arrived with the brother, placed a long letter to the boy's mother and father on top of the casket, and then helped carry the casket to the hearse for the trip to the airport.

A week later, the brother called to tell us that his brother's body had ar-rived home safely and that the burial had taken place at the family cemetery. He added that he had heard about American funeral homes and was thankful that he had a chance to pray and help carry his brother to start his trip home. Funerals are simple in his homeland and he felt he had to attend to all his brother's needs. His parents told him that they had felt very deep sorrow, but because their son had been sent home so quickly, they were able to have their religious service and bury him in the same manner they would have had he died in their home.

The brother further expressed his feelings in a note he wrote to the funeral home: "It is really a great opportunity for me to express my deepest thanks for the funeral home. As a young foreigner, I was very shocked with the situation I was faced with. But thanks to the help of the funeral director, everything was settled. Moreover as a student, I had a financial problem to cover the expenses of the funeral service. Having considered my problem, the funeral director made me to pay the minimum. Hence I owe him a lot. He is a great helpful person."

CASE 3

A woman in her early 40's, well educated, was married to a university pro-fessor. Without a word of warning, after her husband had gone to his first class early one morning, the woman, still in her nightclothes, went to the barn and, with the aid of a chair and piece of rope, hanged herself.

The husband came home around 11 A.M. after his second class to see his wife and to prepare for his late afternoon class. Not finding her in the house, he started to call friends nearby, but no one had heard or seen her all morning. He walked out to a large field where his wife often liked to walk. On his way back, he stopped at the barn where his eyes caught something. He walked in and there was his wife. He freed her and attempted mouth-to-mouth resuscitation to try to save her. A neighbor who had come to the barn ran back to the house and called a doctor. When the doctor came, he examined the woman and pronounced her dead. A coroner was called, as was the funeral home, and thus came about our first meeting with the bereaved husband.

His first statement was that he wanted his wife's funeral arrangements taken care of as soon as possible and that he must notify their families. Then he added that he didn't know whether to have cremation or earth burial or if he should have the remains taken back to Ohio. He even discussed not having a funeral. We suggested that he make no decisions in a hurry. We said that we would remove his wife and that after he had had time to notify the families and time to think about it and talk over all possibilities, he could come down to the funeral home and we would arrange whatever he felt was best.

Later that day, he arrived at the funeral home with his mother, his wife's sister, and a close friend from the university. After discussing the alternatives, the husband decided on cremation and no service. It was suggested that it might help him psychologically if he came in after all the preparations were completed to view his wife. He agreed that he would do this before making his final decision.

When all was ready, the husband and his mother, sister-in-law, and closest friend returned to the funeral home. The husband, going alone into the room, placed a large bunch of wild flowers in his wife's hands. He then came out and told us how much it had helped him to see his wife so peaceful with all the dark color and anguish gone from her face.

He inquired if it would be possible to talk to a clergyman and if he could change the arrangements from cremation to a brief service, followed by burial in the family cemetery in Ohio. He said that after being alone with his wife and seeing her in the casket, his feelings were completely different. By mid-morning the next day, all the arrangements had been made according to the husband's wishes. A local minister had talked to him and had worked out a funeral service that had the meaning the husband was looking for.

The time for the service arrived; most of those attending were from the local university and were close friends and neighbors. The minister conducted his service and at the end announced that the husband would read a poem he had written in memory of his wife. Before the poem was started, the husband said that if by chance he could not finish, his closest friend would finish it for him. In brief, it called to mind the wild field flowers his wife had loved and had gathered each day, the good times as well as the bad, gave a promise to try to understand her deed and acknowledged in public that he forgave her.

Before departing, the friends went up to the casket, then over to the husband and the other family members, offering their help in any way. After this, the family members went and said their last farewells. One by one, they held our hands and though no words were spoken, we felt gratified in our profession.

CASE 4

A 17-year-old boy—a student with long hair and in the typical casual dress of today's youth—liked to write poems and short stories. Some of his friends had talked him into trying pills—uppers and downers. Then he started using heroin. He had dropped out of school and society as a result. However, he was able to stop all drugs for more than a year and was again rejoining society.

One cold night when his family was out, the phone rang. The person on the other end of the line was his old pal, the pusher, who insisted on coming over "for old time's sake." They talked for a while. Later, some more old friends came and asked what the pusher had and what he was going to do.

He had heroin and great pills that would put you in outer space. They decided to try the heroin and persuaded the boy to join them. A few hours later, after having eaten some food, they drove to a deserted area and again persuaded our friend to join them. Because the dose was too strong or too pure, the boy died from an overdose. The pusher got scared, drove him home, kicked him out onto the road, and left him. Someone going to work found him and called the police, who in turn called the coroner.

The mother and brother came to our funeral home to make the arrangements. This was to be a different funeral, with time for friends to call, a nonreligious service, and earth burial.

After the removal and embalming were completed, the boy was dressed in his everyday clothes—jeans, plain flannel shirt, and boots. The mother called and said that photographers from a nearby town's underground paper would be coming over to take some pictures. They came and told us what they had in mind. The pictures would be used for their paper and some would be made up as posters. These posters would be placed around in stores and youth hangouts with the caption, "He gambled on the hard stuff and it won," or words to that effect.

During the calling hours, all types of people came in, one by one or in small groups. Most said a few words to the family and went up to the casket. Gathering together, they discussed the way of death and many commented about not getting involved with drugs of any kind.

On the day of the funeral, the kids came into the funeral home early. The family arrived and invited them to stay, suggesting that they sit on the floor, wanting them to feel at home. There was no formal service, no clergyman. Instead, a local doctor and a prominent attorney spoke. A poet, who had helped the boy with his writing, read some of the boy's poems and some of his own, including one written for the service. The service ended with the boy's brother giving a brief talk addressed to those who used drugs: "Double your effort to avoid their use; if using them, get some help!" And to the older people: "Help support, in person and with money and time, the local drug programs now in operation in our community."

The trip to the cemetery was not what might be called the normal funeral procession. There were VW's and VW buses painted in psychedelic colors, a few old remodeled cars, a few motorcycles, and for the more affluent, big expensive cars.

At the cemetery, after a minute of silent prayer, the brother thanked everyone for their physical and psychological help at the family's time of need. After a long time, a few of the boys came over and asked if we were going to lower the casket. The brother and mother overheard and said to go ahead. Once the lowering device was out of the way, the young people took the shovels and one at a time started to fill the grave in. In the silence, the noise was deafening—the shovels hitting the rocks, the dirt hitting the casket—all sounds of their final act of love. It was as if they wanted to fill the grave in and leave to start their lives over again, to improve their work and to change their priorities so they might grow and lead lives of accomplishment.

DISCUSSION

The first case was a young boy, very active in church, school, and sport activities, his death visually seen by four people very close to him, with resultant feature damage. This was the first death the immediate family had had to cope with. Each family member had deep questions about death, about what it meant and how he or she would be able to pass through this terrible part of life.

The fact that we at the funeral home were able to restore the damaged features and viewable portions of the body enabled the family members to confirm the fact of death of a loved one. The calling hours gave time to communicate with close friends. Later they expressed gratitude for the opportunity to see the deceased and said that the funeral home had actually helped them to accept the hard fact of his death.

The community was allowed to express its own feelings of loss. It is my belief that the calling hours were therapeutic for the immediate family and for the community at a time when the world seemed to come to a sudden and sharp halt.

In the second and third cases, tragic suicides were the deceaseds' answers to their personal problems. Both their families blamed themselves for not having seen the warning signs in time to avert the action taken.

The young man from Ethiopia was survived by a brother here in America and a family in his homeland. Arrangements were made so that everyone could participate, and homeland funeral customs were observed. The parents found it extremely hard to accept the fact of suicide, but because their son's body had been transported so quickly, they were able to have their own rituals of mourning and service, which helped them adjust to the fact of death.

The young woman had left a note in an attempt to tell her husband why she did what she did. Most suicide notes are written by people not in complete control of their faculties. I believe that these notes are written to justify their decision to take their own lives.

The husband saw his wife with the manifestations resulting from a death in this manner. The therapeutic value of viewing the deceased after embalming and restoration was immeasurable. The husband felt that his wife was as beautiful in death as she had been in life. He wanted to forget the memory he had of her in the barn.

Many months after the tragedy, he spoke to me and remembered that the funeral and all the decisions he had had to make at the time had helped him adjust to his loss with a little better understanding of why his wife chose suicide.

The fourth case reflects an aspect of our times—youthful unrest and, for some, the answer of drugs. With his whole life ahead of him, this boy started on drugs and his world became smaller and smaller. He found the strength to kick the habit for a while but the old ties were very strong and resulted in the "just one more time" and a fatal overdose of heroin.

The family's attempt to publicize his death may have stopped some other young person from following in his footsteps; no one knows for sure.

The funeral was different in that his friends participated in the final act of filling in the grave, an act of love for the deceased. Some said in public that they were going to change their lives, and some have.

This funeral, from the funeral director's point of view, was not the "norm," but it stimulated positive responses in a wide range of people. In the end, one could only hope that this would be the last funeral he would have to arrange for a young person who had died because of drugs.

SUMMARY

I have tried to describe four tragic deaths; what each funeral meant to the immediate family, neighbors, and close friends; and the decisions made, and in some cases changed, by the families. The resulting funerals served their needs in a time of sorrow. These four families have returned to thank us for our help in some of the decision-making.

The funeral home provides neutral territory. A man may shed tears and no one will berate him; emotions need not be restrained. It has been said that grief shared is grief diminished. Many bereaved have acknowledged that the use of the funeral home for calling hours and the viewing of their deceased helped them to accept the death and then in a small way understand a little more about life. Death ends life as we know it. We are left with our snapshots, our mental picture, and memories which seem to grow and take on more importance as the days stretch to years.

When death is caused by traumatic events, it may be necessary for the embalmer to employ all the art and skill he possesses to restore a person so that the family will be able to view the remains. Many such families have returned to us after a period of time to tell us how much it meant to them to see their loved one. They all seem to be expressing gratitude for what was done to change the harsh picture of a terrible death and to replace it with a memory picture that they could live with and eventually accept.

The Funeral Home as a Community Resource

Otto S. Margolis

The values of the funeral have been abundantly documented by recognized pastoral scholars such as Bachmann (1964), Grollman (1974), Irion (1954), Jackson (1957), Rogers (1950), and others. These values have, perhaps, been summarized most effectively in a short pamphlet by Irion entitled, "The Funeral— An Experience of Value." To be of value the funeral must meet certain basic needs of the bereaved: the need for support; the need to actualize and accept the death that has occurred; the need to express sorrow, which often includes feelings of hostility and guilt; the need for new relationships; and spiritual needs. To the extent that a funeral meets any or all of these needs it is an experience of value.

During the brief period of the funeral, at best a good start will be made toward meeting these needs. In some cases this start may be sufficient to carry the grief sufferer through the ensuing weeks or months of mourning to an effective resolution. In other cases the group support that proved itself so effective during the funeral is suddenly withdrawn, and the bereaved person feels completely helpless. This is the situation to which we shall address ourselves.

What resources are available to a bereaved person who needs help following the funeral? We think immediately of our religious institutions and the clergy who traditionally deal with these problems with their parishioners. But we are told that possibly as many as half of our population has no religious affiliation. We are also told that some members of the clergy have little time for individual bereavement counseling because of many other pastoral commitments. This is understandable. Some do not have the aptitude or inclination for such counsel-

173

ing. Then there are others—and this is true of people in all walks of life—who prefer to avoid all discussion of bereavement except when duty makes it a necessity.

Who else, then, is to be called on for postfuneral counseling of the bereaved? In prolonged terminal cases within the hospital setting in certain hospitals there is a bereavement team. Its function is to deal with the preparatory grief reactions of the dying patient and the anticipatory grief of the family. Members of the bereavement team generally include a clergyman, a nurse, a psychiatrist or psychologist, a social worker, and a physician.

What are the possibilities of a similar group, to be designated as bereavement counselors or consultants, drawn from the community at large and qualified in their respective specialties, to help bereaved persons with the many problems that require resolution after the funeral? Beyond the central problem of grief management, there are legal problems, insurance, tax, and other financial problems, medical problems, psychosocial problems, and probably others in which the intervention of specialists would be helpful.

In suggesting that such people volunteer their services as bereavement consultants, I realize that most of them could not possibly continue to provide professional services gratis on an individual basis over an extended period of time. As members of the consultant group they could be called upon from time to time to participate in group counseling sessions in their own speciality.

Just how is such a group of bereavement consultants to be organized? What kind of ongoing program is to be developed? And most important of all, who is to take the initiative?

In this context, another question has been asked: What is the single most important attribute of an effective counselor? Two words can answer this—*being there*. Just being there is paramount. It is the obvious prerequisite for any counseling relationship.

In every death that occurs and in every funeral that follows, a funeral director is involved. He is there. In most funerals a clergyman participates. He also is there. This necessitates cooperation and rapport in working together to make the funeral a meaningful experience for the bereaved family. Bachmann (1964) speaks of this relationship between clergyman and funeral director as a cooperative venture. When handled effectively, I have heard it referred to by someone as "a healing partnership." And that is where the process of healing usually begins—at the funeral—even though it may have a long course to run afterward.

Because of this relationship between the clergy and the funeral director and their joint involvement in deaths and funerals, the initiation of some form of group counseling program on a continuing basis falls very naturally into their hands. Their first responsibility will be to recruit an interdisciplinary team of consultants. Working with the consultants, the next job would be to develop a cycle of group counseling sessions. Each cycle would cover a series of typical problems with which most bereaved persons must cope. The emotion of grief along with numerous other problems alluded to earlier would be included. Upon completion of a given cycle, it would then be repeated.

Grief itself encompasses a constellation of feelings and somatic symptoms described in Lindemann (1944). Feelings of anxiety, hostility, and guilt are common. Somatic distress in the form of respiratory difficulty, loss of appetite, physical weakness, digestive disturbances, insomnia, and distorted sensations occurs frequently.

The grief sufferer needs to understand that any of the foregoing are a normal part of the grief reaction. He should be encouraged to ventilate his feelings despite the pain that this causes. This is an essential part of grief work. Someone described grief as "the hurt that heals itself." But this occurs only when the grief is freely expressed. Otherwise the process is delayed, prolonged, or distorted.

As mentioned earlier, grief work will usually have begun with the advent of death, during the arrangements for the funeral, and during the period of the funeral itself. In many cases of prolonged terminal illness, anticipatory grief will have been under way before death occurs. It is important that the bereaved-to-be or the newly bereaved be encouraged to attend the group counseling sessions at the earliest opportune time.

It is not our purpose here to attempt a blueprint of the content of such counseling sessions. However, it does not seem wise that these sessions be highly structured. The needs of individuals within a particular group will vary. They will also change with time. Quite likely the most effective results will be obtained by interaction among the counselees under the skillful guidance of the counselor.

If and when some structuring becomes desirable, this can readily evolve from the experience and expression of the group. The most important thing is that such groups be started and that bereaved persons be informed that they are available. It would also be desirable that the experiences of various groups be reported through some central agency. At the moment, I believe that the Foundation of Thanatology through its periodicals and symposia could serve as an excellent clearing house for the reports and recommendations of various bereavement counseling groups.

There are likely to be a number of problems arising in the implementation of the bereavement counseling programs. Some of them can readily be anticipated. The most difficult of these is likely to be "people problems." It would seem pointless for a group of clergymen and funeral directors who have not previously established a good working relationship in their traditional roles in the funeral to attempt an innovative program of group counseling for the bereaved. Still, it is very possible that rapport between the two groups could be established for the first time in a common endeavor. Whether the impetus comes from one group or the other, the attempt should be made. If just one clergyman and one funeral director in a locality can work together, a counseling program can be started.

What is the optimal frequency with which such counseling sessions should be held? This is likely to be governed by practical rather than theoretical considerations, assuming that such knowledge is available. The time that counselors or consultants can devote to the project is a major concern. We must not lose sight of the fact that "being there" is indispensable. Then, too, we know that in individual bereavement counseling the earlier sessions occur with greater frequency and that the time interval between them increases as grief work progresses.

In group counseling the grief sufferers will be at different stages in their grief work. While this may seem to be a problem, it may actually prove to be an advantage. Through free interaction within the group, those bereaved persons who are in more advanced stages of their grief work can be of great help to the newly bereaved. As they work through their grief the counselees themselves can serve as a significant reservoir of future bereavement counselors and consultants.

This raises a further question concerning the qualifications of counselors and consultants. Obviously, there are not nearly a sufficient number of academically trained and experienced counselors to meet the needs of even a substantial number of bereaved persons who need help. Not all clergymen are trained and skilled in counseling the bereaved, particularly those grief sufferers who have little or no religious orientation and find little consolation in traditional religious beliefs. Most clergymen, nonetheless, have sufficient training and experience to contribute materially to the program.

Then there is the funeral director, whose potential in counseling the bereaved has been largely overlooked. No group has as much contact with death and bereavement as do the funeral directors. Until recent years, his knowledge of bereavement and grief has come largely through the school of experience. This may, indeed, be the best possible vehicle for learning. Today, however, with the advent of a vast body of literature on death, dying, and bereavement and an expansion in the educational programs of the funeral service schools and colleges, the funeral director of tomorrow can and should become an expert in thanatology in the broadest sense of the word.

Funeral service educators are currently expanding their curricula to include more studies in the behavioral and social sciences. In this effort we look for help to the behavioral and social scientists, and such help has been forthcoming. In recent years, more and more college graduates with good backgrounds in the behavioral and social sciences are finding a challenging vocational opportunity in funeral service. The public, in general, and the academic community in particular, are unaware of the changes that are taking place. Whether through experience or through increased formal education, most funeral directors who are willing to participate in group counseling for the bereaved need have few qualms about their qualifications. They will continue to learn by doing, as will other participants, including the counselees themselves.

There will undoubtedly be some grief sufferers displaying delayed, distorted, and morbid grief reactions who will not be helped by group counseling. These will require individual therapy by referral to mental health professionals.

What then are some of the essential qualifications of an effective bereavement counselor? Heading the list I would use the word empathy, defined as sensitivity to other persons' feelings. Second, is the ability to be a concerned listener. The opportunity for bereaved persons to ventilate their feelings of anxiety, anger, guilt, and hostility is of the utmost importance. Third on the list is a sufficient knowledge of the psychology of grief to enable the counselor to inspire confidence in the counselee. And finally, there is the ability to skillfully moderate free interaction within the group. Professional counselors would probably modify or add to this list of qualifications.

The ultimate goals of bereavement counseling as expressed by recognized authorities in the psychology of bereavement and grief are: (1) "emancipation from the deceased" in the sense of severing the emotional bonds that fetter the bereaved, and (2) "learning to live with the image of the deceased." This refers to the ability of the bereaved person to recall memories of the deceased without pain.

Another matter that requires consideration is a suitable locale for holding the bereavement counseling sessions. Here we have a wide choice. There are a variety of community facilities including churches, community centers, fraternal group centers, funeral homes, and others.

Relating our discussion to the title of this paper, I should especially like to emphasize some values that attach to the use of funeral homes in a community as bereavement counseling centers. At the very least, funeral homes should be used from time to time. During the present century in this country we have seen a gradual transfer in the setting of the funeral from the home of the deceased to the funeral home. In most deaths the funeral home is where grief work begins. Revisiting the scene of the funeral will very likely serve as a stimulus for the continuation of grief work that may have been interrupted. That is precisely what counseling sessions are intended to accomplish.

Then, too, there will be instances of prolonged terminal illness in which the bereaved-to-be are working through anticipatory grief reactions and should be encouraged to join a counseling group. One of their major concerns may be the anticipated emotional trauma that attends funeral arrangements. Such feelings can be more comfortably aired within a group that has experienced these same feelings and in an environment in which the funeral is to take place. Anxiety can be eased and, in due course, prearrangement of the funeral worked out.

In addition to the use of the funeral home as a bereavement counseling center, I would recommend that each funeral home that participates in such a program maintain a small library of books that can provide comfort to the bereaved. Clergymen and funeral directors should keep abreast of new titles as they appear.

178   Otto S. Margolis

I am very much aware of the fact that certain of the suggestions that appear in this paper will be unacceptable to many clergymen, funeral directors, and others in the caregiving professions. Some of them may prove to be unworkable. My purpose is to provoke discussion and action. Many, if not all, of the proposals are amenable to constructive alternatives.

In a challenging paper, "Judaism and Bereavement," that appeared in Pastoral Care of the Dying and Bereaved (1973), Milton Matz stated: "Adequate psychological and religious counseling resources to help people at this crucial time are lacking. I hope that this need will be the subject of concern on the part of churches and ministers throughout the country. If I may be so bold as to make a prediction, I will say that within a decade or two people will receive intensive counseling in the area of grief, based on the most modern techniques of psychology in keeping with the most meaningful wisdom of religion. I believe they will receive this counseling as a matter of course, as naturally as mourners today observe the traditional customs of their faith."

The above is a clear statement of the need that exists. I would suggest only that one or two decades is too long a time to wait. There is an abundance of information on the psychology of grief available. Let us start now and continue to learn by doing.

REFERENCES

Bachmann, C., "Ministering to the Grief Sufferer." Englewood Cliffs, N.J.: Prentice-Hall, Inc. (1964).

Grollman, E., "Concerning Death: A Practical Guide for the Living." Boston: Beacon Press (1974).

Irion, P., "The Funeral and the Mourner." New York: Abingdon Press (1954).

Irion, P., "The Funeral: Vestige or Value." New York: Abingdon Press (1966).

Jackson, E. N., "Understanding Grief." New York: Abingdon Press (1957).

Rogers, W. F., "Ye Shall Be Comforted." Philadelphia: The Westminster Press (1950).

Lindemann, E. Symptomatology and management of acute grief. American Journal of Psychiatry, 101:141 (1944).

Matz, M. Judaism and bereavement. In "Pastoral Care of the Dying and Bereaved: Selected Readings." New York: Health Sciences Publishing Corp. (1973).

Funeral Home Environment

J. Sheridan Mayer

Color has a profound influence upon man both psychologically and physiologically. Even though he is not consciously aware of it, color influences what he eats, drinks, purchases, and feels. It has a powerful but silent voice, a voice which the funeral director employs in the funeral-home environment to help in the reclamation of those who mourn. While the clergyman seeks to aid the bereaved spiritually, the funeral director contributes quietly, without fanfare, by employing color psychology in the environment of the funeral home.

Where else do you hear more warm conversations than in and about the funeral home? Relatives who do not see each other regularly seize upon this opportunity to have a family reunion; friends and neighbors refresh their acquaintance. The emotional scene changes fairly rapidly.

You enter the funeral home with your spirits at low key; your respiration is shallow and you wear a serious, somber countenance. As you gaze upon the face of the deceased whom you have known as an active and vital personality, a frustrated hush comes over you; you are looking at a silenced personality whom you will see no more. You turn away to seek the next of kin and pay your respects in muted tones. As you move on, you see someone you know and move to greet him. Following the amenities, a thought about the deceased, and the beauty and number of the floral offerings, talk turns to mutual interests. You move to the foyer or lounge and there meet other acquaintances. The conversation becomes light and perhaps reminiscent. The mood has changed; perhaps there is laughter. You are no longer thinking of the deceased. You are "socializing." Your social behavior does not demonstrate disrespect for the deceased; it is a release from the tensions which engulf you as you peer into the face of the deceased. It is a natural and understandable human reaction. A viewer can tolerate only so much of this depressed feeling and then must find release. Members of the family (and even the next of kin) are similarly affected. After the first part of the viewing period they too need release. Conversation with friends may become smiling and animated. Sometimes it is possible to induce the spouse to join you in the lounge where the conversation dwells on less morbid things. It is not beyond the realm of possibility that he or she may break into laughter. This too is good.

The decor of the modern funeral home is intended to encourage these releases. The evolution from past practices to current ones has been slow. In great-grandfather's day, when more people died at home, the deceased was embalmed in bed and viewed in the "front parlor." The presence of the remains in the house until the time of burial was a great hardship on the emotions of the family. Moreover, it gave problems to the funeral director in regard to the trucking of the equipment and lighting; he was also constantly apprehensive that someone might draw a shade or turn on another light when he was absent.

In grandfather's day, the funeral director saw the wisdom of isolating the funeral from the private home. He bought a property and converted it into a funeral home. It was usually a house which, like those of his neighbors, had small rooms and was architecturally inefficient. But it was still an improvement over the private-home funeral.

The first funeral homes continued the austere Victorian atmosphere which had been simulated in the private home. The shades were drawn, the lights were dimmed, and the mourners sat on hard, wood-slat folding chairs. In some funeral homes it was impossible to distinguish the faces of the immediate family as they sat side-by-side against one wall during the viewing. The atmosphere of the funeral home was depressing and perpetuated the strain of grief.

Gradually the funeral director broke away from the Victorian tradition. Interior decorators were called in to suggest changes in the funeral-home decor. They recommended the use of warm, moderately energizing colors which would provide a desirable atmosphere of cheering calm and physical comfort. New floor plans were suggested which required the tearing down of old walls and the construction of new ones which would efficiently organize the flow of staff and group traffic. There followed expansion with new wings, face-lifting of the exterior, planned parking facilities, and landscaping. The delivery entrance was redesigned and freight elevators were installed where needed.

Notwithstanding their valuable contributions, the interior decorators did not fully understand all the problems of the funeral establishment. The funeral setting with all its inherent problems of illumination was perhaps their greatest weakness. Torchiere lighting with amber-colored lamps still remained. Today there are several organizations which specialize in funeral-home decor and illumination for both established premises and new construction. They are aware of the problems of funeral homes and of the presentation of the remains for viewing.

These funeral-home specialists advocate a decor which is slightly more opulent in its appointments than the homes of the people who will form the clientele; they decry any lavish treatment of the decor, with perhaps one exception—the ladies' powder room. A crystal chandelier in this area, when employed in the foyer, seems to give a distinctive impression.

Today's model funeral homes continue to be decorated in warm, pleasant colors—muted tones of red, yellow, yellow-orange, and red-orange as in light, warm browns, tan, beige, and taupe. The cool colors (blue, green, and so on) are not excluded; they are seen as tiny, vivid accents which complement the duller dominant colors of the interior. The one exception may be the casket-selection room. Since this room is likely to reinstate the finality of death in the minds of the family, it avoids as much as possible any atmosphere of depression. To this end, a background of the greenery of nature has been recommended. A scenic wallpaper of a landscape in subdued gray-green provides a fitting background; it is located on the longest wall. The other walls may be painted with a light gray-green or prepared with gray-green upon which a subdued pattern of white is imprinted. Since the casket woods (and metal finishes) are usually red, orange, or yellow in basic hue, these warm colors stand out pleasantly from the background. Bright and bold background colors are avoided; so also are very warm wall colors such as gold or rose. A slightly warm, neutralized color such as ivory or warm silver-gray may be employed effectively; varied wall textures or designs are also effective.

The funeral parlor is designed as either a churchlike chapel or a living room. The chapel is normally decorated with a single color; it appears drab and monotonous until the center of focus (the casket, flowers, and so on) is in position. In a livingroom decor, the appointments are the same as those found in a private home: sofas, armchairs, tables, lamps, pictures, and so forth. The folding chairs which are added are padded and comfortable. Eliminated are ornate fireplaces, hanging tapestries, and Oriental rugs, which formerly distracted attention from the funeral service. The folding velvet back-drapes, so necessary for the private-home viewing, has largely been retired. Many funeral homes have replaced them with ceiling-to-floor drapery across the entire wall; others employ the greenery of artificial ivy, ferns, and cybotiums as a background against a "natural" wall. Where architecturally possible, the casket-alcove has become very popular. The lights and controls are hidden from view behind the side and top proscenium walls which mark the setting for the casket; this eliminates the need for illumination from visible torchieres.

The most effective colors in the livingroom-type of funeral homes are conservative and pleasant; they provide a friendly atmosphere and add the comfort of a homelike environment. There is one dominant color to which all others are subordinate; this dominant color is repeated in its tints, tones, and shades. The colors which have the greatest ability to unify the colors of objects set before them are the weak tints and tones of yellow, yellow-orange, and orange. One funeral home decorated three parlors in its new establishment. The one finished in powder-blue was not selected by any family for two and one-half years. Cool hues do not unify the colors of objects set before them; they tend to be depressing and cold under artificial illumination. This does not mean that cool colors are eliminated. They are necessary to the color scheme as accent colors to be repeated in rugs, upholstery, furniture, and accessories.

The office may be formal or informal, but both styles strive to relax tensions with a simple decor, comfortable upholstered chairs, and an uncluttered appearance. To appear less stiff and conventional, a table may substitute for the formal desk, and the filing cabinets may be located out of sight in an adjacent area. The walls may be plain or paneled and hold a framed diploma and license.

An interview or conference room may substitute for the formal office. It may include an upholstered sofa and easy chairs. The drapes on the windows may be parted to let in daylight. Several oil paintings may grace the walls. A water carafe and glasses are available. State law permitting, some funeral homes make available hot coffee or tea. It is in the office or conference room that necessary information is sought and emotional control is essential.

The family room, where architecturally available, is the small wing adjacent to the chapel; here the family can witness the service without being observed by others. It is also available for visitation by friends before the service. French doors with glass curtains hide the interior when not in use. The room is equipped with comfortable overstuffed furniture and repeats the decor of the chapel. After the friends are directed to their cars following the service, the family can pay its last respects alone.

A reposing room is available in some funeral homes for visitation of the family before the scheduled visiting hours. The family can come to this small room to be alone with their loved one. In some funeral homes, the reposing room resembles a bedroom and includes the usual bedroom furniture.

The lounge is one of the most important areas of the funeral home. It creates an entirely different atmosphere from other parts of the establishment. It is remindful of what is generally called a "rec room" or a "family room" in the private home. Here there are smoking accommodations, relaxing furniture arranged for intimate groupings, floor and table lamps, tiled floor, and pictures (or a mural design of tropical vegetation) on the walls. The walls may be paneled in part or in all. The lounge is a relaxing, smoking, and visiting area where people can escape from the tensions of the funeral parlor.

And so it is seen that the funeral director goes hand-in-hand with the clergyman in his effort to aid those who mourn. The funeral director may be responsible for the care of the deceased but, far more important, he serves the living.

Why Are We? What Are We? Where Are We?

Sumner James Waring, Jr.

In service to all, regardless of race, creed, color, or financial circumstances—
the responses stimulated by the questions of the title will certainly suggest that
the role of the licensed funeral director is among the most intimate and sensitive
of those relating one individual to another. We serve the living during their hours
of most immediate need as they express their feelings of grief, start the process
of positive personal adjustment, and attempt to rejoin society.

The more technically oriented disciplines of the funeral director relate to
receiving the body and responsibility for its preparation for burial, together with
sheltering it prior to the funeral rites and transporting it to the cemetery. The
funeral director accepts and is thus guided by the framework of licensing requirements set forth in the various jurisdictions to which he is responsible before both
he and his facility are licensed. Thus, licensure assures that certain qualifications
have been met and grants the director the privilege of serving the general public.

These licensing requirements have evolved as a part of society's recognition
of the need to care for its dead in the proper manner.

Many would add that they provide us with reassuring evidence of the funeral director's willingness to cooperate with government and society. There is
considerable reason to believe that such licensing requirements came about
because of other than mandatory reasons. All should know that the profession of
the funeral director involves practice and experience which respond to man's
feelings and preferences during times of grief.

183

THE FUNERAL DIRECTOR'S COUNSELING COMMITMENT

We care for the dead in service to the living. We function as coordinative counselors during an interval which is frequently among the most depressing and desperate in the lives of the living. Other than within the realm to which our training and skills are most particularly directed, ours is not so much the responsibility to know or be expected to know in-depth answers as it is the responsibility to recognize our client family's need to be in touch with these answers and to see that they are guided or coordinated—the responsibility of knowing when, how, and to what extent to intervene within their crisis; the responsibility of knowing where such answers may be obtained so that those who place confidence in us may be directed and served.

Sharing our immediate involvement are likely to be those functioning within the disciplines of religion, medicine, and law. We share with them as we continue to counsel within the realms to which our knowledge and experience most directly apply. More specifically, we coordinate the involvement of our client families with the various other disciplines with which they are involved when we recognize there is unrecognized or unattended need.

Care, concern, tribute, ceremony, and coordinative follow-up continue to be cornerstones of that which we pursue, with no limit except the limit of our respective sights and abilities.

Recognizing our responsibilities, implied and otherwise, we use our education and training together with the counseling "practicals" of experience, judgment, and leadership in justifying the value of our being.

Counseling the Bereaved
Robert J. Volk

A mortician, funeral director, undertaker, or practitioner of mortuary science—whatever we may wish to call him—may in essence be someone else. Perhaps as we read through these pages, we will recognize that through his experience and the fact that he serves the living and the dead, he is also a person con-
versant with thanatology, psychology, and sociology. He also faces the challenge
of changing in order to continue to meet true human needs. This is a challenge
that must be accepted by the funeral director and by the other helping professions.

"The funeral director must become more of a caretaker—a caregiver. He
must continue to develop his sensitivity to the various levels or degrees of loss
that death creates in our present-day society. The funeral director must always
realize that after he has done what he does he is at a point of no return. What is
done cannot be changed. What is not done will remain undone. Neither the
funeral director nor the family he is serving will have a second chance." (Raether,
1971).

On Dec. 14, 1973, I was privileged to direct a two-hour seminar for
mortuary science students on the importance of the director's being sensitive
to the true needs of the people he serves and not just to their surface requests.

In the seminar we first had to understand the challenge to the profession—
to be different from present-day funeral service. We briefly discussed: Why we
chose funeral service as a profession; How funeral service started, where it is
now, and where it may be going; The public's image of the funeral director and
the funeral; The challenge to the funeral director to meet the human needs of

185

those involved through proper counseling; The need for us to understand ourselves and death before we attempt to help others.

The overall method of explaining to the group how to have a learning experience on counseling the bereaved was organized as follows:

(A) We broke into five individual discussion teams with nine members on each team.

(B) A team leader was appointed for each team. Each team had a different problem situation to solve within a period of 35 minutes.

(C) The instructions for each problem situation were: You are to write down on this paper how you feel you would help the family at their time of loss. Use your own thoughts and try to forget how you know someone else would handle the situation. Remember, your main objective is to help all those who are experiencing bereavement to return to a productive and satisfying life. When you have completed your thoughts, wait for the rest of your team to complete their thoughts. Then, as a team, come up with a unified solution which the team leader will report to the overall group. If you wish to have this paper returned to you, please write your name in the upper right-hand corner.

(D) One of the situations discussed was of a family which included:

Mother, 33   Brother, 10
Father, 36   Brother, 8
Sister, 16

A third brother, 13, drowned with a friend while swimming in a river. When the father is making the arrangements, he insists that the casket be closed— no one, absolutely no one, is to see his son, not even his wife or children.

THE GROUP DECISION

Reported by the team leader the group decision was that the father should be approached and asked why he wanted the casket closed. This would be done with the realization that the father's thinking at this time might not be normal because of his feelings of deep grief. The group said that the father had not indicated that the closed casket was family thinking. It felt it advisable to try to get the family together, feeling that from this might come a trial viewing by the wife and the husband together or by the wife alone with the husband's consent. In this way all members of the family would be part of the final decision.

After this there were individual comments from the students. Some of these students were members of the group assigned to this situation, but for the most part they were nonmembers. Their observations, in brief, were as follows:

"Husband is the head of the family, it is his money that pays the bill."

"There is a lot more than paying the bill, believe me."

"We have been told by funeral directors, inside and outside of school, not to argue with families—give them what they want."

"Later on he can't say, 'If you had told me about the alternatives maybe I would have thought differently.' "

"Something he will have to live with forever."

"That's not the business of the funeral director."

"At a time like this people are not aware of alternatives. You're not telling them what to do, you're just telling them the advantages of the different avenues."

There was an additional spontaneous comment by one student. It is quoted here as it expresses awareness, sincerity, dedication, and a desire for personal education and direction:

We were talking about making people aware, talk of death and what the funeral business is all about. Now, when you allow a person—let's say if a person comes into the funeral home and he tells you lock, stock, and barrel that this is what he's insisting on and this and that—one thing you have to do, that you are obligated to do, is to at least open his mind up enough to the point where he has other things he has to consider. You see, people run through life—we have fun, games, and parties, this and that, we hide behind. As far as you're concerned this man is possibly hiding behind his grief and not accepting the fact of what happened. This is just as much reality as the passing of his son, no matter how horrible it was. You have a right, you have an obligation to get that man together and bring one thing to his attention. To do that you may possibly be able to open the channel for them to discuss this whole thing again and that is the fact that they *love* that child and you get everybody at that time—you call a private counseling session. The father gets a chance to listen to one of his sons speak as to how he felt about one of his brothers, and you get a chance to see a sister speak about how she felt about her brother, you get the mother to speak out, and the father hears how the mother felt about her son. You see, then, that the father is given the opportunity to speak his feelings—how he felt about his son; and at the same time you are guiding these people and making them realize that there is a family love there—that even though they all loved that particular son individually, that he still belonged to that family as a unit, but at the same time he had other friends outside the realm of that family who loved him and respected him also—that it is an obligation to allow these people to reclaim some of the friendship, some of the love they had for him, too. You see, when you bring up enough of a challenge to people, you'll be surprised, it will almost act as though it's a steam valve. This man who almost changed 360 degrees would be willing to talk to you. Thus, if you were to ask him after the meeting is over, "Would you be willing to view the body now, would you be willing to take a look?" Now that you've opened this man's mind up and he's not as hostile, set on his purpose . . . then you let him see his son that everyone has spoken of, spoken about . . . you see, when he gazes on that child— then the realization of everyone's words, my feelings toward the child,

I'm feeling what my wife will probably feel . . . I'm feeling what my daughter feels, if she comes. You see, then, he may realize that he does owe a little bit more . . . it changes the situation altogether. But the other thing you have done is act as a catalyst; you've been able to take a situation and open it up where the family has been able to pool on nothing more than that family love they had. And people are afraid . . . some guys are ashamed, a father is sometimes ashamed to tell his son, "I love you," you see. But you are putting him in a position where he has to say it at that particular time—he'll say it—he may say it as he stands there by himself, he will say, "I love you." He may never have said it to that boy before, but you have put him in a position now that the feeling he is feeling, what he may never have been aware of riding on a train day-by-day. You put him in a position now where he thinks, and that is what you are there to do—you're not there to push him, probe him, nothing else, you are just there to work with those things which you're trained to know, and when that family walks out of that funeral home, they will have to respect you, because of one thing—that you were aware enough of what love is—love is the most amazing factor that permeates everything as far as a funeral is concerned. The reason why you do it is because of love. . . .

We can see by the reaction of these students that this area of involvement may be in the distant future for many of them. This is a loss for them, the public, and the profession.

These students have shown that the need for the development of the ability to be of additional help to the bereaved among those in funeral service is greater than ever. Their understanding and desire to meet the needs of the public with deeper insights into the situations they may encounter are encouraging, as are the concern the students have for the problems of complacency within our profession and their desire to meet the challenge. With the proper awareness of the funeral profession and the aid of the other helping professions their visions will be realized.

This actual situation had occurred approximately eight years before. I told the father that I thought I could understand how he felt, but had he given any thought as to what his wife or other children might want? Perhaps his wife would like to see her son—maybe his children would like to see their brother in the casket? However, Mr. Jones responded that he wanted the casket closed and no one was to see his son. All I asked of Mr. Jones was that he think about what we discussed. And, to remember, whatever decision was made, it could not be changed in the future. He did not have to see his son. If his wife and other children wished to see him, we could let them and then close the casket.

He went home saying that he would call me in the morning to let me know if there were any changes. I told him that was not necessary because we would take care of his son as we would anyone else, and he would be ready to be seen by the family that afternoon. If, when he came in, he still did not want to see his son, the casket would be closed.

The next morning, Mr. Jones called and informed me that his wife and the other children wished to see his son, but he still did not. When they came in that afternoon, the family went into the room and Mr. Jones stayed in the counseling room. His wife and children came into the counseling room and asked him to see his son—"He is at peace with God."

Mr. Jones joined his family in the room—they cried, they talked, they cried, they gave support to one another. Mr. Jones came to me and said, "Thank you, we will leave the casket open."

Later, when we were alone, I asked him, "Would you mind sharing with me why you wanted the casket closed?" His reply was, "First, I did not want my family to have any more grief. I wanted them to remember him the way he was. But in all honesty, I felt he would look like this." He placed his hands on his throat as if gasping for air, his mouth open and his eyes looking upward. I thanked Mr. Jones for being so open and sharing his thoughts with me.

When we first think of this type of reaction, we have trouble understanding why the person would not be aware of the ability of the embalmer with his skill and expertise in most cases to erase any traces of the manner in which a person died but not death itself. Upon deeper reflection we realize that this is understandable when the first stage of grief includes denial, shock, and agitation.

There is a tremendous amount of work to be done in order to educate the public, the other helping professions, and those presently in funeral service to the importance of change and how to meet the challenge of providing additional help to the bereaved.

In order to be of greater help to the bereaved, the funeral profession must concern itself with the following:

(A) The public—with emphasis upon information and education the public will become aware of what funeral service is presently doing and of its future capabilities.

(B) The helping professions—the other helping professionals (psychiatrists, psychologists, physicians, educators, social scientists, clergy, nurses, and so on) as a group have not been aware of what funeral service has been doing and its capabilities for improving upon their services by being of greater help at the time of bereavement.

(C) Funeral service—this is where the problems of change and meeting the challenge originate. Is the funeral director willing to look at himself? What is he? What is he doing? Where is he going? Is he willing to become educated with new knowledge—thanatology, psychology, and sociology? Does he realize that he has been effective at being one of the original encounter leaders,* and will he

*The funeral director is one of the original encounter leaders. Just about every death involves more than one person, and he strives to meet the needs of all involved. If he is serving properly, he is able to help all those who have a need to express themselves through words or actions. He achieves this by his natural sensitivity to others. This seems to be the type of person attracted to the profession.

seek additional education to improve his effectiveness in helping the bereaved?

It would be very wrong for anyone to feel that the funeral director has to be a psychologist or sociologist. However, he should be a person who seeks more knowledge, understands his present abilities, and applies them in the area of helping families with understanding and bereavement counseling. His additional education in thanatology and the problems arising from dying, death, and bereavement will aid him in becoming a crisis intervenor. If counseling is provided after the funeral, he should be able to help the bereaved and guide them to other professionals.

The funeral director is already a representative of death in his community. His records and his practical experience reflect the needs of people. As he receives additional education and as he shares with the other helping professions, is it not logical that he should become a bereavement counselor? Is it not practical that his facilities should be utilized as a bereavement center which involves representatives from the other helping professions and to which the public may come for information on death; individual and group counseling on dying, death, and bereavement; resource information, similar to that provided to the helping professions; and education for both the public and the professions on dying, death, and bereavement.

These goals can be achieved if those in the helping professions who are interested in death share experiences and information to a greater extent by relating more closely to one another.

REFERENCES

Raether, H. C. The place of the funeral: the role of the funeral director in contemporary america. Omega, 2:148 (1971).

GRIEF AND THE PUBLIC IMAGE

The Media and Grief

Howard F. Barnard

Certain types of communications can play an important role in helping to assuage grief. Conversely, other types can prolong it. An urgent need has long existed for publicized helpful information on all aspects of death—not half-truths or distortions used to sell books, newspapers, and radio or television time.

Some newspapers, as well as some radio and television programs, have continued to treat funeral service as a whipping boy. Others have carried articles or produced programs designed to be of genuine service in aiding survivors. Unfortunately, there is still too much of the wrong kind of funeral service publicity. Feature writers have jumped at the slightest provocation to accuse funeral service of charging outrageously high prices. They have pandered to those who urge "cutting to the bone" services for survivors or eliminating them altogether.

Such publicity frequently has shared in the responsibility for the elimination of funerals. Human remains have been offered to medical schools, unceremoniously buried, or immediately cremated. In some instances there have been cold, barren memorial services, devoid of flowers or any other kind of sentiment, held weeks after the death; in other cases there has been nothing.

The survivors, hastened into such actions by well-meaning friends or influenced by what they have read or heard, have been left with deep emotional scars. They have been denied viewing the body, which would help them realize the finality of death. Some have memories of loved ones who have been ravaged by long periods of suffering or by disfigurement from accidents. They have been denied the memory of faces at peace and rest, with the marks of suffering removed by skillful restorative art.

On the reverse side of the coin there have been other types of publicity which have helped to comfort those who have suffered the loss of a loved one.

One such program even has won an Emmy award. Here, I refer to a series of television programs prepared for local viewing in the Minneapolis-St. Paul area. Because of its excellent public reception, portions of the series were broadcast nationally by CBS. These broadcasts centered on the reactions and courage of people as they approach death. The focus was the waning life of a young high school athlete stricken with an incurable ailment which gradually wasted his body.

With the permission of the youth's parents, which took time and patience to obtain, numerous interviews were conducted with the fatally ill boy and broadcast. The series concluded with the type of funeral which could give comfort to survivors.

The unique series of television interviews was originated and conducted by Don Kladstrup of station WCCO-TV.

This type of program ties into the efforts to assuage the physical and emotional suffering of terminal patients in which researchers such as Dr. Elisabeth Kübler-Ross have played a prominent part. The periodicals which have publicized the work of Dr. Kübler-Ross and other research on impending death are injecting a positive factor into material relating to death.

It is unfortunate but true that articles designed to help the dying and those who will survive them do not sell newspapers to the extent that exposé stories do. Many people are excited by the sensational. They like to read of scandals, regardless of what or by whom committed. The stories of families being sold funerals considerably in excess of their means, wiping out savings or meager life insurance policies, make spicier reading than stories of how the suffering of the dying can be alleviated or how families can be comforted by viewing and funerals—conventional or humanist.

Some exposés can serve a useful purpose. A group of funeral homes recently were accused in articles in The New York Times of "body snatching," fraudulently obtaining possession of human remains in welfare cases in order that they might profit illegally. It was alleged by the newspaper that these funeral homes employed the names of nonexistent friends or relatives of the deceased or made use of the names of living persons without their knowledge, or committed forgery to gain possession of remains for improper disposition. Funeral service will be the better for having such alleged practices given full publicity and thus eliminated.

Fortunately, the average funeral director is conscientious and honest, but it goes without saying that every profession, including funeral service, has a few dishonest persons in practice.

There is a long and growing list of books designed to comfort the bereaved.

Professional and lay people have grieved deeply and, when rays of hope penetrated their grief, perpetuated this hope on the written page so that they might help others to work through their grief and find inner peace. Again, these helpful books have received far less publicity than the books of the detractors of funeral service like Ruth Harmer, Jessica Mitford, and other writers who have accomplished little or nothing in helping the survivor work through his grief.

Fortunately, various bibliographies of useful books for survivors have been compiled. It is to be hoped that the nation's librarians will have access to and consult these lists when ordering books for their patrons so that books offering solace can be made readily available to those who grieve.

Numerous funeral homes are attempting to meet this need. Several useful bibliographies have been compiled by mortuary representatives. One funeral home organization, Thomas M. Quinn & Sons of Long Island, N.Y., has provided a library in each of its funeral homes where patrons can borrow books which may help them reestablish useful and happier lives. Other funeral directors are donating books to libraries which stress the positive side of funeral service together with other publications useful to survivors.

In conclusion, may I say that I spent years as a daily and weekly newspaperman and I realize the public responsibility of the press. I only hope that more representatives of my former calling will come to understand that they have a responsibility to help their readers rather than to cater to sensationalism which can help no one but instead directly or indirectly inflict deep hurt.

The changing attitude of the public may become a factor in bringing greater restraint into the reporting practices of various newspapers and radio and television stations. Many persons are becoming weary of reading or hearing sensational news in the same way as they have had their fill of sexually explicit and sadistic movies. Such people are searching for more inspiring reading and visual presentations.

Newspapers as a Mirror of Death

Martin L. Kutscher

Although the editors of The New York Times attempt to maintain objectivity in their coverage of the news, bias often is evidenced, unconsciously or consciously. Emotion-laden words, the style of writing, the length and format of an article, and the deliberate exclusion or inclusion of facts are a few of the methods by which a newspaper can slant a news story. According to S. I. Hayakawa, "We cannot attain complete impartiality while we use the language of everyday life . . . Nevertheless, the best newspapers . . . try to tell us as accurately as possibly what is going on in the world, because they are run by newspapermen who conceive it to be part of their professional responsibility to present fairly the conflicting points of view in controversial issues" (1).

To a great extent, the events themselves control the language and format of an article. In its reaction to the death of a prominent American leader, a good newspaper generally reflects the grief, anger, and remorse of society at that specific time.

The following are descriptions of The New York Times' coverage of the deaths and funerals of five American leaders. Comparisons of the treatment of each news event will be made with the above considerations in mind, with the comparisons extending over a wide range of contrasts and covering as many facets as possible.

MALCOLM X
MARTIN LUTHER KING, JR.

The tone of the New York Times' coverage of the deaths of Malcolm X and Martin Luther King differed markedly. The article on Malcolm X failed to draw forth the emotional response from the reader provoked by the coverage of Martin Luther King's death. Sentences in the front-page stories about Dr. King such as "Dismay, shame, anger, and foreboding marked the nation's reaction last night to the Rev. Dr. Martin Luther King, Jr.'s murder" and words such as "forlorn hope," "urge," "deplore," "stunned," and "brutal" (2) found no counterparts in the articles on Malcolm X. Sub-headlines, such as "Dismay in Nation" and "President's Plea" were matched only by "Malcolm Knew He Was a 'Marked Man.' "

In his autobiography, Malcolm X wrote: "When I am dead—I say it because from the things I know, I do not expect to live long enough to read this book in its finished form—I want you to just watch and see if I'm not right in what I say: that the white man, in his press, is going to identify me with 'hate.' He will make use of me dead, as he has made use of me alive, as a convenient symbol of 'hatred' —and that will help him to escape facing the truth that all I have been doing is to hold up a mirror to reflect, to show, the history of unspeakable crimes that his race has committed against my race" (3).

Articles in the Times contained subheadings concerning Malcolm X such as "Told of Hate," and he was constantly called the "militant black leader." Although this was true, the Times failed to point out that he was a militant black leader who used violence only when there was no other way to obtain peace and racial equality. There was also inadequate mention of his complete change from racism. (Incidentally, he did not live to see his autobiography in its finished form.)

The Times pointed out in both cases that the men knew that their lives were endangered. Dr. King was quoted as saying, "It really doesn't matter what happens now. I've been to the mountaintop." An unnecessary editorial comment by the reporter ruined Malcolm's equally brave statement. The article stated: " . . . and Malcolm leaned forward to give emphasis to his words. 'It [death] doesn't frighten me for myself as long as I felt they would not hurt my family" (4).

Both men were described as being eloquent, but Malcolm X was "bitterly eloquent," while Dr. King was "eloquent and beloved by crowds."

On the day of their assassination, there was a story about the life and career of each man. The story about Dr. King started: "To many millions of American Negroes, the Rev. Dr. Martin Luther King, Jr. was the prophet of their crusade for racial equality. He was their voice of anguish, their eloquence in humiliation, their battle cry for human dignity." Although Malcolm X could have been described in the same manner, his article started: "He was Malcolm

Little, alias Big Red, a marijuana-smoking, cocaine-sniffing, zoot-suited, hip talking hoodlum when he went to prison in 1946." Malcolm's article started with and continued to present most of his negative traits; the article devoted only one sentence to explaining Malcolm's new philosophy. Dr. King's news story presented all of his good characteristics. Furthermore, Malcolm X's life story occupied less than 20 paragraphs; Dr. King's was a full newspaper page.

Control over the length and format of an article is one way in which a newspaper can pass judgment on the importance of a news event. Only about 15 paragraphs were devoted to Malcolm's assassination on the first page, whereas more than half of the front page was given to Martin Luther King's death.

Perhaps these differences were due in part, at least, to the events which had surrounded each man's death. Yet since a newspaper is the mirror of the society for which it writes, the differences in The New York Times' coverage of the deaths of Malcolm X and Martin Luther King, Jr. reflected our society's scorn for violent people and actions.

MARTIN LUTHER KING, JR.
ROBERT FRANCIS KENNEDY

The New York Times reported the deaths of Martin Luther King and Robert F. Kennedy in almost the same way, except that several things said about Robert Kennedy were said in a stronger manner. Ever since Dr. King's death, the desire to bring back the dead was already at a heightened intensity.

Fear, brought on by a trend of violence, was becoming all too clear by June 6, 1968, when Bobby Kennedy was assassinated. Only three months earlier Dr. King had been shot, and this second Kennedy assassination was one more to be added to the list of assassinations of the decade. The headline "JOHNSON APPOINTS PANEL ON VIOLENCE" appeared in one-inch caps on the front page of the newspaper on the day of Mr. Kennedy's death. On page 6, there was a full-page article under the heading "Europeans, Seeing a Growing Climate of Violence, Express Fears for the U.S."; and an article entitled "World Morality Crises" appeared in the same issue. The Times quoted Arthur Schlesinger, Jr. as saying that the United States was a land of "violent people with a violent history." Schlesinger wrote that Americans should realize that "the evil is in us, that it springs from some dark, intolerable tension in our history and our institutions" (5). There were also articles about fears over the stability of American society at the time of Dr. King's assassination, but the point was not made as strongly.

The story of Dr. King's career was most complimentary, and so was the life story of Bobby Kennedy: ". . . in his brief but extraordinary political career. . . ." A great deal of emotion was evoked from the reader by reminding him of the "near-martyrdom of the Kennedy family, which has now lost two sons to assassins' bullets . . . Wherever he [Bobby Kennedy] went, he drew crowds by evoking, through his Boston accent, his gestures, and his physical appearance, a remarkable and nostalgic likeness to his elder brother."

There was a tremendous desire expressed in the paper to bring these dead men back to life. This was one common link among all the people studied. For example, on the front page of the June 6, 1969, issue there was an article stating that: "It [Robert Kennedy's assassination] removed forever one of the most promising young political leaders in recent American history, one with particular appeal for the poor, the downtrodden and the alienated inhabitants of the Negro slums." Martin Luther King was described similarly: "He was their [the poor] voice of anguish, their eloquence in humiliation, their battle cry for their human dignity. He forged for them the weapon of nonviolence that withstood and blunted the ferocity of segregation." Both men were missed greatly.

The Rev. Martin Luther King, Jr. and Robert F. Kennedy were both heroes of the poor and downtrodden, and there was little difference in the events surrounding these men's assassinations. America's deep anger and remorse for the death of these two men were reflected in The New York Times.

ROBERT F. KENNEDY
JOHN F. KENNEDY

John F. Kennedy was President of the United States; Robert F. Kennedy was not. This simple fact explains most of the differences in the ways that the Times reported their deaths.

Literally the entire first 16 pages were dedicated to the death of the late President Kennedy (6). In the Nov. 23, 1963, issue of The New York Times, not one word was said about any of the other activities going on in the world until page 17. The lead article was printed in large size print. Bobby Kennedy's assassination was reported in the front page headlines, but did not preempt the whole front section. The length and format of the coverage of John Kennedy's assassination was one way in which the Times expressed its judgment on the importance of the event.

A comparison of the headlines of back-page stories shows one important similarity in our society's reaction to the deaths of the Kennedy brothers. On the day of the President's assassination, the following headline appeared: "First, Is It True? Then Anger and Anguish Among New Yorkers and Visitors." On the day of Bobby Kennedy's death, an almost identical headline appeared: "New Yorkers Awaken in Shock to a Day that Many Would Prefer to Forget." However, a President is a President, and Bobby Kennedy's article could not match sentences such as: "Another cry quickly took its place as the news of the death of President Kennedy swept with stunning impact: 'My God!' Women wept, and men wept. A refusal to believe the report was the immediate reaction, but swiftly came the horror, then anguish, and then, among many, both city residents and visitors, deep anger."

A fear of violence was also obvious with both assassinations. People were shocked, and most importantly, surprised about the possibility of assassination at the time of John Kennedy's death. Assassination was basically a new and horrible thought. People were equally shocked and fearful at the time of Bobby Kennedy's murder, but for a slightly different reason. People were afraid of a trend of continued violence.

An attempt to draw forth nostalgia and remorse from the reader was obvious in the life stories of both men. An old picture of John Kennedy was captioned: "At ten, John F. Kennedy smiled warmly through the freckles of his boyhood." Later the author describes him at the age of 28 as being "scrawny . . . and shy about meeting people." On the front page, he was called the "dead young President." The same happened with Bobby Kennedy. Besides the previous quotes cited above, which showed the editor's attempt to provoke a feeling of remorse, there were descriptions such as Senator Kennedy's reaction to his brother's murder: "The assassination plunged Mr. [Robert] Kennedy into a deep grief that amounted virtually to melancholy. His face was a mask; sadness enveloped his eyes; he seemed to have shrunk physically. He often walked alone, his hands dug into his jacket pockets. And for the remainder of his life he lived with thought of his dead brother never far from the surface of his mind."

The world missed both men; the United States had great plans for both of them. The fact that people wanted to cry out and scream at the time of the deaths was made painfully evident in the Times. Robert F. Kennedy received a hero's attention; it would only be proper that the assassination of a President receive the newspaper coverage that the late President John F. Kennedy's assassination did receive.

JOHN F. KENNEDY
DWIGHT D. EISENHOWER

John F. Kennedy was an American hero, and his death was considered tragic. Dwight D. Eisenhower had been an even bigger hero. Yet since his death had been foreshadowed for months, its emotional impact on the public was not nearly as great.

Since there were hardly any details concerning Eisenhower's death, almost everything written about him concerned his career and personality. Using the first four paragraphs to explain the conditions by which he "died quietly," the main article made a quick transition and shared with the reader some of "Ike's" experiences (7). Later in the issue, four pages were devoted to his life, lingering on his military career for the most part. This lack of specifics about his death was in sharp contrast to the articles about John Kennedy's assassination, which gave a great many details.

The main concern of the newspaper was to make sure that everyone should know that Mr. Eisenhower had died peacefully and without anguish. "END IS PEACEFUL" was printed in caps above the main article on the front page. The article itself started with "Dwight David Eisenhower, 34th President of the United States, died peacefully at 12:25 P.M."

The funeral coverage of both men contained the same tone. "The body of John Fitzgerald Kennedy was returned today to the American earth" (8). Eisenhower's article said "Long lines of average citizens from whom he drew his strength filed past his bier beneath the Capitol dome in a farewell salute" (9).

However, on the day of Mr. Kennedy's funeral, the shock of a sudden death to Americans was shown by the words "New York Like a Vast Church" which appeared in large print on the front page of the Times. In contrast, no one was appalled by Eisenhower's foreshadowed death, and this was made obvious in The New York Times. "It was like the passing of a beloved great uncle. . . . Sadness was in the faces yesterday of the generation that knew him as the general and the President, but there was no anguish, no deep shock." Perhaps, people were relieved that the former General Eisenhower's discomfort had ended.

There are thus many methods through which a newspaper can edit the facts to give a news story a desired tone. "Slanting gives no explicit judgments, but it differs from reporting in that it deliberately makes certain judgments inescapable" (10). As Hayakawa said, complete impartiality is impossible, and the above is presented to illustrate, and to show the existence of, some of these methods, not to condemn The New York Times.

As shown, a careful choice of words is very important. The certain connotation of just one word can change the tone of the entire passage which contains the word. For example, about a year before Malcolm X was shot, he had left a religious group called the Black Muslims. His breaking from the group was explained in at least three different articles. One article said that he "left" the group, another said that he "split" from the Muslims, and the other used the word "defected." "Defected" carries a quite different connotation from "left"; a defection is usually considered wrong and immoral. The difference in the connotation causes a difference in the tone.

A reporter can also add bias by stressing certain points. For example, while writing an article about Elijah Mohammed, the leader of the Black Muslims, the author referred to the man's luxurious "19-room mansion . . . worth at least $50,000" four times in the first eight paragraphs. It is possible that the reporter was trying to say that religious leaders are not supposed to be rich. The only quote of the Muslim leader that was contained in the article had improper grammar.

But most of the differences in The New York Times coverage of the deaths of the men studied were caused by a lack of impartiality in American society's reaction to their deaths. A newspaper is merely a mirror of our society—a peephole. By its very nature it must reflect a society's biases as well as a nation's grief and reactions to death.

REFERENCES

1. Hayakawa, S. I., "Language in Thought and Action." New York: Harcourt, Brace, and World, Inc. (1964), pp. 47-49.
2. The New York Times, excerpts from the Apr. 5, 1968 issue. New York, New York.
3. Malcolm X, "The Autobiography of Malcolm X." New York: Grove Press (1964), dustjacket.
4. The New York Times, excerpts from the Feb. 22, 1965 issue. New York, New York.
5. Ibid., June 6, 1968.
6. Ibid., Nov. 23, 1963.
7. Ibid., Mar. 29, 1969.
8. Ibid., Nov. 26, 1963.
9. Ibid., Mar. 31, 1969.
10. Hayakawa, S. I., op. cit., p. 48.

Stripes and Grief

Robert W. Ninker

I have experienced the lasting impact of a grief situation three times, each time under vastly different circumstances.

I shall never really understand the first experience. It occurred in Mannheim, Germany, in October 1952. Louis, a Puerto Rican friend, and I, both of us with the humble rank of private first class (PFC), had just returned from Amsterdam, Holland, after a ten-day leave. We were both due to be considered for a rank increase to corporal which meant a $26 increase in monthly pay to $129 a month.

We both knew that with cessation of the Korean conflict, the number of available promotions would be curtailed. I knew that my performance, including the fact that I represented Headquarter's Company as "Soldier of the Month" and had helped win a bowling tournament for our division, gave me a distinct edge for the promotion over Louis.

As we returned to the barracks from the train station via Volkswagen taxi, I tried to cushion any disappointment my friend Lou would have if he missed his promotion by chatting about several openings that would probably occur before the end of the four months remaining in his tour of duty. Lou seemed to even understand my preconsoling comments!

Our mutual anxiety to see the posted promotions was evidenced by our walking through dark halls in the early morning to check results before we went to bed. There was the posting:

205

William A.

Louis G.

Fred P.

Even in the dim light, I could not believe that my name could possibly have been omitted. William was in the captain's office, so that was understandable, but Fred was a queer one and how could that "damn" Puerto Rican—Louis—be made a corporal over me? There was no answer, only deep hurt, humiliation, and emptiness. Yes, in the truest sense, grief was what I experienced for weeks, even after I, too, was granted the same rank a month later. At age 20, I knew things weren't always done the fair way. Logic failed as evening after evening I skipped going to the mess hall to lie on the still-made GI cot with my cheek buried in the coarse OD blanket which served as a dust cover on the pillows. No one ever noted my borderline acts of depression. It was my problem, all bottled up and gnawing away at the vital youth and energy of a kid who took a routine lump very poorly. Not wanting to discuss it and unable to write home about a failure, I just lived with it for weeks until the matter was less distracting, but acceptance never really came. Silly? Unbelievably. True? Absolutely. Grief? Undeniably. Today, more than 20 years later, I still remember the sorrow of missing one stripe for just for one month.

The second traumatic experience and the resulting grief occurred in April 1949 when my mother received a panic call from our neighbor. His wife, Ann, who was just recovering from the birth of their second child apparently was dying and could barely breathe. He had called the clinic but was told to get the fire department to come with a respirator. Before it arrived, my mother watched wholesome, always hearty Ann die. Later, it was determined infection resulting from incomplete discharge of the placenta had caused the lovely young woman's death.

Her husband couldn't help her. His Ph.D in biology prepared him to teach that subject and general science, which I had taken a year earlier, but he could do nothing more logical than call my mother when the tragedy occurred. Doc and Ann were much more to us than teacher, neighbor, and friend. Both were counselors at our church youth group.

What fun we had at Pfitzinger's farm cooking stew over an open fire and trying to eat persimmons, still a bit green, without puckering. Rosemary Platt's family had let us use their three-acre homesite in the autumn of the year before, too. Marshmallows, a few hotdogs, and some unsuspected necking with Judy Williams, behind the garage, were part of the many fun outings where Doc and Ann had acted as chaperones for our impetuous group.

Those recollections were painful enough for a 16-year-old. It was really startling to be asked if I would be a pallbearer for Ann with some others from the congregation. I remember my concern that we'd look silly carrying the casket on our shoulders. Unless we stooped, little Gene B. wouldn't be touching.

While I had been to a couple of visitations, somehow I had the erroneous impression that caskets were always carried on the shoulder. What troubled me most, though, was how to greet Doc as we attended the visitation. How do you express the deep affection a teenager develops for those who really invested their time and life to bring a bit of order into the unsettled world of youth? I groped, awkward as most teenagers are, and blurted something about being sorry we couldn't bake potatoes in the leaf fires any more. Strangely, incoherent as the message seemed, Doc understood. He sniffed a couple of times, but that didn't mean much because he always sniffed. At college he had inhaled too much formaldehyde and his breathing had been affected. It was a peculiarity which would have caused any other teacher unmerciful kidding, but with Doc, we hardly ever noticed it—except now. How I wrestled for an explanation as to why God took this wonderfully sensitive person away from her children who needed her, Doc, us, and, specifically me. No explanation was really possible, but I grew up a bit that night because it hurt to look at Ann. I cried, and then I felt better. Sad, but better.

My tears weren't ended though. The next day was the funeral. It took place at 4 PM so those of us who wanted to could be there. It cost me two dollars, too. That's what I earned after school working at the grocery store. It didn't matter to the owner when I asked for time off. He understood. Everyone seemed to—except me.

The funeral service seemed to vanish quickly. I can't recall anything except that I was sure worried how we'd look with the casket hoisted on our shoulders with little Gene trying to walk four inches taller. It was a relief to see we were just to walk it down the aisle on the wheeled casket bearer. Strange how you worry about such things at a time like that.

At the cemetery, we were assigned a casket position. Then we had to lift and carry the casket to the graveside. Somehow, the exertion broke down my camouflaged composure and I cried right through the entire service. Even as the casket was being lowered and a few dropped a handful of dirt in the open grave, I remember a distinct emotional change. It was all over. If I'd ever thought something was going to happen to cause a change, such as Ann maybe waking up, the realization came suddenly that this was the end. Nothing more.

My third and most tragic experience with grief occurred on my thirtieth birthday. My wife had made Herbie Moeller's mother's chocolate cake. We always had that. She inherited the recipe from my mother when we were married. The original was part of a handmade recipe book made when I was in the first grade. Each of us brought our favorite food recipe from home and it was assembled in a little book. Mine had a purple, finger-painted cover with a yellow mushroom. It was sewn with green yarn across the top. Mom treasured it. Because each recipe was that of the student's mother, they were identified as "Wendell Blanton's mother's cupcakes" or "Herbie Moeller's mother's chocolate cake."

Once, when I was 27, we decided to call Herbie Moeller's mother to let her know how her cake had become a tradition at our house. She still lived just a few blocks from school. When I identified myself, she remembered our family and me.

What was particularly significant this year was that we weren't celebrating my thirtieth birthday together. My father had had a heart attack and was in the hospital.

Since it was just a 20-minute drive from home, Mary and I decided to take a large slice of cake for each of us and visit Dad. Mom had been there all day and had just returned home. We took an extra slice to drop by for her when we came back from the hospital. We parked at the hospital, caught the elevator to the eighth floor and, holding the chocolate cake slices, walked to room 807, Dad's.

When we entered, we saw him lying on his bed with his false teeth protruding from his mouth. He wasn't sleeping. He didn't seem to be breathing. I caught a nurse who paged for the respirator and a physician and then began respiration. Before they arrived though, it was clear Dad would not have even one more piece of Herbie Moeller's mother's chocolate cake.

In a few minutes, the doctor nodded and we just wept.

It was an agonizing drive to Mom's. When we got there, she was at the door to greet us. Before we got out of the car, her smile faded and she said, "What's wrong?" My answer was a choked, "Dad has gone to heaven."

After a few minutes of family crying and recalling precious moments that would be no more, we called the pastor, who said he wanted to come over, and Larry White, the funeral director and friend. When Larry answered, all I could think of was his generous loan of chairs when we had a high school party at home and his kind manner whenever we met at church suppers and picnics. Larry said he would send for Dad at the hospital and arranged for us to come to the funeral home in the morning.

The pastor arrived in a few minutes. He had called on Dad several times at the hospital. He sensed a need to help us organize our thinking and made several suggestions. He said that Larry would take care of Dad and be helpful as we made arrangements. He was eager to get us involved in our need to plan. After a prayer, he asked some questions to help him make some suggestions for the funeral. Dad's old favorite songs were selected. "Rock of Ages" had been meaningful to him. His mother had died when he was 14 and he had gone to work in a packing house splitting hogs when he was 15. He finished the eighth grade by a home correspondence course. As a service theme, I suggested Revelations 2:10, "Be thou faithful unto death and I will give thee a crown of life." It was my confirmation verse and truly described Dad, always faithful to his Redeemer. What a wonderful inheritance of faith he left all of us.

The next day, we met at the funeral home. Larry White was in charge, and we appreciated that. He was quiet in manner. In a few minutes, we had given him information for the newspaper notices and other details. Then it was his turn. He wanted us to talk about Dad, how we felt and what we hoped for in the funeral so that some of the older people, like 85-year-old Aunt Carrie, would not be inconvenienced. He asked if we would move to the church for services. While Lutherans always try to, it was almost 90 degrees and the humidity meant we had to seek an air-conditioned facility. The church had the ducts in, but we hadn't found the $12,000 needed to finish the job, so we decided to have the pastor conduct the service from Larry's chapel.

We had two evenings of visitation. How could a simple, fragile man have so many friends? It became apparent as those he had supervised came by to say he was the fairest man they had ever worked for. We knew him, but it was encouraging to see others who sensed his qualities, too. A black man who appeared to be in his 60's stopped. All he said was he had wrestled with Dad at noontimes when they had split hogs together, over 40 years ago. "Your Dad was the best," he said. Nothing more was needed.

There were dozens more who came with some precious nugget of their experiences with Dad to share with Mom and our family. She was proud. Everyone really knew how wonderful a guy he was. It was a marvelous comfort to know our deep loss was shared. Somehow it helped.

The funeral service, too, was well attended. The pastor had prepared his sermon specifically for us. Dad's faithfulness was blended into the Revelations 2:10 passage, so there was no doubt that he had graduated to a heavenly home. Quietly, peacefully, the pastor helped us accept and spiritually rejoice.

A procession of many cars accompanied us to the cemetery. Just knowing friends would drive another eight miles to share their support with us was comforting.

As we came to the grave, I remembered the finality of Ann Watson's burial and now knew what to expect. It was simple and dignified, a quiet interment of a man, great . . . to his family.

Today, while my birthday is never quite as joyous an occasion, our family still enjoys Herbie Moeller's mother's chocolate cake and someone always says, "Wouldn't Dad have loved to have met all of his five grandchildren?"

Death and the Young Woman

Frances I. Delany

Give me your hand, my fair and tender child,
As a friend I come and not as a foe.
Be of good cheer! I bring you rest;
Hasten to sleep softly within my arms.

My background and culture allow me to view death as cessation of the body experience and liberation of the spirit into a community of spirits united in goodness and faith after a stay on the earth. This belief softens the stress of death. But death represents a crisis which is not only more easily handled with professional help, but often requires professional help to heal the hurt. The death of a colleague whose understanding of children with developmental difficulties was sensitive and skillful has given me much to reflect over. It is this experience, which took place over a period of two years, that I wish to share. My association with the tragic circumstances and the ways in which they were handled has made me question just who the caregiver should be.

An attractive young woman had applied to my institution for a position and was interviewed by me. After teaching school for several years, she had entered a master's program and earned her license as a school psychologist. Her internship was largely spent evaluating habilitation potentials of young, institutionalized, handicapped children. Her credentials, background, and reports seemed topnotch and she was hired in mid-August to start working in September. A health plan, a benefit of employment at our institution, required a physical examination. The laboratory blood count report revealed certain abnormalities and the attending physician asked her to return for further tests. A young internist urged her to enter a hospital so that more detailed tests could be performed and evaluated. All the medical personnel assured this now uneasy young woman that although her blood count was unusual, there was no cause for alarm. However, she was hospitalized for several weeks and missed the month of September at school and the first month of a graduate program in which she had enrolled. There was no informative communication from the medical staff, and this further aggravated her anxieties.

Although she was independent and self-sufficient, she wanted more data so that she could make plans for the immediate future. She was given medication and told to have blood counts done at regular (monthly) intervals. The internist, in addition to overseeing her medication, was to be responsible for her general health management. Over the Christmas recess she became ill and was hospitalized again at a prestigious medical center. She received excellent care; her illness was given a name, and she was informed that blood transfusions were required. Unfortunately, hepatitis developed as a result of a transfusion.

By February she was pronounced fit, and after a brief vacation returned to work looking well. Everyone showed concern about her health, but she laughed and said that she appreciated our thoughtfulness but that with proper medical supervision she would be all right. Her work with the children was superior. Everyone relaxed as her vigor returned. Our own physician was most supportive but informed her that she faced a very serious picture. She expressed confidence in her hospital internist but was most grateful for our doctor's frankness. In fact, she began to research her own diagnosis and found many gaps in the medical knowledge about her illness. With an optimistic air she decided to carry on as though her problems would be solved. Her professional progress continued and she seemed well.

In early December (her second year at the school) she told me that her waistline was expanding and that she could not wear some of her clothes. She had returned to her doctor who explained that fluid seemed to be accumulating in the abdominal area, a condition the hospital would deal with if further discomfort should occur. In the meanwhile, she should just carry on. Suddenly one weekend in March, she had to be hospitalized for a transfusion. This helped her for a few weeks, but then her vision became impaired. Again, she entered the hospital. After surgery, intense pain, both physical and psychological, followed. She reported to me, "I've been violated!" No definitive medical statement about her prognosis was revealed.

Her mother, who lived a thousand miles away, arrived in April and sat by her bedside day after day. She was completely immobilized and was of little help to her daughter. It was an eerie sight for a visitor who, after changing into sterile gown and gloves, entered the patient's room and saw the mother withdrawn and silent and the daughter suffering but fighting with courage and common sense.

My colleague would tell me what all the doctors said, individually and collectively; then with textbook precision she would discuss her own symptoms and feelings and beliefs. We discussed our own reactions to what was happening. Dying and death were not seen as imminent by this brilliant, warm person.

A temporary improvement in May was followed by a relapse with fever. After many telephone talks, I visited with her and for the first time found her conversation dispirited and discouraging. I poured each of us a small sherry; we toasted her good sense. While I was there, her doctor arrived to inform her that although he had promised she could return home, it was not possible. Tears rolled down her cheeks. She remonstrated that she could not pay the bills or replenish the blood bank; she became angry and indignant. He became upset and said that as he had told her many times, there would be no financial pressure on her and she would continue to receive good care. Not one of us sitting there was satisfied with this response. It was incomplete. The tension of both doctor and patient led me to believe that both had relinquished hope that normal living conditions would be reestablished, but that as yet neither was speaking openly of finality or death. The doctor left and both the mother and I advised her to remember his kindness. She looked at us as if we had abandoned her. I grabbed her hand and said, "Let's say some four letter words!" She said several as if delivering bullets to those who had hurt her. Finally, her humor returned and she began giggling. She turned to me and said, "I'll never get well in this damn place. I have to sleep. Then I can consider what has happened to me."

Both she and her mother had decided that the hospital food was delaying her recovery, and this aspect was used projectively. There was no mention of all the signs of physical debilitation caused by severe illness. However, she told me that one beautiful day in June the nurses had put her in a wheelchair, taken her outside to see children playing in a park, and bought her a popsicle. She said, "I really broke down and bawled like a baby. It was so wonderful to be out!" So I understood the idea of getting out of a hospital room meant freedom to her. I also recognized that although her doctor was very concerned about her illness, his concern was now met with resentment. Her mother then surprisingly took a stand with her daughter against the authority figures and said that somehow they would go home. Interesting, too, the mother had arrived in the spring wearing mostly warm clothing. She never changed into lighter clothing but continued through the heat of a New York summer in wool suits. The mother talked about "Daddy's wanting to see his little girl," their daughter. I discussed with her the loneliness of this man, so isolated from his wife and daughter. The mother believed he understood and added that there were relatives with whom he regularly conferred. In a very touching way, she talked about the flowers and vegetables he planted and how the plants were being readied for the daughter's return.

My friend then told me that several health insurance checks had failed to arrive and could I help her secure what was due. I promised immediate help and said that I would continue calling and be available. This was mid-July. I called in 2 or 3 days at her apartment. Her mother informed me that the daughter had been discharged from the hospital, felt wonderful, and wanted to talk to me. However, at the moment she was at the hospital as an outpatient undergoing treatment for a lump in her throat. After two more treatments, Daddy was taking them home (an airplane trip of over 1,000 miles). I was speechless! Mother sounded euphoric.

In the days that followed, I tried several times to telephone my friend but received no answer. Finally, the operator informed me that the service was disconnected. A substantial check covering May, June, and July arrived at the school, and I sent it to the mother's address, which I obtained from the hospital. Receiving no response, I sent a letter containing multiple choice items:

I am better
I am worse
I am returning
I received the check

along with best wishes in a self-addressed envelope. Near the end of September, the envelope came back. Inside was my letter marked, "I received the check," and as I looked at it, a card fell out of the envelope announcing that my friend had died in mid-August.

I was shocked and saddened. Would I, could I have done more? Had she suffered less or more as a result of the lack of frankness in her physician's skilled professional manner? She was a direct, intelligent, sensitive human being. She believed her person had been violated. Yet she maintained "guts" and finally with a supreme effort, signed herself out of the hospital and went home to sleep.

Her mother was almost depersonalized in the process. In fact, not until the end of December did she acknowledge our remembrance to her daughter. Again I wrote. The last message came six months later from another state further west advising that she and Daddy still cannot believe that their daughter is gone and cannot understand why she had to die. In fact, they had been unable to continue living in the house which they had shared together for so many years.

Did my friend know? I think not. Yet our knowledgeable, helpful neurologist felt sure that she knew. He said her courage is a tribute to the human race and only an indefatigable spirit like hers could have managed to sign herself out of the hospital and go home in peace to rest her torn, weary body.

Some considerations occur to me; principally, that most hospitals are less prepared than most individuals anticipate in dealing with the business and feelings surrounding death. The practical obligations surrounding death or even temporary removal from the mainstream of daily routines ought to be outlined for any adult wage-earner who is hospitalized. Hospital administrators and personnel might jointly prepare a small checklist containing monthly budgetary items for the patient with a friend or some professional knowledgeable about the hospitalized person's responsibilities. Social workers often assume this responsibility for those obviously isolated or on welfare, but there is a much larger population which is not served. Pain often causes indifference to other pressures; this may be a therapeutic aid for the hospitalized one, but subsequent financial pressures often harm those closest to the hospitalized person. These generally are the family members who must seek emotional support in their period of acute grief and often, thereafter.

Keeping sick persons somewhat involved in daily routines relevant to outside hospital affairs would be a more appropriate recognition of the individual's maturity and sense of responsibility. A checklist can serve many purposes: all those concerned about the hospitalized one's condition have at least some common reference point.

When there is general or majority opinion that the patient, whether or not he survives, must face a curtailed or unsure life-style, someone must bear the burden of informing the patient. Already, I can hear rumblings. We do not understand why some survive and some do not, and we do not want to alarm needlessly. This is a normal human response, but it is not a useful response. Life-styles are not enhanced or enriched by professionals' withholding information; much more to the point is how information is communicated. It is mutually beneficial to keep the lines of communication open. A hearty bombastic optimism deceives only a few. We are not wise enough to predict with assurance, but trends and knowledge strongly indicate directions. Why should hospitalized persons be treated as if their physical ills had robbed them of reason? Trust is built with truth and valid experiences, not with general remarks, however optimistic, which cause increasing disbelief in oneself as well as in others. Not all medical personnel can handle communicating unfavorable information; perhaps this aspect of patient care requires specialized training with those whose skill in this area appears extraordinary. Certainly, there is considerable room for improved communication between medical personnel and hospitalized patients. Patients, however ill, remain individuals and respond to warmth and commonsense treatment. They are not easily deceived, but an almost imperceptible intuition about withheld facts seems to increase dependency and regression. Individuals handle these feelings in different ways, but the management of the feelings benefits neither hospital personnel nor patient.

My plea is for a compassionate, realistic procedure which routinely and regularly reaches hospitalized persons. Pressured promises and professional perfection are not available in any walk of life, and this reality should be emphasized in dealing with persons suddenly and almost completely dependent on what the doctors say.

My friend received superb medical treatment. Her doctors cared and maintained interest in her case. Somehow, she became a patient, a case, and lost something of herself as a person. Friends tried to help but found her situation a sticky and unwelcome involvement. Procedures can be improved if enough of us care. My hope is that through thanatology improvement will occur.

Death, an inevitable interface of being, can be handled with majesty and dignity, not only as a ritual but as an experience which strengthens with sharing. These qualities can be cultivated through experience when death comes to a friend, a relative, a neighbor. Each of us, in his own particular way, can serve as a model for others and as a comfort and source of compassion when a finality occurs.

OVERVIEW

The Sociology of the Mortuary: Attitudes to the Funeral, Funeral Director, and Funeral Arrangements
Baheej Khleif

Although there have been several outspoken critics of the funeral and funeral director in recent years, there has been very little empirical research investigating how the bereaved define the situation. Moreover, prior to this, no sociological study had been done investigating the behavior of the bereaved inside the mortuary in the process of making funeral arrangements. The purpose of this paper is to report the findings of a study on attitudes of bereaved persons to funerals, funeral directors, and funeral arrangements. This paper focuses on what importance the bereaved give to the funeral during bereavement and on how the bereaved define the role of the funeral director in making funeral arrangements. Findings are presented on how the bereaved feel about many specific items in the funeral arrangements, including casket selection, funeral cost, and restoration work. This material is part of a larger survey which also analyzes differences in attitudes to funerals related to age, sex, family position (parent, spouse, sibling, and so on), income, education, and religious groups. (Ph.D. thesis, University of Colorado, Boulder, 1971).

It is important to emphasize from the start that the findings of this study strongly contradict critics of the funeral and funeral director—such as Mitford, Bowman, Harmar, and others. The bereaved surveyed in this research generally held the funeral and funeral director in very high esteem. Most were satisfied with the cost of the funeral and reacted favorably to the restoration work. These results were somewhat surprising to me. At the beginning of the project I held very critical opinions on several aspects of the funeral and services offered by

219

the funeral director. I rather suspected that the data would reveal many dissatis-factions among the bereaved—especially with regard to cost, restoration, and the role of the funeral director in planning the funeral. This simply was not the case. Quite the contrary, the bereaved were extremely supportive of both funerals and funeral directors. These are the results reported here.

COLLECTION OF DATA

The data for this study were collected by questionnaire mailed to bereaved persons in La Crosse, Wisconsin, in December 1970. A saturation sample was taken of all the obituaries which appeared in the La Crosse Tribune in 1969. The year 1969 was chosen because it was distant enough to allow for detailed inquiry but recent enough to enable clear recollection of the funeral process. The questionnaire was mailed to the next of kin listed in each obituary notice. Addresses were given in the notices. When a choice had to be made among next of kin (e.g., when a brother and sister were equally close relatives), the draw alter-nated by sex. A follow-up card was sent to each respondent ten days after the questionnaire was sent. The final sample totaled 189 respondents. The complete questionnaire for the survey, including the questions for data reported in this paper, is given in Appendix A.

Prior to mailing the questionnaire, a good deal of preliminary work was done to investigate how willing bereaved persons would be to talk in detail about the funeral and funeral arrangements. Moreover, it had to be determined how this type of data could be collected effectively. These preliminary steps were taken:

(1) Funeral directors in the La Crosse area were interviewed about funeral arrangements with the bereaved. At first these interviews were conducted at a meeting with the funeral director in the funeral home. This, however, proved un-satisfactory; it appeared that the funeral directors were somewhat confined by their professional role in giving the needed information. After that, steps were taken to meet the funeral directors outside their professional setting. I joined a local service organization to which several funeral directors belonged. This enabled me to meet funeral directors informally and socially—and to arrange for inter-views which yielded more information.

(2) Interviews were conducted with bereaved persons in which I received clear indications that they would be very willing to talk explicitly about the death and the funeral arrangements.

(3) Interviews were held with florists who provide flowers for funerals in the area.

(4) The owner of a local firm for grave markers was interviewed.

(5) A pathologist and several doctors and nurses at the major hospital in La Crosse were interviewed concerning attitudes of the bereaved.

(6) A pilot project was conducted which pretested many of the questions and demonstrated that bereaved would be willing to complete a mail questionnaire asking very direct and specific questions on the topic. Also, this pilot project indicated that the funeral director was highly regarded by the bereaved. Since the final questionnaire contained a long section on the professional performance of the funeral director, I decided to inform the funeral directors about these preliminary results. Local funeral directors were mailed a letter telling them about the pilot project and the favorable response of the bereaved to the services they provide. I thought this would minimize the possibility of any interference or negative reaction to the study on the part of the funeral directors.

(7) During the week just preceding the mailing of the final questionnaire, news releases were dispatched to the local radio stations and newspaper announcing that a study of attitudes to the funeral was being conducted in the La Crosse area. The study was fortunate to be given very good coverage by the local news media. This was centered on preparing the public for receipt of the questionnaire on this "taboo" topic.

SAMPLE DESCRIPTION

All respondents were next of kin to someone who had died in 1969. Sixty-three percent of the bereaved persons in the sample were women, and 37 percent were men. Their ages ranged from 20 years old to over 80 years old: 10 percent of the bereaved were 20 to 39 years old; 48 percent were 40 to 59 years old; 38 percent were 60 to 79 years old; and 4 percent were 80 or above. Most bereaved in this sample were between the ages of 40 and 79.

The education of the bereaved, according to the highest level completed, was as follows: 22 percent grade school; 11 percent junior high school; 41 percent high school; 15 percent some college; 7 percent college graduate; and 4 percent graduate degree.

Most of the respondents were living on an approximate annual income of under $10,000: 34 percent on less than $4,000; 16 percent on $4,000 to $5,999; 25 percent on $6,000 to $9,999; 10 percent on $10,000 to $14,999; 6 percent on $15,000 and over; 8 percent just answered "retired" without giving an amount; and one percent gave no response to this survey question.

Occupations of the bereaved (at the time the questionnaire was completed) were the following: 31 percent housewife; 20 percent retired; 2 percent elementary or high school teacher; 12 percent white collar, clerical, or sales; 6 percent technician, craftsman, or the trades; 5 percent business manager or executive; 10 percent laborer or factory worker; and 10 percent other (including unemployed).

The religious background of the bereaved was 40 percent Catholic, 32 percent Lutheran, and 26 percent other Protestant—including Methodist, Presbyterian, Congregational, and unspecified Protestant—and 2 percent answered None or gave no response on this question. Most of the bereaved were either widowed, 51 percent, or married, 42 percent. Only 4 percent were single; 2 percent were divorced; and one percent gave no response.

The age, sex, and family position of the deceased relatives on whose death the bereaved respondents reported were as follows: 67 percent of the deceased were 60 years old or above; 25 percent of the deceased were 30 to 59 years old; and only 8 percent were younger than 30 years old. Fifty-eight percent of the deceased were men; 42 percent were women.

A check on kin-relationships showed that in 38 percent of the cases the deceased was the husband of the respondent; 13 percent, wife; 28 percent, parent (father or mother); 6 percent, child of the respondent; 9 percent, sibling (brother or sister); and 6 percent, other. The great majority of respondents, 79 percent, had lost either a spouse or a parent.

FINDINGS

Attitudes to the Funeral. There has been much debate over whether the funeral is a valuable event. Briefly stated, some central issues in the controversy have been these: On the one hand, many criticisms have been directed against the funeral. In 1926, Puckle attempted to demonstrate in his "Funeral Customs" that the funeral is an outdated social and religious activity. Puckle argued that the funeral is primitive and superstitious. He wrote, "When we have stripped any one of our funeral observances of its crapes and tinsel—those grave clothes of convention in which they have been preserved and embalmed—we shall find very little that is worthy of continuance" (1). This position has had a number of advocates. For instance, in "The American Funeral," Bowman contended that the funeral is largely irrelevant to the needs of the bereaved. One reason for this irrelevance, according to Bowman, is that the urbanization process had eroded the supportive function of the funeral—the geographic mobility which has accompanied urbanization has diminished the value of the funeral as a territorial ritual (2). In "The American Way of Death," Mitford criticized both the funeral industry and the funeral itself. She also suggested that the funeral is no longer worthwhile (3). In "The High Cost of Dying," Harmer criticized the American funeral, arguing that it generates a feeling of unreality which intensifies the shock rather than alleviates the pain of mourners (4). On the other hand, many social scientists have argued that the funeral is extremely important—both for the mourners and for society at large. For example, Van Gennep considered the funeral and mourning period to be an important rite of passage. In 1906, he observed that the funeral is "a transitional period for the survivors and they enter it through rites of separation and emerge from it through rites of reintegration" (5). Warner expressed a view similar to Van Gennep when he wrote, "The

Funeral as a *rite de passage* . . . symbolically translates the body from the world of the living to that of the dead and helps to reestablish the relations of living members of the group to each other and to the memory of the dead (6). Fulton also stressed this point, emphasizing that as such the funeral "not only marks the completion of a life but also reaffirms the social character of human existence" (7).

Becker and Bruner contended that the funeral is an important ritual of social control—whereby society enforces the behavior it considers to be appropriate (8). Durkheim, in 1926, argued that mourning behavior serves to enforce the solidarity of the group (9). Parsons argued, "In the case of bereavement, there may be a loss of incentive to keep on going. Ritual on such occasions serves to organize the reaction system in a positive manner and to put a check on disruptive tendencies." Moreover, rituals assert "the importance of the survivors going on living in terms of the value system, redefining the solidarity with the deceased in these terms: 'It is what he would have wished' " (10). Mandelbaum suggested that the funeral has a coping function for the survivors (11). In their work "Funeral Customs the World Over," Habenstein and Lamers argued that "funeral ceremonies satisfy basic needs, allay suffering, and help to rescue death from the horror of meaninglessness" (12).

The bereaved respondents in this study were asked a series of questions to investigate what they think about the worth of the funeral. For instance, they were asked how important they believe the funeral is for the survivors. The results are given below in Table 1:*

Table 1. How Important Do You Believe Funerals Are for the Surviving?

Extremely important	41%
Somewhat important	34
Undecided	12
Not very important	7
Not important at all	3
No answer	3
Total	100%

The great majority, 75 percent, felt that the funeral was "extremely" or "somewhat" important for the survivors. In another question, bereaved persons specified whether they considered the funeral to be more for the living or for the deceased: 39 percent answered "more for the living"; 51 percent "more for the deceased"; 8 percent said "both"; and 2 percent gave no response or "other." Still another aspect of the problem was to explore how people feel about the funeral in terms of an expression of care for their dead. People in the study were asked, "Do you feel that the funeral was a meaningful way to express love for

*Results throughout this chapter are presented as percentage distributions based on a sample size of 189 respondents.

the deceased?" Nearly 60 percent answered "very much." The complete results are given below in Table 2:

Table 2. Whether the Funeral Was a Meaningful Way to Express Love for the Deceased?

Very much	59%
Somewhat	30
Not at all	9
No response or other	2
Total	100%

Here it is interesting to note that bereaved persons who found death very difficult to cope with valued the funeral most highly. Most of the bereaved felt it was "very difficult" (38 percent) or "somewhat difficult" (43 percent) to "cope with this death in the family."* Eighteen percent felt it was "not difficult at all"; and one percent gave no response or "other." It was within the category "very difficult to cope" that the greatest proportion of the bereaved believed the funeral was "very much" a meaningful expression of love for the deceased. See Table 3:

Table 3. "Funeral Was an Expression of Love for the Deceased" vs. "How Able the Respondent Was to Cope with This Death in the Family"

	Funeral was a meaningful expression of love for the deceased			
Ability to cope with the death	Not at all	Somewhat	Very much	Totals
Very difficult	4%	19%	77%	100%
Somewhat difficult	6	41	53	100
Not difficult	26	23	52	100

Two themes are quite striking in these data. First, there was a strong feeling among the bereaved that the funeral is indeed a very important experience for the living. Second, most people do value the funeral as one way to show their love for the dead and consider the funeral to be a meaningful expression of that concern. The more difficult death is to cope with, the more meaningful the funeral is considered.

Arrangements Inside the Funeral Home. The bereaved were asked the following three questions to determine the setting where the funeral arrangements took place (Tables 4 to 6):

Table 4. Did You *Go to the Funeral Home* to Make Plans for the Funeral?

Yes	84%
No	13
No response or other	3
Total	100%

*Throughout this chapter, quotations such as these indicate the specific wording of questionnaire items.

Table 5. Did You Make Most of the *Arrangements* for the Funeral During the *Meeting with the Funeral Director* in the Funeral Home?

Yes	83%
No	15
No response or other	2
Total	100%

Table 6. Did You Go to the Funeral Home to *Select a Casket?*

Yes	86%
No	12
No response or other	2
Total	100%

According to these data, the transaction of making funeral arrangements took place in the great majority of cases (over 80 percent) inside the funeral home. The bereaved planned the funeral and selected a casket during a meeting with the funeral director inside the mortuary.

In most cases, 78 percent, the deceased had not left instructions on burial details for the bereaved. Only 17 percent had left written instructions or told someone his or her wishes.

In "The American Funeral," Bowman contended that the pressure of limited time when arranging for the funeral puts the bereaved family at a bargaining disadvantage with the funeral director (13). The bereaved in my study were asked if they felt the pressure of limited time while they were selecting the casket and vault. Table 7 shows the results:

Table 7. When You Were Selecting the Casket and Vault, Did You Feel the Pressure of Limited Time in Your Decision?

Yes	11%
No	74
I did not select the casket	15
Total	100%

The findings in Table 7 do *not* support Bowman's contention. They indicate that the great majority, 74 percent, did not feel the pressure of limited time when selecting a casket. Moreover, most of the bereaved (over 70 percent) answered in response to two further questions that they did not feel foreign or strange in the mortuary setting.

The bereaved were asked very directly what they took into consideration or what influenced them in the selection of the casket. The results are charted below; each item in Table 8 was a separate question in the study and responded to by the total sample:

Table 8. In the Selection of the Casket, Did You Take into Consideration or Were You Influenced by the Following?

	Yes	No	I did not select the Casket or No Response	Totals, N=189 on each item
Style of casket	68%	16%	16%	100%
Color of casket	67	17	16	100
Cost of casket	62	24	16	100
Funeral director	12	70	18	100
Grief at the time	31	51	18	100

It was found that the majority of the bereaved (62 to 68 percent), were influenced by style, color, and cost when selecting the casket. However, most bereaved did not feel they were influenced by grief or by the funeral director. Seventy percent said that they were not influenced by the funeral director in their selection. This stands contrary to those critics of the funeral director who suggest that the bereaved are subject to strong influence or manipulation from the funeral director in choosing a casket (14). The bereaved in this sample did not define the situation that way. Furthermore, it is worth noting in this context that the bereaved did not claim to be as "upset" while planning the funeral as is often thought to be the case. When deciding the details of the funeral, 38 percent claimed they were "not upset at all"; 31 percent said "somewhat upset"; only 23 percent felt they were "very upset"; and 8 percent gave no response.

The bereaved did not go to the funeral home alone—87 percent of bereaved persons in this study went in groups of two or more to plan the funeral. Over half the bereaved were in a group of three or more persons. The size of the group that went to the funeral home to make the funeral arrangements is charted below:

Table 9. How Many Went to the Funeral Home to Make the Funeral Arrangements?

Alone	6%
With one other person	31
With two other persons	30
With three others	15
With four others or more	11
No answer	7
Total	100%

Another question was posed asking who the people were that went with the respondent to the funeral home. See Table 10 below:

Table 10. Who Were the People Who Accompanied You to the Funeral Home to Make Funeral Arrangements?

Friend(s)	3%
Relative(s)	79
Friend(s) and relative(s)	1
No response or not appropriate (went alone, did not go personally to funeral home or other)	17
Total	100%

Seventy-nine percent of the bereaved said that they were accompanied by relatives to make funeral arrangements; only 3 percent of the sample were accompanied by friends; and only one percent by both friends and relatives.

An attempt was made to determine whether those who accompanied the respondent to the mortuary influenced decisions on funeral arrangements. The findings were as follows (Table 11):

Table 11. Did the People Who Accompanied You to the Funeral Home Help Make the Decisions Regarding Funeral Arrangements?

Yes	70%
No	17
No answer or not appropriate	13
Total	100%

Seventy percent of the total sample answered, "Yes, those who accompanied did help to make decisions."

It was found in this study, then, that most bereaved were accompanied to the funeral home by relatives and, furthermore, that these relatives participate in planning the funeral. It was predominantly relatives — rather than friends — who assisted the bereaved.

THE FUNERAL HOME AND ROLE OF THE FUNERAL DIRECTOR

Habenstein is one outspoken proponent of the idea that the funeral director plays an important role in contemporary American society. He emphasized that the strategic location of the funeral director in the mourning process makes him invaluable "as an active agent for the fostering of a normal process of grief." Habenstein maintained that "in a society notable for a lack of integrated 'death-ways,' . . . he [the funeral director] must stage, direct, and participate in a performance having both social and personal significance. . . . He has assumed the major role in defining situations in such a way that people can act toward the phenomenon of death." Moreover, Habenstein maintained that the funeral director is in relatively constant contact with the bereaved during the week of the funeral and that his contacts with them are often more frequent than those of the minister (15).

Fulton and Geis argued that the funeral director is caught between contradictory societal demands: "On the one hand, he is encouraged to disguise the reality of death for the survivors who do not possess the emotional support once provided by theology to deal with it; on the other hand, he is impelled to call attention to the special services he is rendering. Thus he both blunts and sharpens the reality of death" (16). In this context, Habenstein and Lamers have observed that the funeral directors in the United States have been seeking professional recognition — seeking to minimize the commercial aspects of their vocation and to emphasize the social service they provide (17).

This study inquired into how the bereaved selected a funeral home and the type of services received from the funeral director, including both comforting and making funeral arrangements. It was found that less than half the sample had any prior experience in arranging for a funeral. Most, however, had at least been inside a funeral home for visitation at some time (Table 12):

Table 12. Prior to the Loss of the Deceased, Had You Visited a Funeral Home?

I had never been inside a funeral home	2%
I had only visited a funeral home during visitation hours	46
I had visited a funeral home to arrange for other funerals	47
Other or no response	5
Total	100%

The bereaved were asked how they chose a funeral home, the results were as follows (Table 13):

Table 13. How Did You Select a Funeral Home?

The funeral home contacted me	1%
Clergyman's recommendation	1
Hospital's recommendation	1
Coroner's recommendation	1
Physician's recommendation	1
Religious affiliation of the funeral home	3
Knew the funeral director	51
The deceased had specified a preference for a funeral home	17
Other (including respondent did not personally make the selection)	24
Total	100%

Sixty-eight percent of the bereaved indicated that they selected the funeral home either because they knew the funeral director or because their relative who died had chosen that funeral home. It is of significance that bereaved persons in this sample were not contacted by funeral homes or referred to particular funeral homes by hospitals, doctors, clergy, or coroners (only 1 percent each). Fifty-one percent said specifically that they chose the funeral home because they knew the funeral director.

The bereaved were asked where they had met the funeral director. The findings were the following (Table 14):

Table 14. Where Did You or Your Family Get Acquainted with the Funeral Director?

Church activities	6%
Civic organizations	5
Friend of the family	29
Past funerals	48
No answer or other	12
Total	100%

Many (48 percent) of the respondents met the funeral director at past funerals. Another 29 percent answered that they had met the funeral director as a "friend of the family." In answer to a further question, most of the respondents (80 percent) indicated that they knew the funeral director personally — either as a "casual acquaintance" or "friend" (Table 15):

Table 15. How Well Did You Know the Funeral Director Before the Death?

Not at all	14%
Casual acquaintance	44
Friend of mine or of the family	36
No answer or other	6
Total	100%

It has been suggested that due to lack of preparation for dealing with death, the bereaved may abandon several roles which the funeral director must assume (18). This study attempted to investigate role abandonment by bereaved persons in the funeral transaction. The bereaved were initially asked a general question probing the extent to which they had been willing to pass responsibility for the funeral plans to the funeral director. The results are given in Table 16:

Table 16. How Did the Funeral Director Assist You in Making Funeral Arrangements?

I asked him to take over all possible arrangements	41%
I asked him to take over several arrangements	30
I asked him to take over very few arrangements	21
No answer or other	8
Total	100%

The data show that 41 percent of the bereaved in this sample asked the funeral director to take over "all possible arrangements." Another 30 percent asked him to take over "several arrangements." This certainly indicates a reliance on and confidence in the funeral director. With respect to certain specific arrangements, we determined whether they were handled by the funeral director. Results are given in Table 17 (each item was responded to by the total sample):

Table 17. Did the Funeral Director Perform Any of the Following Services for You?

	Yes	No	Other or no answer	Total sample
Order flowers?	67%	28%	5%	100%
Contact pallbearers?	22	68	10	100
Send thank-you cards?	11	78	11	100
Notify any friends?	5	84	11	100
Notify any relatives?	4	86	10	100
Select a grave marker?	2	91	7	100

One service which is frequently taken care of by the funeral director is the ordering of flowers (67 percent). One florist (who does a large business in the area) maintained that the big problem he faces is that some bereaved "don't know what they want or what is the right encasement" when they come in to order flowers for the funeral. He also said that sometimes the family "is so stunned by the death and so busy that they forget all about the flower pieces." The data in this study indicate that the bereaved rely heavily on the funeral director for his professional knowledge of what is needed and what is proper.

In some cases the funeral director contacted pallbearers (22 percent) or sent thank-you cards for the bereaved (11 percent). Very rarely, however, did the bereaved in this sample rely on the funeral director to help in notifying friends or family about the death (only 4 to 5 percent). In only 2 percent of the cases did the funeral director select the grave marker. One reason for this was suggested by a major monument dealer in the area. He said that the monument firm contacts the bereaved personally five to six days after the obituary is listed in the paper — rather than work through the funeral director. Moreover, he pointed out that the marker is often not even selected until five to six weeks after the death.

Respondents were also asked where the funeral was held. The findings were these (Table 18):

Table 18. Where Was the Funeral Service Held?

Funeral home	34%
Church	28
Both funeral home and church	35
Home	0
Other	3
Total	100%

A sizable proportion (34 percent) of the funerals were held in the funeral home instead of in the church. Sixty-nine percent of the respondents in the study reported that the funeral service was held exclusively in the funeral home or in both the funeral home and the church.

This study also inquired into the role which funeral directors perform in comforting the bereaved. For instance, bereaved persons were asked the following question (Table 19):

Table 19. Did the Funeral Director Succeed in Comforting You During the Funeral Week?

Yes	63%
No	31
No answer	6
Total	100%

Sixty-three percent of the bereaved felt that the funeral director succeeded in comforting them during the funeral week. This supports, to some degree, the position of those who suggest that the funeral director fulfills an important function as a "grief therapist" in contemporary American society (19). It is important to stress in this context that when bereaved were asked "Did the funeral director seem like a member of the family during the funeral week?" 54 percent answered "Yes"; only 38 percent said "No," and 8 percent gave some other response or no answer. Traditionally, the comforting role has been assigned to the clergy or to relatives. These data suggest·that the funeral director is sharing roles that were formerly within the domain of the family.

In order to further verify the way in which the bereaved defined the comforting role of the funeral director, they were asked whether he continued to offer his help after the funeral (Table 20):

Table 20. Following the Week of the Funeral, Did the Funeral Director Continue to Offer His Help and Sympathy?

Very much	38%
Somewhat	28
Not at all	31
Other or no response	3
Total	100%

Most bereaved (66 percent) indicated that the funeral director continued to be "very much" or "somewhat" of a help — even after the funeral week was over. Furthermore, in answer to another question a sizable minority (33 percent) expressed the belief that the funeral director "helped very much" in "making them aware of their new status as a widow, widower, or member of the bereaved family"; 34 percent felt the funeral director had "helped somewhat" in that process; 33 percent maintained he "did not help at all" in making them aware of their new position; and 7 percent gave no response or some other.

Two additional questions were included in the survey to investigate the general image which the bereaved held of the funeral director. In one question, bereaved persons were asked to indicate how the funeral director impressed them in terms of his interest in the people he serves (Table 21):

Table 21. How Did the Funeral Director Impress You?

He does not seem at all interested in the people he serves	2%
He is somewhat interested in the people he serves	14
He seems very interested in the people he serves	80
No answer	4
Total	100%

The great majority (80 percent) felt that the funeral director seems "very interested in the people he serves." In response to the other question, 61 percent of the bereaved replied that the funeral director went "very much" out of his way to help them in their time of grief. The results are charted below (Table 22):

Table 22. Did It Seem That the Funeral Director Went out of His Way to Help You in Your Time of Grief?

Not at all	8%
Somewhat	25
Very much	61
No answer	6
Total	100%

These data suggest that the funeral director is, indeed, succeeding in minimizing the commercial part of the transaction and emphasizing the service aspects of his role. The funeral director appears, according to these data, as a comforter who goes out of his way to help the people he serves. The bereaved tend to define him in a very favorable manner. Moreover, the funeral director seemed to be known by the bereaved as an acquaintance or friend of the family. There is an indication that the funeral director is sharing the clergy and family's traditional roles of making funeral arrangements and comforting the bereaved in time of grief.

FUNERAL COST AND RESTORATION

There has been much criticism leveled at funerals regarding the presumed unexpected high cost and subsequent dissatisfaction with the expense by the bereaved. This study investigated whether the bereaved were dissatisfied with the cost of the funeral. A series of three questions probed whether the funeral cost more than expected, whether they would have preferred a less expensive funeral, and whether the casket was more than they could really afford. The results are given in Tables 23, 24, and 25 below:

Table 23. How Much Did the Funeral Actually Cost?

Less than expected	12%
The same as expected	55
More than expected	22
Don't know	7
No answer or other	4
Total	100%

Table 24. When You Think It over, How Much Would You Have Liked to Have Spent on the Funeral?

Less than was spent	22%
The same amount	68
More than was spent	3
No answer or other	7
Total	100%

234   Baheej Khlief

Table 25. Concerning the Cost of the Casket You Selected, Was It:

More than you could really afford	12%
Just what you could afford	70
Less than you could afford	10
No answer or other	8
Total	100%

The findings of this study were that 67 percent of the bereaved paid "the same as expected" or even "less than expected" for the funeral (Table 23). Furthermore, most of the bereaved were satisfied with the cost of the funeral — 68 percent said that the amount spent was the same amount they had wanted to spend (Table 24). It is interesting to recall at this point that the bereaved in this study were surveyed a full one to two years after the death — and still held that opinion. Contrary to the popular belief that the bereaved often buy a casket that is more expensive than they can afford, 70 percent of the respondents in this study felt that the casket was "just what they could afford." Another 10 percent even thought the casket was "less" than they could afford. Only 12 percent thought they had selected a casket that was more than they could really afford (Table 25). The main theme throughout these data is that the great majority of people in this study expressed no regrets about the cost of the funeral.

The survey also inquired into financial and pragmatic preparations for the death — such as means of payment for the funeral and prepurchase of a cemetery lot. The findings are listed below in Tables 26 and 27:

Table 26. By What Means Were Funeral Expenses Paid?

Savings account	39%
Loan	2
Special burial funds (burial insurance, public assistance, veteran's benefits, etc.)	25
Relatives shared cost	3
Both savings and special burial funds	14
Other or no response	7
Total	100%

Table 27. Prior to the Death in the Family, Did You Own a Cemetery Lot for the Deceased?

Yes	65%
No	34
Total	100%

The majority of bereaved persons had money set aside with which they paid funeral expenses: 49 percent paid funeral costs in whole or part by special burial funds and insurance; 40 percent relied on money in their savings; only 2 percent had to borrow money to pay for the burial. Sixty-five percent of all bereaved persons had a cemetery lot for the deceased prior to the death. Although the bereaved may not have been emotionally prepared to deal with death, they seem to have made the pragmatic preparations. This suggests a cultural paradox in American society — on the one hand, the culture manifests an attitude of death denial, and on the other hand, it manifests quite a bit of financial preparation for death.

Finally, bereaved persons in this study were asked about their reactions to restoration work. Some critics of the American funeral have contended that restoration work is a masking process — for example, that restoration makes the deceased look much younger than he or she actually was at the time of death. Bereaved persons in this sample, however, did not think that was true (Table 28):

Table 28. How Did You Find the Deceased in Regard to Restoration Work?

The deceased looked much younger	9%
The deceased looked somewhat younger	12
The deceased looked about the same as when alive	64
Other	12
No response	3
Total	100%

Most bereaved (64 percent) maintained that the deceased looked "about the same as when he or she was alive." Furthermore, most bereaved persons in this study reacted positively to the restoration work (Table 29):

Table 29. How Did You React to the Appearance of the Deceased Regarding Restoration Work?

I was pleased with the appearance	65%
I was not pleased with the appearance	7
Undecided	8
Other	8
No answer	12
Total	100%

Most bereaved (65 percent) indicated that they were "pleased with the appearance of the deceased regarding the restoration work."

Since the sample of bereaved respondents for this study was drawn exclusively from one midwestern community, generalizations from the study must be limited to the population studied. It should be stressed, however, that the sample seems rather typical of American society in general with respect to such demographic characteristics as age, sex, income, occupation, and religion of the bereaved and the deceased. Moreover, La Crosse, a town of about 50,000 located on the Mississippi near the Minnesota border, is similar to many others throughout this country, with its economy based on a combination of small business, a state college, light industry, and a surrounding farming community. Thus, on the basis of this study, it is interesting to suggest that many of the attitudes and trends in these data exist in American society at large.

APPENDIX A: QUESTIONNAIRE*

This questionnaire is a study about American attitudes toward death which is being conducted by the Sociology Department at Wisconsin State University — La Crosse. Please do not sign your name, so that we may be sure that all replies will be confidential. *In addition, please do not reveal the name of a funeral home, funeral director, clergyman, or other persons.*

Each of these questions or statements is followed by several choices. We would appreciate it if you would please check ONE answer most nearly expressing your way of thinking, your attitude, belief, or opinion.

Your name was selected at random from the obituary columns of the La Crosse Tribune as next of kin to one who died during 1969.

1. Your age: _____
   ___ 1. 20-39
   ___ 2. 40-59
   ___ 3. 60-79
   ___ 4. 80 and above
2. Your sex:
   ___ 1. Male
   ___ 2. Female
3. Your education:
   ___ 1. Grade school
   ___ 2. Junior high school
   ___ 3. High school graduate
   ___ 4. Some college
   ___ 5. College graduate
   ___ 6. Graduate degree
4. What is your religious background:
   ___ 1. Catholic
   ___ 2. Lutheran
   ___ 3. Methodist, Presbyterian, Congregational, other Protestant

5. Your marital status:
   ___ 1. Single
   ___ 2. Married
   ___ 3. Separated
   ___ 4. Divorced
   ___ 5. Widowed
6. Your approximate annual income:
   ___ 1. Less than $4,000
   ___ 2. $4,000 to $5,999
   ___ 3. $6,000 to $9,999
   ___ 4. $10,000 to $14,999
   ___ 5. $15,000 and over
7. Your present occupation:
   ___ 1. Elementary or high school teacher
   ___ 2. White collar, clerical, or sales
   ___ 3. Technician, craftsman, or the trades
   ___ 4. Business manager or executive
   ___ 5. Professional
   ___ 6. Laborer, factory worker

*This is the questionnaire for the complete study, including questions for the data reported in this chapter.

___ 7. Housewife
___ 8. Retired
___ 9. Other (including unemployed)
8. Occupation of the deceased relative:
    ___ 1. Elementary or high school teacher
    ___ 2. White collar, clerical, or sales
    ___ 3. Technician, craftsman, or the trades
    ___ 4. Business manager or executive
    ___ 5. Professional
    ___ 6. Laborer, factory worker
    ___ 7. Housewife
    ___ 8. Retired
    ___ 9. Other (including unemployed)
9. What relation to you was the deceased?
    ___ 1. Husband
    ___ 2. Wife
    ___ 3. Parent (father, mother)
    ___ 4. Child
    ___ 5. Sibling (brother, sister)
10. Age of the deceased? _____
    ___ 1. 1-29
    ___ 2. 30-59
    ___ 3. 60 and above
11. Sex of the deceased:
    ___ 1. Male
    ___ 2. Female
12. What were the circumstances surrounding the death?
    ___ 1. Sudden death – accident
    ___ 2. Illness – not exceeding 6 months
    ___ 3. Illness – over 6 months
13. How did you select a funeral home?
    ___ 1. The funeral home contacted me
    ___ 2. Clergyman's recommendation
    ___ 3. Hospital's recommendation
    ___ 4. Coroner's recommendation
    ___ 5. Physician's recommendation
    ___ 6. Religious affiliation of the funeral home
    ___ 7. Knew the funeral director
    ___ 8. The deceased had specified a preference for a funeral home
    ___ 9. Other
14. Where did the death take place?
    ___ 1. At home
    ___ 2. In the hospital
    ___ 3. In a nursing home
    ___ 4. At work
    ___ 5. In a traffic accident
    ___ 6. Other

15. Did the deceased leave instructions as to the burial details?
    ___ 1. Yes (left written instructions or told someone his wishes)
    ___ 2. No
16. Where was the funeral service held?
    ___ 1. Funeral home
    ___ 2. Church
    ___ 3. Both funeral home and church
    ___ 4. Home
    ___ 5. Other
17. If you are a widow or widower, who made most of the financial decisions during your marriage?
    ___ 1. I did
    ___ 2. My spouse
    ___ 3. My spouse and I jointly
18. Do you feel that the funeral was *more* for the living or for the deceased?
    ___ 1. For the living
    ___ 2. For the deceased
    ___ 3. Both
19. How important do you believe funerals are for the surviving?
    ___ 1. Extremely important
    ___ 2. Somewhat important
    ___ 3. Undecided
    ___ 4. Not very important
    ___ 5. Not important at all
20. How able were you to cope with this death in the family? It was:
    ___ 1. Very difficult
    ___ 2. Somewhat difficult
    ___ 3. Not difficult at all
21. Prior to the loss in the family, did you discuss death with friends or relatives?
    ___ 1. Frequently
    ___ 2. Seldom
    ___ 3. Not at all
22. Since the loss in the family, do you find yourself discussing death with friends or relatives?
    ___ 1. Frequently
    ___ 2. Seldom
    ___ 3. Not at all
23. Emotionally, how prepared do you feel you were to cope with this death?
    ___ 1. Very prepared
    ___ 2. Somewhat prepared
    ___ 3. Undecided
    ___ 4. Not very prepared

_____ 5. Not prepared at all

Have you been involved in discussions about death in any of the following situations?

24. At church?
_____ 1. Very much
_____ 2. Somewhat
_____ 3. Not at all

25. At school?
_____ 1. Very much
_____ 2. Somewhat
_____ 3. Not at all

26. At work?
_____ 1. Very much
_____ 2. Somewhat
_____ 3. Not at all

27. In the family?
_____ 1. Very much
_____ 2. Somewhat
_____ 3. Not at all

28. With friends?
_____ 1. Very much
_____ 2. Seldom
_____ 3. Not at all

29. With physicians?
_____ 1. Very much
_____ 2. Seldom
_____ 3. Not at all

Did you know that you needed:

30. A burial vault?
_____ 1. Yes
_____ 2. No

31. A death certificate?
_____ 1. Yes
_____ 2. No

32. Prior to the death in the family, did you own a cemetery lot for the deceased?
_____ 1. Yes
_____ 2. No

33. Was it easy for you to get off work during the funeral week?
_____ 1. Very easy
_____ 2. Somewhat easy
_____ 3. Not easy at all
_____ 4. Do not work

34. Did friends help out with routine tasks like cooking and babysitting during the funeral week?
_____ 1. Yes
_____ 2. No

35. In general, how do you feel that people expected you to express your grief?
_____ 1. In a very open way
_____ 2. In a somewhat open way
_____ 3. Not tolerant of openly displayed grief

36. Following the week of the funeral, did the funeral director continue to offer his help and sympathy?
_____ 1. Very much
_____ 2. Somewhat
_____ 3. Not at all

37. Did the funeral director help to make you more aware of your new status as a widow, widower, or member of the bereaved family?
_____ 1. Did not help at all
_____ 2. Helped somewhat
_____ 3. He helped me very much

38. Did the funeral director succeed in comforting you during the funeral week?
_____ 1. Yes
_____ 2. No

39. Do you feel that the funeral was a meaningful way to express love for the deceased?
_____ 1. Not at all
_____ 2. Somewhat
_____ 3. Very much

40. Did the expectations of your friends affect you in the selection of type of funeral, flowers, and extra services?
_____ 1. Very much
_____ 2. Somewhat
_____ 3. Not at all

41. Did you go to the funeral home to make plans for the funeral?
_____ 1. Yes
_____ 2. No

42. Did you go to the funeral home to select a casket?
_____ 1. Yes
_____ 2. No

43. Did you make most of the arrangements for the funeral during the meeting with the funeral director in the funeral home?
_____ 1. Yes
_____ 2. No

44. Prior to the loss of the deceased, had you visited a funeral home?
    ___ 1. I had never been inside a funeral home
    ___ 2. I had only visited a funeral home during visitation hours
    ___ 3. I had visited a funeral home to arrange for other funerals
    ___ 4. Other

45. How much did you expect the funeral to cost before the prices were quoted?
    ___ 1. Less than $500
    ___ 2. $500 to $799
    ___ 3. $800 to $999
    ___ 4. $1,000 to $1,199
    ___ 5. $1,200 to $1,499
    ___ 6. $1,500 and over
    ___ 7. Had no idea of expected cost

46. How much did the funeral actually cost?
    ___ 1. Less than expected ($_____)
    ___ 2. The same as expected ($_____)
    ___ 3. More than expected ($_____)
    ___ 4. Don't know

47. When you think it over, how much would you have liked to have spent on the funeral?
    ___ 1. Less than was spent ($_____)
    ___ 2. The same amount ($_____)
    ___ 3. More than was spent ($_____)

48. By what means were funeral expenses paid?
    ___ 1. Savings account
    ___ 2. Loan
    ___ 3. Special burial funds (burial insurance, public assistance, veteran's benefits, etc.)
    ___ 4. Relatives shared cost
    ___ 5. Savings and special burial funds
    ___ 6. Other

49. Concerning the cost of the casket you selected, was it:
    ___ 1. More than you could really afford
    ___ 2. Just what you could afford
    ___ 3. Less than you could afford

50. When making arrangements, how did the atmosphere of the funeral home make you feel?
    ___ 1. Very foreign
    ___ 2. Somewhat foreign
    ___ 3. Not foreign at all
    ___ 4. I did not make the arrangements

51. When making arrangements within the funeral home, did the setting (the music, furniture, carpeting, decor, etc.) make you feel:
    ___ 1. Very strange
    ___ 2. Somewhat strange
    ___ 3. Not strange at all
    ___ 4. I did not make arrangements

52. How many went to the funeral home to make the funeral arrangements? I went:
    ___ 1. By myself
    ___ 2. With one other person
    ___ 3. With two other persons
    ___ 4. With three others
    ___ 5. With four others or more

53. Who were the people who accompanied you to the funeral home to make funeral arrangements?
    ___ 1. Friend(s)
    ___ 2. Relative(s)
    ___ 3. Friend(s) and relative(s)

54. Did the people who accompanied you to the funeral home help make the decisions regarding funeral arrangements?
    ___ 1. Yes
    ___ 2. No

55. If the funeral was for your spouse, whose relatives were more influential in the funeral arrangements and planning the funeral?
    ___ 1. My relatives
    ___ 2. My spouse's relatives
    ___ 3. Deceased was not my spouse

56. When deciding on the details of the funeral, were you:
    ___ 1. Very upset
    ___ 2. Somewhat upset
    ___ 3. Not upset at all

57. How well did you know the funeral director before the death?
    ___ 1. Not at all
    ___ 2. Casual acquaintance
    ___ 3. Friend of mine or of the family

58. Where did you or your family get acquainted with the funeral director?
    ___ 1. Church activities
    ___ 2. Civic organizations
    ___ 3. Friend of the family
    ___ 4. Past funerals

59. When you were selecting the casket and vault, did you feel the pressure of limited time in your decision?
____ 1. Yes
____ 2. No
____ 3. I did not select the casket

In the selection of the casket, did you take into consideration or were you influenced by the following?

60. Style of casket?
____ 1. Yes
____ 2. No

61. Color of casket?
____ 1. Yes
____ 2. No

62. Cost of casket?
____ 1. Yes
____ 2. No

63. Relatives or friends?
____ 1. Yes
____ 2. No

64. Funeral director?
____ 1. Yes
____ 2. No

65. Grief at the time?
____ 1. Yes
____ 2. No

66. Did the funeral director seem like a member of the family during the funeral week?
____ 1. Yes
____ 2. No

67. How did the funeral director impress you?
____ 1. He does not seem at all interested in the people he serves
____ 2. He is somewhat interested in the people he serves
____ 3. He seems very interested in the people he serves

68. Did it seem that the funeral director went out of his way to help you in your time of grief?
____ 1. Not at all
____ 2. Somewhat
____ 3. Very much

69. How did the funeral director assist you in making funeral arrangements?
____ 1. I asked him to take over all possible arrangements
____ 2. I asked him to take over several arrangements
____ 3. I asked him to take over very few arrangements

Did the funeral director perform any of the following services for you?

70. Order flowers?
____ 1. Yes
____ 2. No

71. Contact pallbearers?
____ 1. Yes
____ 2. No

72. Notify any relatives?
____ 1. Yes
____ 2. No

73. Send thank-you cards for you?
____ 1. Yes
____ 2. No

74. Select a grave marker?
____ 1. Yes
____ 2. No

75. Notify any friends?
____ 1. Yes
____ 2. No

76. How did you find the appearance of the deceased (in regard to the restoration work)?
____ 1. The deceased looked much younger
____ 2. The deceased looked somewhat younger
____ 3. The deceased looked about the same as when alive
____ 4. Other

77. How did you react to the appearance of the deceased?
____ 1. I was pleased with the appearance
____ 2. I was not pleased with the appearance
____ 3. Undecided
____ 4. Other

We wish to thank you for your cooperation in completing this questionnaire. If you would like a copy of the results, please send us a card with your name and address:

Attention: Mr. Khleif
Department of Sociology and Anthropology
Wisconsin State University — La Crosse
La Crosse, Wisconsin 54601

If there are comments or additional information you wish to add, please use the space below and the back of the questionnaire.

REFERENCES

1. Puckle, Bertram S. "Funeral Customs." London: T. W. Laurie (1926), p. 253.
2. Bowman, L. "The American Funeral: A Study in Guilt, Extravagance, and Sublimity." Washington, D.C.: Public Affairs Press (1959), p. vii.
3. Mitford, Jessica. "The American Way of Death." New York: Simon and Schuster (1963).
4. Harmer, Ruth M. "The High Cost of Dying." New York: Crowell-Collier (1963), p. 225.
5. Gennep, Arnold van. "The Rites of Passage." Chicago: University of Chicago Press (1961), pp. 146-147.
6. Warner, W. Lloyd. "The Living and the Dead." New Haven: Yale University Press (1959), pp. 31-32.
7. Fulton, Robert. On the dying of death. In "Explaining Death to Children," E. A. Grollman (Ed.). Boston: Beacon (1967), p. 44.
8. Becker, Howard, and D. K. Bruner. Attitudes toward death and the dead and some possible causes of ghost fear. Mental Hygiene, XV:828-837.
9. Durkheim, Emile. "The Elementary Forms of the Religious Life." London: Allen and Unwin (1954).
10. Parsons, Talcott. "The Social System." New York: Free Press (1951), p. 304.
11. Mandelbaum, David G. Social uses of funeral rites. In "The Meaning of Death," H. Feifel (Ed.). New York: McGraw-Hill (1965), p. 189.
12. Habenstein, Robert W., and William M. Lamers. "Funeral Customs the World Over." Milwaukee: Bulfin (1963), p. 772.
13. Bowman, op. cit.
14. See, for example, Bowman, op. cit., pp. 29-35, and Mitford, op. cit., pp. 22-38.
15. Habenstein, Robert W. Group psychotherapy and the social psychology of grief. A paper presented at the Fourth Annual Meeting of the Inter-American Society for Psychology. University of Puerto Rico, Dec. 29, 1956, pp. 5-6.
16. Fulton, Robert, and Gilbert Geis. Death and social values. In "Death and Identity," R. Fulton (Ed.). New York: Wiley (1965).
17. Habenstein, Robert W., and William M. Lamers. "The History of American Funeral Directing." Milwaukee: Bulfin (1955), pp. 591-594.
18. See, for example, Habenstein and Lamers, "The History of American Funeral Directing," op. cit., and Fulton and Geis, op. cit.

A Monograph on Embalming

Murray Shor

Since my original affiliation with funeral service over 30 years ago, I have been asked questions many times on the subject of embalming. It is my assumption that this is the experience of every funeral director. Since these questions came from laymen, I have enjoyed the opportunity to dispel some long-held and widespread myths about embalming. In answering these questions, I have also tried to remove the aura of the occult and the bizarre which seems to be associated with the funeral profession.

Those engaged in the care of the dead are not unique in being regarded with an attitude of something less than suspicion yet not with complete trust. In a similar twist of logic, the precursor of the modern chemist, the alchemist, was equated with the practitioner of witchcraft. More germane, however, to the theme of this discussion are the early scientific medical investigators, those who pioneered studies in anatomy and pathology and did so under the threat of arrest and persecution. However lofty the intentions of these scientists, public attitudes forced them into clandestine methods.

Obviously, time has improved their image. Physicians, in particular, sharing their hopes, aspirations, and achievements with the public by way of biographies, autobiographies, and the novel, had been brought to a position of public adulation by the late 1930's. By the 1960's, lay publications were publishing detailed descriptions of surgical procedures as sophisticated as heart transplants and enterotomies. Public knowledge of the surgeon's objectives and the complexity of his work has brought to him great esteem.

243

This monograph is not a bid for public esteem, but it is an effort to remove the mystery that surrounds the work of the funeral director and to establish a basic understanding between him and the public he serves. For a better perspective, we should dispel some of the false impressions about ancient embalming which are still regarded as true facts by many lay people.

The term "embalm," in general usage, means the preparation of dead human bodies for funeral purposes. This is a valid concept with which to begin this discussion.

The word is derived from the Latin "em," meaning "in" or "into," and "balm," meaning "resinous products." Thus, the term "to embalm" describes ancient Egyptian embalming more accurately than it does modern embalming. There are tremendous differences between ancient and modern embalming methods. The former procedure closely resembled taxidermy, requiring the removal of all organs, while modern embalming does not. The widespread myth that the techniques of the ancient Egyptian embalmers have been irretrievably lost is not true. It has been said that the modern embalmers envy the work of their ancient predecessors, wishing that they could duplicate their methods. This too is untrue. It is a fact that the type of embalming practiced by ancient Egyptian embalmers does not lend itself for application in the modern practice of the funeral service. Modern embalming has three major objects: sanitation, preservation, and restoration to a lifelike appearance. The almost complete dehydration inherent in ancient embalming precluded the possibility of restoring a lifelike quality to the features of the corpse.

Knowledge of the true nature of ancient embalming has come to us from many sources. Herodotus, the early Greek historian (circa 484 BC), visited Egypt, and in his "History of Herodotus" (Book II, paragraphs 86-88) he gave a very detailed description of ancient Egyptian embalming. About 400 years later, another scholar and historian, Diodorus of Sicily, writing of the customs of the Egyptians, gave an almost identical description of Egyptian embalming. In addition to the writings of these and other historians, there is physical evidence to verify the facts in their works.

In 1925 the tomb of Tut-Ankh-Amen, a king of the 18th Dynasty (about 1350 BC), was opened and examined carefully. Incisions on the body and materials within the mummy matched the descriptions of Herodotus and Diodorus. From these sources we have learned that the ancient Egyptian embalmer made an incision on the left side of the abdomen through which he removed all of the internal organs, except the heart and kidneys. The organs were then bathed in palm wines and sweet-smelling oils such as oil of rosemary and oil of eucalyptus. The body was then soaked in a salt solution called "Natron" for a period of 70 to 90 days. This caused such dehydration that the features of the face no longer resembled the original countenance. Dehydration, which was assisted by the warm, dry climate of Egypt, discouraged decomposition and made the ancient method so successful that the mummies have remained intact for more than 3,000 years.

Contrary to other opinions, I believe embalming to be the oldest profession extant. Mummies found in Fezzan Province, Libya, are 6,000 years old. Although these mummies were not prepared in accordance with the best traditions of later Egyptian embalmers, definite efforts to preserve the body are evident. If one considers that these first efforts were made so many thousands of years before the birth of Christ and that the practice continues to this day, he must realize that preservation of the human body after death has a certain significance for man.

With the decline of ancient Egyptian culture, the practice of embalming fell into disuse in that country. However, the urge to preserve the dead never disappeared. According to the book of St. John, the body of Christ was cared for by Joseph of Arimathea and Nicodemus. It was they who anointed His body with myrrh and aloes, the former an odorous resin, the later a scented wood, and then wrapped His body in bandages saturated with these compounds. Whether or not this can be considered an "embalming" treatment is really a matter of semantics. Wrapping bodies in scented materials masks the odors of decomposition, thereby giving the impression of preservation.

At approximately the same time, during the Western Han Dynasty in China (206 BC to 24 AD), the body of Lady Li was placed in six coffins that were packed in five tons of charcoal. The innermost coffin, containing the body, also contained mercuric compounds. This body was discovered in 1973 and was in excellent condition. Modern embalmers know that the salts of mercury are good preservatives and that charcoal serves to dry the environment, which also discourages decomposition.

Embalming was practiced on the Canary Islands, which are located about 67 miles off the northwest African coast, within a few centuries of the birth of Christ. The method utilized was similar to the Egyptian process. It included evisceration of the body and a period of drying, either on the warm sandy beaches or in stone ovens. The bodies were then wrapped in goatskins which were painted in a variety of colors and returned to the deceased's family for burial. Writing in 1835, Jean Nicolas Gannal, a French chemist and embalmer, stated that the Neolithic Guanche people who inhabited the Canaries had been embalming bodies for about 1,500 to 2,000 years.

The antiquity of embalming has been irrefutably established, and its widespread use is meaningful. From Changsha in Central China to Fezzan Libya to the Canary Islands, people unknown to each other and as remote from each other culturally as they were geographically were all impelled to embalm their dead. The literature describing embalming procedures in the early Christian era is scarce and undetailed. The descriptions that have been passed down to us are often offensive to contemporary sensibilities. There are reports that the bodies of great men who died far from home were boiled to clear the flesh from the bones; the bones were then returned to their native soil for burial. Henry I of England, who died in 1135, was "embalmed" after his brains, eyes, and entrails had been removed. The embalming of King Henry consisted of soaking his eviscerated body in spirits of wine, camphor, or turpentine, a method which persisted until late in the Middle Ages.

Not until the 17th century was a method of embalming approaching acceptability by the general public discovered. Gabriel Clauderaus, a German anatomy professor, in his "Methodus Balsamandi Corpora Humana" (published in 1670) described a method of preparing bodies without evisceration. With a long, hollow needle he injected the body cavities with sal ammoniac and cream of tartar. However, even this so-called new method required that the body be immersed for five or six weeks in the same fluid with which it had been injected. This waiting period is hardly acceptable in modern funeral practice. However, it must be understood that Clauderaus did not intend to embalm bodies for funeral purposes but, rather, for the long-term preservation of anatomical specimens. During this period, the first serious studies of anatomy began. Such studies required various types of bodies for investigation of specific areas of the human body. There are organs, systems, and conditions indigenous only to the male, the female, the very young, or the very old. Because of strong religious sentiment against dissection, bodies in general, and the bodies of females and children in particular, were difficult for the early anatomist to acquire.

Careful dissection and study of a single organ may take days. To protect his rare and costly material against the ravages of decomposition the early anatomist had to find a method by which his specimens could be preserved for long periods of time. Within three to four decades after Clauderaus, Dr. Frederick Ruysche, a Dutch anatomist, made what is probably the greatest single contribution to embalming. He demonstrated that bodies could be embalmed via the vascular system. Except for the contributions of modern chemistry, virtually nothing of significance has been added to the practice of embalming since this discovery. But Ruysche's failure to commit his newly discovered embalming process to writing diminished his position in the annals of embalming history.

Among important early medical embalmers are William Hunter and his younger brother John. They did leave written records of their embalming process. In a paper read on Jan. 13, 1776, to the students at his school on Great Windmill Street in London, William Hunter described how he injected the femoral artery (a large blood vessel in the upper third of the thigh) with oil of turpentine and oil of lavender. Following the arterial injection, all the organs were removed from the chest and abdominal cavities and soaked in palm wines and sweet-smelling oils. After the organs were returned to the body cavities, the entire body was laid on a bed of plaster of Paris, where it remained for months.

As effective as Hunter's embalming process was, it contained elements unacceptable to 20th-century funeral service. Removing the organs is not a procedure followed in routine embalming by modern embalmers. Nor would embalming have a place in contemporary funeral service if it required storing bodies on plaster of Paris beds for several months. (It was recorded that Dr. Hunter embalmed the wife of his dentist friend, Martin Van Butchell, and kept her embalmed remains on display at specified hours in the widowers' reception room of his establishment for many years.)

By committing arterial embalming techniques to writing, William Hunter paved the way for a host of others. Most significant among those who experimented with his method was a French chemist, Jean Nicolas Gannal. Although he originally was interested in perfecting a method for preserving cadavers for scientific study, he eventually gave great impetus to the practice of embalming for funeral purposes. In 1831, having successfully prepared bodies at the request of a Monsieur Strauss, "an anatomist of well known merit," M. Gannal proceeded to accept assignments from the lay public. An example of his skill is the case of Dr. Oudet, a dentist of 24 Daupine Street, Paris. According to a statement signed by a Monsieur H. Petit, the body was embalmed on Mar. 6, 1837, and exhumed on the 28th day of May of that year, at which time it "resembled a man asleep."

In the introduction to his book on embalming Gannal wrote, "I have desired to offer to persons groaning under an afflicting loss, the means of preserving all that death has left them. With this intention I have founded an 'Embalming Society' and have placed the price of this operation within the reach of the majority of persons." For those who could not afford this service, funds accrued from the membership dues paid for the preservation of "those who honor and are useful to society."

We can state now, without making a value judgment, that after 6,000 years of effort, there is available to the general public today a practical and economical method of preserving the dead. The paradox that presents itself at this point is that although all those contributing to embalming techniques were European and their contributions were made on European soil, the United States is now the land where embalming is practiced almost universally and Europe is the area in which the practice is rare.

There is an explanation for this phenomenon. Soon after Gannal wrote his book it was translated into English by an American physician, Richard Harlan, who hoped that embalming would be effective in controlling epidemics. (This is still a controversial issue.) However, in 1837, Dr. Harlan embalmed a body at the Philadelphia Hospital, following more closely the method of an Italian physician of that era. The chemicals used in this process were wine, arsenic and carmine. It was a fairly successful procedure. The body assumed a natural complexion (owing to the carmine, a red dye) and lasted for three weeks before it started to decompose. This is probably the first written record of a body being embalmed in America by an American. By 1840, a text on embalming had been published in this country, and subsequently embalming became a widespread practice here.

Why did it become so deeply rooted in this country? Perhaps it was because the nation was still young and growing and therefore able to adapt easily to new ideas. Perhaps, too, the Civil War created a need for the acceptance of the custom.

In the last week of May 1861, Colonel Elmer Ellsworth, a personal friend of President Lincoln's, was killed while removing a Confederate flag from the flagpole of a secondrate hotel in Alexandria, Virginia. The saddened President ordered the body embalmed and laid out in the East Room of the White House for the funeral. Following the White House service, the embalmed body was started on its journey by train to Colonel Ellsworth's home town in Mechanicsville, New York. Because Colonel Ellsworth had been a famous entertainer prior to enlisting in the Army, his embalmed and colorfully uniformed remains were taken off the train and viewed by thousands in New York City and Albany en route to upstate New York. Perhaps, then, for the first time the American people saw the funeral of a hero, the first officer killed in the Civil War, transported from city to city without the ice and icebox previously part of all such funerals.

An indication that the new art was gaining rapid acceptance is gleaned from "Boyd's Directory of Washington, D. C., Georgetown and Alexandria." This publication was analogous to the modern telephone book. From 1860 to 1862, inclusive, there are 13 "Undertakers" listed in the Directory, but not one embalmer. The issue for the year 1863 listed four embalmers in the business and professional section.

During the Civil War many of the practicing embalmers were physicians. One of these, a Dr. Bunnell, set up shop in an old barn near Fredericksburg, Virginia, and devoted his efforts solely to embalming soldiers who had died in battle. Other embalmers established themselves in the cities of Washington, Alexandria, and Georgetown, offering their services to undertakers or directly to the families of the deceased. Among the latter was the firm of Drs. Brown and Alexander, twice called upon by the Lincoln family for its services. In 1862, the firm was hired when the Lincolns' son Willie died and again when the President was assassinated.

The actual embalming of Lincoln was delegated to an employee of the firm, Harry P. Cattell, who did his work so well that the body traveled 1,700 miles, was displayed in six cities, and was viewed by 1,500,000 people before being interred in Springfield, Illinois, on May 4, 1865, 20 days after death. Unsolicited praise for Lincoln's embalmer and for embalming in general came from a close friend of the late President, David R. Locke, who viewed the body and later wrote: "The face was the same as in life. Death had not changed the kindly countenance in any line."

For the second time within five years the value of embalming had been demonstrated. Bodies could be transported for thousands of miles and for many days without an attendant to replace the ice and empty the water bucket. Prior to the general introduction of embalming, bodies frequently had to be taken off trains halfway to their destination because fresh ice was unavailable and decomposition had started. After 6,000 years and the efforts of religious innovators, scientists, and quasi-scientists, a fast, effective, and economical method of preserving the dead had evolved. The method required very little surgery and relatively small amounts of chemicals and other material.

How is the new art, devised chiefly by physicians for the use of physicians, applied in the 20th century? Basically, there are three phases. First, the embalmer endeavors to restore the facial features to a lifelike appearance. In death, the muscles are completely relaxed so that the mouth and eyes tend to remain open. To keep the mouth closed, the embalmer sutures tissues of the lower jaw to structures of the upper jaw. These sutures may be removed after the embalming is completed. The eyes are then closed and restored to a natural contour by placing a pledget under the eyelids. In most cases, the embalmer will complete the restoration by supporting the cheeks and lips with artifacts.

The second phase is the most complex. It involves the injection of the preservation fluid (embalming fluid) under pressure into the arteries and the drainage of most of the blood via a vein. When the vascular system, which is filled with blood, receives additional liquid in the form of embalming fluid, pressure is created in much the same manner as pressure is created when water is allowed to flow into a closed garden hose. Therefore, when a vein has been open by an incision, the blood will flow out. Because blood is a source of decomposition and discoloration, the embalmer makes every effort to remove as much of it as possible.

In the final phase, the embalmer must preserve the contents of the hollow organs, such as the stomach and the intestines. These organs receive blood during life and, therefore, will receive embalming fluid after death via the arteries. But the partially digested food and the bacteria within these structures have no arterial supply so that the embalmer must reach them with a long, hollow needle passed through the abdominal wall.

For all practical purposes this is a complete description of modern embalming; but one must appreciate the fact that many years of formal and informal training are required to produce a competent embalmer.

Knowledge of embalming's history, its art, and its practice leads to a number of questions: Does embalming have social value? Does it contribute to society? Does it make any contribution to the comfort of the bereaved? In my opinion, it does all of these.

Medical students and medical researchers require embalmed bodies for study and investigation. Many newly devised surgical procedures are tried on legally acquired embalmed bodies to test their practicality and to improve operating techniques. A more hidden benefit derives from the fact that embalming keeps the body intact so that chemicals or trauma administered prior to death remain unaltered and may be examined months or years later. In some recent notorious murder cases, the bodies of the alleged victims were autopsied many months after death and interment. In these instances chemicals administered before death were retrieved. Had the bodies been buried unembalmed, decomposition would have reduced them to liquid and gases which would have drained into the earth. The bodies, kept intact by embalming, served as containers for compounds injected before death.

By far the greatest contributions of embalming, however, are the options it offers bereaved families. It permits them to repatriate their dead regardless of how far from home death occurred. There are no two points on earth so far apart that a body cannot be preserved for the travel time between them. Embalming permits the family to delay the funeral for the arrival of loved ones who must come from distant areas. Embalming offers the family an opportunity to view the deceased restored to a lifelike appearance in cases where disease has destroyed the normal appearance.

Yet despite these positive features the art of embalming has been much maligned. Looking into the future, I do not feel that these attacks will have much effect on the custom or its practitioners. Other professionals have also been the objects of such negativism, and none of these targets (such as the clergy, the police, the optometrist, or the manufacturer of pharmaceuticals) has been relegated to oblivion. Although embalming is being attacked, its practice has spread to Puerto Rico, Canada, England, and France. The facts seem to indicate that in the future embalming will serve more people and fulfill its basic function in our society — to relieve the stresses of the period of acute grief and give comfort to the bereaved.

Grief and Its Katharsis
William M. Lamers

When one has lived more than 70 years and has himself witnessed many funerals, as I have, he should have some personal foundation on which to construct a few tentative, perhaps superficial, judgments concerning the cycle of death, funeralization, and bereavement. In addition, when he has collaborated in the writing of two books concerning funerals, he should be able to supplement his experiences and observations with insights. To illustrate my position in this paper I would like to begin with examples from each of these sources.

When I was 13, I served as a pallbearer for an eighth-grade classmate, John, who had died suddenly. As his casket was being lowered into the ground, John's father shouted, "I want to be buried with John," and lurched toward the grave. Strong hands seized and restrained him. But his anguished cry still rings in my ear.

When my coauthor, Dr. Paul Habenstein, and I were doing the research for our second book on funerals, we were provided with an account of Rumanian peasant funerals by Professor Adrian Fochi of the Folklore Institute in Bucharest. From his personal experiences, he related an incident which we did not have adequate space to include in the book. As he was strolling down a dusty road in the back-country of Rumania, he saw a peasant ahead of him walking in the same direction. Suddenly, the man halted, leaped high into the air, threw himself down, screamed lamentations, and began to tear his hair and beard and rend his garments. Professor Fochi hastened to the man's side. He found him weeping, anguished. His strange conduct apparently had been triggered by the sight of a

251

funeral crepe hung on the gatepost of a nearby cottage. The professor asked solicitously, "Is it your wife that died?" "No." "Your child?" "No." A parent?" "No." "Then a dear friend or neighbor?" "No." It was none of these. Nor did the peasant know the name of the deceased, nor whether the dead person was a man, woman, or child. He was just a stranger passing by.

His recovery was as swift as his grieving had been turbulent. He quieted down, rose, brushed his garments, straightened his hair, regained his composure, and casually continued on his way.

There was strange erratic behavior in both cases. I am certain that members of the health and funeral service professions could supply from their own experiences many equally bizarre incidents. One is stimulated to read deep meanings into these events. When I recently began to think again about extreme grief and its therapy, these two cases were recalled to my mind. Crowding after them came an observation made by that wise ancient Aristotle.

During my high school and university courses, I was exposed to many years of classical Greek language and literature. The method was disciplinary — word for word translation, analysis, "gerund grinding" — and something of the grandeur of Greek tragic drama seeped through the parsing. The language was magnificent, orotund; the plots were epic in their capacity to inspire one; the themes were heroic. On the stage the human characters walked and talked with the Olympic deities. The settings were designed to enhance the mood of gloom that hung like a dark cloud over the whole performance. As I read the chanting of the chorus, I wished that I could be out of the classroom and into the theatre of Dionysus, under the beauty of the Grecian sky. What a way, I thought, for 25,000 Athenians to spend a few hours!

However, as I learned later from the Poetics of Aristotle, Greek tragedy was more than entertainment. According to Aristotle, its ultimate function was the "purgation of the passions of the audience through pity and terror." "Purgation" may also be translated as "catharsis" or "purification"; "passions" as "emotions"; and "terror," as "awe" or "fear."

It is probable that Aristotle also wrote about funerals. Although he wrote approximately 300 books, only a few have survived. However, it is reasonable to suppose that he would have set the emotional purgation of the bereaved in his interpretation of the funeral above the disposal of the dead as the foremost and most difficult task of funeralization. Greek tragedy and the funeral — especially contemporary American funeralization practices — have many more features in common than they have differences. They both have the capacity to stir the emotions deeply and thereby to cleanse them. Only the catharsis problems are more real and difficult to solve for the funeral. My thinking long ago progressed away from the naive belief that the major business of the funeral was the disposal of the remains. As death terminated all the personal problems of the dying, it created massive emotional and other problems for the survivors which persisted through the period of the funeral and often troubled individuals for the rest of their lives.

Similarities between ancient Greek tragedy and today's funeralization are not hard to discover. The Greek hero or heroine is basically an individual locked into a hopeless struggle against man, the gods, fate, his own mortality, and his own weaknesses. The deceased had fought his battles and lost. Both have the same terminus. Whatever anyone's eschatological beliefs may be, death, in the words of Sir Walter Raleigh, is "eloquent, just and right." To this I would add, it is solemn in its silence, awe-inspiring, common, and final for this comfortable world. The Greeks made no effort to soften this picture.

Perhaps we are wise in attempting to moderate the effects of death. But not even the substitution of white vestments for black in the Roman Catholic church, to use an example, nor the elimination from the funeral mass of the Dies Irae, that 13th-century catalogue of the terrors of the day of judgment, can altogether exorcise the chill and vapors of the open, waiting grave. Both Greek tragedy and today's funeral rites are rooted in religion and draw dignity and beauty from this fertile soil. Greek tragedy was enacted against a simple, solemn setting. The skene, the background screen (from which we derive our word "scenery"), stood boldly and simply against the sky. Whatever the origins might have been for this arrangement, the aesthetics of the Greek theatre were consciously selected to reinforce the dramatic message. We can discern a similar purpose in the arrangements of our funeral homes, chapels, and churches today. While modern taste has put aside some of the grim symbols of death — for example, the jawbone and the skull and crossbones prominently displayed as on the 18th- and 19th-century tombstones of Ireland — other symbols of death still persist. Greek actors wore highly tragic, metaphoric masques, simple and deeply pleated robes, and elevated sandals, all of which was good showmanship. This was tragedy, and stern dignity was required in all things. While the American funeral director has generally put aside certain similar aspects of costume, such as the Prince Albert coat worn by the undertaker many years ago, his dress remains conservative, in keeping with the solemnity of the occasion. Today, most clergymen still dress as clergymen. Greek tragedy also gained dignity from the alternations of commentary and the slow chanting of the chorus — strophic and antistrophic — even as today's funeral, less solemn perhaps, remains impressive in its praying and musical backgrounds.

The list of correspondences might be continued at some length. But it should be emphasized in any discussion of these two time-separated ceremonial and dramatic functions that in one major matter they are not identical, not even to be compared. The funeralization cycle, particularly for the deeply bereaved, is real. This is not playacting, playviewing, or an experience that the involved bereaved can ignore or brush aside. Nor is it an academic exercise for them, and therein lies the greater challenge and burden for its cathartic, purgative, and healing functions.

Edmund Burke spoke of the difficulties of "restoring order to a great and disturbed empire." The spirit of the bereaved person may not loom large like an empire on the world map, but when it is deeply disturbed, it too demands a restoration of order. Emotions can be in disastrous rebellion. Funeralization cannot and does not entirely ignore this fact; nor does it ignore the fact that it can assist in bringing some sort of emotional order out of the disorder. This is the funeral's cathartic function. We are thus led to consider emotions. Emotions, or passions, are affective psychic reactions or any of the feelings, among them joy, grief, fear, hate, love, which are aroused by pleasure or pain, activity or repose, and so on. Emotions rise, climax, and subside. They are not stable like ideas.

While for seven decades I have consistently maintained that two and two make four, during the same period, I have experienced changes in emotions — temporary spasms of fear, joy, anger, sorrow, and other feelings. It is impossible to maintain an emotion at its peak for a prolonged period. While it persists, an emotion tends to fix attention and whatever fixes attention determines action. Because emotions are dynamic, the energy they release causes people to "do something," to find an outlet either through communication activities, most often speech, or through motor activities of many kinds. Anger, for example, moves the fist to strike, while fear moves the legs to run away from danger. These, of course, are simple illustrations.

Emotion can be dealt with in one of three ways. It can be expressed, that is, allowed to take its normal, direct outlet. It can be suppressed, that is, denied this outlet. Or it can be sublimated, that is, diverted from direct expression to another outlet. Sublimation provides a most useful means for converting the dynamic energy released by an emotion from a possibly harmful to a more useful purpose. Complete suppression may be injurious. When this takes place the emotion is pushed down into the subconscious, where it storms around like a tiger in a cage. When a person's emotional life is persistently disturbed or out of balance, he is said to be mentally ill.

Normal living has its ups and downs, and normally people survive and keep on moving along. Under great stress they may seek professional help or muddle through by their own devices. When someone near and dear to them dies, it is normal that the bereaved should suffer severe emotional reactions of a very complex character. Involved are grief, fear, sense of loss, love, and possibly anger, remorse, guilt, and traces of other feelings. Some of these reactions may be the result of psychic impediments consciously or unconsciously carried into the crisis situation. In any event, normally and with some help persons suffering from severe loss struggle with the first difficult spasms of mourning and then, little by little, regain composure and are restored to a state of functioning good order to resume a comfortable pattern of life.

It should be emphasized that catharsis does not imply the elimination in whole or in part of the emotional nature of man. It does imply the reconstitution of the person; the restoration of the proper order among his faculties, with the higher controlling the lower. When we have restored such order, happy creative living is again possible.

In setting goals for providing catharsis for the seriously bereaved, we should distinguish those goals which can be assigned to the brief death and funeralization cycle from those which are properly to be served in the days, weeks, months, and even years beyond. The short-range goals relevant to the funeralization period should look to the prevention or amelioration of such short-range negative phenomena, such as extreme grief, panic, hysteria, confusion, immobility, anger, and the like. They should seek to prevent the bereaved from taking action which might injure themselves or others. At the same time, they should encourage positive thinking and action and provide entry into programs for achieving long-range goals. All should center around the gradual healing of the damaged spirit of the bereaved and the structuring of an integrated, well-adjusted personality. Merely to try to return the bereaved to his or her former state of emotional health is to assume either that that state was good or that it cannot be improved upon.

Individual differences in the need for catharsis are as wide and widespread as they are in other matters affecting human conduct. Seeking catharsis, the bereaved will turn to two major outlets, communication and action. While it is convenient to speak of these as though they were distinct from each other, actually they so interlock that it is generally impossible to find either in complete isolation. Communication is addressed to an audience. That audience may include other people, generally real people, although they may also be imaginery beings, God and his saints and angels, one's dog or cat, or — as in the case of a soliloquoy — one's self. It may take the form of direct, face-to-face address, telephone conversations, telegraphed, taped, or recorded messages, or mere inarticulate groans, grunts, and screams. It may be conveyed by bodily action also, with or without sound. These multiple communication outlets are all available during the stress period.

An infant screams because, in need or discomfort, he lacks the ability to articulate his thoughts. When he learns to talk, the child does tell us what he wants, and his screams grow less and less and are less and less tolerated by his elders. I think that it is safe to say, however, that the occasional desire to scream may not altogether be lost for an adult, and that a few screams on rare occasions may even provide a therapeutic outlet, despite our Puritan tradition which scorns public display of emotion.

The bereaved should be encouraged to use the many means of communication. They should be urged to write letters, to make telephone calls, and to send telegrams. They should be allowed to talk themselves out. Small talk and scattered courtesies during the funeralization period have much cleansing power for the bereaved and should not be limited to the few hours of public viewing. Monologues or dialogues – general conversation to release pentup emotions – create a sense of social solidarity, carry messages of hope and sympathy, help to fill otherwise vacant minutes, and emphasize the reality of death.

I have heard sophisticates deplore the repetitiousness of funeral parlor conversation and the simple language in which it is couched. Such persons fail to realize that in elementary life situations, plain language and simple talk are most appropriate. The language of great loss, like the language of deep love, gains power through simplicity. For the deeply bereaved such stereotyped statements such as "You have my sympathy" or "John was a good man" or "We will all miss him" or "Tell me about his last illness" stimulate healing responses, provide present support, and call the bereaved's attention to the realities of death and loss. In all these ways and many others, they assist the bereaved to build a safe bridge across the deep emotional chasm created by a death.

The communications sciences and arts place much emphasis on the expressive value of nonvocal elements, such as general appearances, gestures, and posture. All people constantly signal meanings by ways other than articulate, voiced speech or other verbal transmissions. In some bereavement situations the warm handclasp of friendship or the silent tear of sympathy proves more eloquent than a cascade of words.

In times of crisis the herd instinct, gregariousness, or the desire to gather into a close group, comes to the fore. Family and friends gather to give support to the bereaved. Even without words a message can come through: "We are one with you in your trouble and suffering."

When we turn to identify a program of activities designed to assist the bereaved to experience catharsis, we meet confusion and frustration. What to do or not to do is difficult to decide. We live in a highly mechanized society in which few home chores remain; in which there is an extensive division of labor, including indispensable professionals such as funeral directors who have the best facilities for public viewing and for other aspects of the ceremonial function of the funeral; in which there are serious problems relevant to urbanization; and in which social standards limit the conduct of the bereaved. Society limits such conduct according to two considerations. The first is the socially perceived need for rules, sometimes expressed in law, to prevent bereaved individuals and groups from doing violence to themselves or to society at large. The second is "fashion." Present fashions for the conduct of the bereaved during funerals did not always prevail.

Custom can determine much of public propriety. During the Middle Ages in certain places, funerals were climaxed with sham battles. Perhaps the clanging of swords and some bloodletting were highly therapeutic for everyone, fighters and spectators both. These must have drained off the latent anger that sometimes develops in the bereaved. When the combatants began to kill one another, the church thought the medicine too strong and put an end to the fun. We also know that wives have mounted their husbands' funeral pyres to burn with the corpse and that mourners flung themselves beneath crushing wheels and were considered by their peers to be heroic and admirable. However, in contemporary American culture, any wife who attempted to be consumed in the crematorium with the remains of her late spouse or any husband who tried to throw himself beneath the wheels of the hearse would likely be referred by a court of law for psychiatric treatment.

To say this much is not to say that in America today profound grief does not sometimes express itself through socially aberrant and individually damaging outlets. Some of these outlets for a person may be one-time only acts; others may represent new departures for the bereaved or old habits carried into new life situations. Among such reactions are suicide, withdrawal from all social conduct or a frantic reentry into it, hypochondriasis, religiosity, and immobility. Widows have been known to draw the shades and to live like wraiths in hush and shadow. Death has sometimes transformed a normal spender into a spendthrift — until the money ran out. Sometimes death has motivated the bereaved to eat or diet to excess; to grow slovenly; to withdraw from normal relationships; to be on the move constantly, wandering to the ends of the earth; to quit a good job; or to become sexually promiscuous. One does not need to look far to find illustrations of such questionable conduct.

After his wife died, the apparently stable father of a friend of mine seemed to be able to discover no outlet for his consuming sense of grief. So he threw himself in front of a moving train. He left behind three young orphans. When a university professor with whom I had close ties learned that his father had died and had been buried in Europe, he went on a roaring spree. And I recall a neighbor, now dead himself, who left the cemetery after his wife's burial and hurried to the baseball park to watch a baseball game. Then there was the family who returned home after a burial to erupt into a violent two-generation brawl, with much damage to persons, furniture, and general surroundings and a pair of black eyes for the widow. These compulsive, aggressive responses stand at one extreme. At the other stands the person who foreswears the joy of active living and sinks into silence or inactivity. The Aristotelian maxim is pertinent here: "Virtue stands in the middle place."

One cannot expect entirely normal (in the sense of "usual" or "totally natural" or "wholly controlled") conduct by the bereaved in the period of acute grief. Grieving is normal. Sometimes strong grieving is normal, healthy, sanative, and purgative. In the first hours after a death, many large and small chores must be performed to get funeral arrangements under way. Inescapably, the bereaved must be involved. Although at the moment some of these may seem to be insignificant irrelevancies compared to the burden of loss and grief, they frequently prove helpful in breaking an emotional deadlock, even if only temporarily. The psychological truism that it is difficult to think of more than one thing at a time applies here. I remember a widow saying, "After John died, I was so busy herding the children together and consoling them, and in wiping the grandchildren's noses, and in doing whatever else seemed needed at the moment that I had small time to indulge myself in self-pity."

A psychiatrist friend of mine tells his patients, "When the black mood comes on, do something. Do anything. But be sure that it won't hurt you or anyone else. Dig a hole. Cut a board in two. Clean out a dresser drawer. Write a poem. But move yourself. Don't just sit there." Perhaps in today's urbanized society we do not find or make enough tasks to keep the bereaved busy, and we thereby deprive them of at least one immediate means of achieving some emotional catharsis. The civil defense slogan and formula, "Self Help and Mutual Aid," seems to suggest a rationale for an activities program for the bereaved, particularly as they enter the funeralization cycle. Doing something, anything, is the best antidote against the whole range of feelings which afflict the bereaved. If activity accomplishes nothing more than release (catharsis) and distraction, it justifies itself. But often it accomplishes useful work as well. The message here to the funeral staff, the clergyman, relatives, neighbors, and friends is: "Try to help the bereaved to be reasonably involved, active. Don't let them become part of the funerary furniture or catharsis will not take place." While the purgation task is much more difficult to accomplish for the bereaved than it was for the spectators watching Greek tragedy, the bereaved have one major advantage: They can become active members of the performing team.

In the matter of keeping the seriously bereaved communicating and reasonably active, the funeral director is in a strategic position to program an important part of therapy. He can give wise counsel. Obviously, he cannot remain with the bereaved 24 hours a day, but out of his professional training, particularly in the field of counseling, and from his background of actual experience, he can draw much serviceable wisdom. While he is closely involved with the bereaved, he occupies an intimate, prestigious function. He speaks with authority concerning professional matters. To the confused bereaved he presents as a "father image." In addition, in typical situations, the same funeral director or his organization is likely to have provided repeated service to members of a family or group. Moreover, he can suggest that persons who need it should seek help from professionals in other fields. It is essential, then, that the funeral director should be prepared not only to undertake the functions of disposing of the dead but within the limitations of his training and his logically and legally assigned duties give counsel to the living. With such counsel the bereaved can make maximum use of the opportunities for catharsis involved in the death and funeralization cycle.

It would not be reasonable to suggest that the funeral service staff should attempt to supply medical and psychiatric services as part of their package or that, if they did so, in three days of ceremony and treatment the healing of grief could be accomplished. Deep wounds of the body or the spirit do not heal overnight. Nor are stresses produced by bereavement likely to respond to any therapy if they are complicated by long-established habits. An alcoholic is likely to merge from his wife's funeral much as he entered it, still an alcoholic. Yet as John Brown advised his judge, "Don't you know? One man and God can change the universe." Perhaps one funeral director and God acting synergistically can quietly heal someone's grief.

Through the whole funeralization cycle the professional calmness of the funeral service team tends to be quieting. The multiple contacts with religion, whether they be through clergymen, religious presentations, familiar texts, dominant philosophical viewpoints, or rites, all tend to create an image of quiet order and control. The mood of the funeral home, chapel, church, or other place of worship is one of hushed reverence. These are places where from childhood people habitually speak softly if at all. The linked social-psychic forces of suggestion and invitation come into strong play as relatives and friends visit with the bereaved. While for the most part our culture shuns the strong expressions of emotions, on this and most other occasions such a pattern can become a two-edged sword for the bereaved. It can give them moral support to ease them into a return to rationality or it can so stifle their reasonable and valid expressions of grief that catharsis is hindered. I remember that as a child I heard repeatedly in family and neighborhood discussions of funerals that "he or she had a good cry, and it helped" or some variance of much the same thought. Perhaps the acceptability of this "good cry" has been too much reduced. If so, it is reasonable to ask whether or not a valuable and legitimate outlet has not been placed beyond the pale of today's polite funeral conduct.

Tragedy on the Athenian stage was ceremonial and ritualistic. It followed a prescribed form. In funerals today there is ceremony in the reading of familiar, comforting passages from the sacred and other literature. We find it too in the religious, fraternal, and other rites conducted in churches, chapels, and synagogues, at the graveside, and elsewhere. The ceremonies, the situations, the familiar order of events, the supportive music, the hushed and dignified atmosphere, the traditional readings and language, the reverent patterns of conduct of the participants, the solemn alternations of response between leaders and audience — all create an atmosphere within individuals and within the group for orderly emotional purgation.

Cosmetology may likewise contribute to the cathartic function of funeralization by creating a final image of the deceased that is correct and comforting. Skillfully performed, that image should be recognizable; clumsily performed that image can impede catharsis. Full identification of the deceased and full acceptance of the fact of death are necessary preliminaries to the full cathartic function. But if cosmetology insinuates the disturbing idea that it is not Grandpa in the casket (too young? too handsome?) such concealment works against proper purgation.

Viewing, of course, is paired with cosmetology; without some cosmetology, ordinarily no viewing; without viewing, why cosmetology? When the deceased is not viewed, death may leave some lingering, unresolved problems. The bereaved may hope and feel that ultimate reunion will take place hereafter but that, for the present, they must accept the vacant chair as an established fact. Viewing reinforces the fact of death and, therefore, strengthens its acceptance.

Funeralization involves more for the bereaved than silent viewing of a tragic story acted out by actors. Here is not a representation of tragedy; here is tragedy in fact. Here is not passing identification with half-fictitious, half-real characters out of history and mythology; here is stern reality. The Greeks did not bid a final farewell to King Creon of Thebes, nor did they return to their homes to resist an impulse to set the supper table for his niece, Antigone, or pull out a vacant chair for her sister, Ismene.

As for the two illustrations with which this paper began, my intent should be clear by now. Each distraught person, the father and the peasant, faced a situation of overbearing emotional impact. In the case of the father, the lowering of the casket triggered a violent reaction; in the case of the peasant, the sight of the symbol of death provoked his demonstration. Both men probably derived emotional cleansing from their outbreaks.

In life the drama of death and funeralization and the emotional problems of the bereaved begin with the births of all the persons involved and end only with their deaths. A funeral is a tragic time of crisis in which many events and many lives meet briefly. It is a highly disturbing crisis. It is neither playacting nor playwatching. It is a drama in which the bereaved and the large group of fringe mourners, together with the professional funeral service staff and all other participating individuals and groups, are involved at one and the same time. There is no simulated mourning, no array of superficial grief, no easy therapy. Bereavement is too deep, too personal, too real for silent grieving and silent observation. It is not the tragedy of epic drama; it is the tragedy of life.

Index

Lucia Bove and Elaine A. Finnberg

261